CLASSICAL ARCHITECTURE IN 30 MINUTES

Illustrations are not necessarily exact 1:1 copies of that which they are intended to depict. When available, please refer to text and captions for exact proportions.

References are largely from the material citied in the Further Reading (page 129).

Whilst this book may be explored in '30 minutes' as an introduction to classical architecture, the portfolio of images and their extended captions may take more time to cover properly. I encourage readers to take as much time as necessary, and to flip to whatever page is required.

For book queries and educational downloads, please email: ed@anvilsquare.co.uk

Version (PAPERBACK) v1.34
Edition I

Paperback ISBN: 978-1-0369-2028-9
Hardcover ISBN: 9798-284829-233

PREFACE

When tasked with designing and building a classical temple almost entirely from reclaimed materials, I knew there were certain design principles I should be following to ensure the structure looked historic and was worthy of being called a *Temple*. However, in my search for a concise, well-illustrated guide to classical architectural design, it became clear that no such resource existed, not one that laid out all the rules I needed, all in one place. To my frustration, most websites on the topic either contain plenty of photos accompanied by mismatched or even plainly false information, or they consist of pictureless essays with limited guidance on how to actually apply classical elements and theory. Then there are the long, esoteric academic journals and books, most of which seem to cost far too much and unfortunately spend most of their time debating the finest architectural and historical details, often ignoring the basics. Lastly, there are the original source materials written by architects long ago, which, though very beautiful, can be somewhat tedious. In amongst all the dialogue, arguments, dedications and archaic typesetting, where every 's' is instead written as an 'f,' making it sound as if you have a lisp whilst reading, it can be difficult to find exactly what you are looking for.

The absence of a clear and practical guide led to countless hours of research grounded in historical sources, and ultimately to the writing of this book: a well-illustrated, easily accessible introduction to the key elements of classical architecture. It is my hope that you too can use, understand and even design with the classical language, and I have aimed to give you the resource I wished I had found at the beginning of my classical architectural journey.

ETH.

TEMPLE OF THE SECRET MESSENGER (2025)

Project available at: www.anvilsquare.co.uk/secretmessenger/

CONTENTS

CONTENTS

To my Brother
and the dream of building

INTRODUCTION

THE TEMPLE OF PORTUNUS, ROME (~80 BC)

INTRODUCTION

Classical architecture isn't just about grand marble buildings; it is a language of form, proportion, and meaning, deeply rooted in historical precedent, mathematical harmony, and our culture. Understanding classical design allows us not only to appreciate the technical, psychological, and mathematical brilliance behind the architecture, but also to perceive the subtle messages a building may convey and to admire the effort and pride once invested in our built environment. Developed over two thousand years and optimised for beauty, endurance, and practicality, the classical language has profoundly shaped the Western world. From Rome to Paris, London to New York, and from town halls to terraces, banks to boulevards, its influence is everywhere, and it reminds us to consider these classical principles going forward.

This concise visual guide, designed to be efficient and accessible, introduces the key elements of classical design through 3D models, illustrations, annotated diagrams, and simple explanations. It is structured primarily as a guide to the foundational design elements of classical architecture rather than a complex historiographical discussion, and provides a comprehensive introduction to the endless variations of classical forms and methods. It aims to serve as a design reference anyone can turn to for their own creative work. Whether you are a builder, designer, artist, architect, or enthusiast, I hope this guide gives you a solid foundation in the world of classical design and helps you understand both how and why the beautiful old buildings around you work.

- The **Introduction** includes a general overview of historical classical styles, including **Greek, Roman, Renaissance, Baroque, Palladian** and **Neoclassical.** The principles and theory discussed throughout the rest of the book are relevant to all of these classical architectural styles unless stated otherwise.

- **Part I** introduces basic terminology and concepts that are used throughout the book, from columns to cornices, fluting to entasis and pedestals to dentils. Part I also covers the important art of classical mouldings; their uses, shapes, effects and decorations.

- **Part II** covers the five Orders of Architecture: the **Tuscan, Doric, Ionic, Corinthian** and **Composite** Orders. These Orders are systems for proportion and form the backbone of classical architectural structures. This section includes a concise historical introduction to each Order, detailed measurements of their proportions, and descriptions of their comparisons and variations. Part II also introduces the fractional systems for proportioning used in classical buildings, called 'diameters' and 'minutes.' This section relies heavily on references drawn from the historical literary works of **James Gibbs** (1682-1754) and **Sir William Chambers** (1723-1796).

- **Part III** discusses classical building composition and theory, such as the spacing of columns, the dimensions and designs of doors and windows, and the use of balustrades, pediments and arches. This section also covers various ornamentations such as urns, finials, statues, coffering and rosettes, as well as the practice of rustication and more. Lastly, Part III briefly outlines the key theories and arithmetic ratios used for classical proportion and measurement.

- **Part IV** contains a summary of key guidelines for classical architectural design, suggested further reading and lastly, an indexed glossary of terms.

INTRODUCTION

The five Orders form the foundations of classical architecture. They are explored in more detail throughout this book, but it is important to understand their names and differences from the outset. The Orders are architectural systems that establish proportion and structural design for classical buildings. Each has unique proportions, decorations and histories, originally rooted in Greek and Roman traditions. The Orders, first recorded by the Roman architect Vitruvius, have since been refined and adapted by countless architects over thousands of years, ensuring aesthetic harmony, structural balance and enduring beauty. The have, in turn, shaped Western architecture and society profoundly.

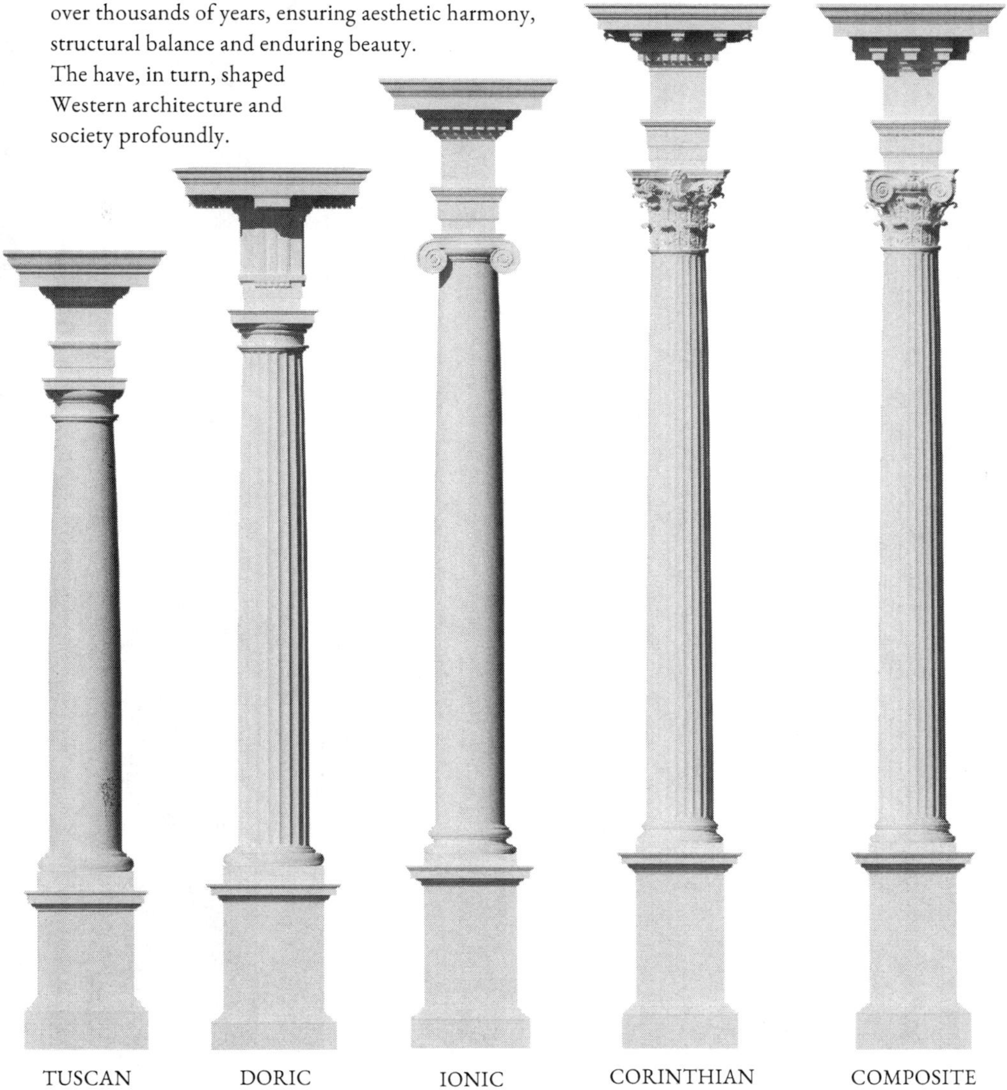

THE FIVE ORDERS OF ARCHITECTURE

GREEK & ROMAN

GREEK ~ 7TH CENTURY BC – 146 BC

- Invented the Doric, Ionic and Corinthian Orders, though primarily favoured the Doric and Ionic Orders.
- Emphasised symmetry, pure idealised forms, simple proportions and visual harmony.
- Primarily built temples, often adorned with richly decorated friezes and pediments.
- Greek architecture was based on post-and-beam construction, and featured no structural innovations like arches or domes.

THE PARTHENON (~438 BC)

Famous examples: *The Parthenon, Temple of Hephaestus, The Erechtheion, Temple of Ilissus, Temple of Athena Nike, The Treasury at Delphi.*

ROMAN ~ 509 BC – 476 AD

- Refined and adapted the Greek Orders, slimming columns and adding additional ornamentations and mouldings.
- Addition of the Tuscan and Composite Orders, though these were not yet considered canonical.
- The use of Roman concrete enabled complex structures like arches, vaults, and domes. These structural innovations allowed for larger and more complex buildings compared to Greek architecture.
- Placed an emphasis on monumental structures and sophisticated engineering.

Famous examples:
The Pantheon, Maison Carrée, The Colosseum, Temple of Portunus, The Roman Forum, Aqueduct of Segovia, Arch of Titus.

MAISON CARRÉE (~2-7 AD)

RENAISSANCE & BAROQUE

RENAISSANCE ~ 1400–1600 AD

- Undertook a detailed inspection and refinement of the classical Orders, establishing the canonical five Orders of architecture.
- The Renaissance brought a conscious revival of classical (Roman) forms, incorporating columns, classical entablatures, arches, arcades and domes.
- Reinstated classical principles with a strong emphasis on symmetry, proportion and perspective.
- Demonstrated an interest in mathematical order and spatial harmony, with less drama and rigidity than in later styles.

SAN GIORGIO MAGGIORE (~1566 AD)

Famous examples: *St Peter's Basilica, San Giorgio Maggiore, Biblioteca Marciana, Villa La Rotunda.*

BAROQUE ~ 1600–1750 AD

- Richly ornamented buildings that accentuated classical motifs and forms, and taking the basic elements of Renaissance architecture and making them taller, grander, more ornate and more dramatic. Designs frequently employed strong contrasts of light and shadow.
- Interiors were highly decorative, designed to overwhelm and draw the eye upward, with intricate plasterwork, gilding and frescoes. Note: Rococo is a later, even more intense form of Baroque.

CHATSWORTH HOUSE (NORTH FAÇADE ~1689 AD)

Famous examples: *St Peter's Square, Chatsworth House, Palace of Versailles, Castle Howard, Blenheim Palace, St Paul's Cathedral, Les Invalides, Palazzo Poli (Trevi Fountain).*

PALLADIAN & NEOCLASSICAL

PALLADIAN ~ 17TH–18TH CENTURY AD

- As a reaction against the complexity and drama of Baroque architecture, Palladianism returned to balanced, classical ideals. Featuring simple, geometric, symmetrical forms with balanced layouts based on Andrea Palladio's interpretation of classical Roman principles.
- Feature projecting temple fronts and porticos, typically of the Ionic or Corinthian Order.
- Ornamentation is restrained, with a focus on elegant simplicity.
- Palladianism is a variation of Neoclassicism.

NOTE: *The term* ***'Georgian Architecture'*** *refers to the period during the reigns of King George I to IV of Great Britain (~1714-1830). Though the style encompasses Baroque influences it is chiefly characterised by Palladianism and Neoclassicism.*

STOURHEAD HOUSE (~1725 AD)

Famous examples: *Stourhead House, Chiswick House, Holkham Hall, Wentworth Woodhouse (east façade).*

NEOCLASSICAL ~ 1750–1850 AD

- Emphasised grandeur, simplicity, geometric regularity and classical authenticity.
- Featured a strong use of repetitive motifs and imposing facades, that were often employed in civic buildings to reflect ideals of democracy and order.
- Influenced by a cultural interest in classical Greek architectural forms, alongside the Roman forms revived during the Renaissance.
- Though more austere and monumental than Palladian architecture, Neoclassicism also avoided the drama and ornamentation of Baroque architecture in favour of disciplined classical purity. Although typically dated to 1750-1850, its principles were still used in the early twentieth century.

BUCKINGHAM PALACE (CURRENT FAÇADE ~1913 AD)

Famous examples: *U.S. Capitol, Buckingham Palace, British Museum, Panthéon (Paris), Brandenburg Gate, Royal Scottish Academy, The White House, Stowe House (south façade).*

PART I
INTRODUCTORY ELEMENTS AND TERMINOLOGY

A CORINTHIAN CAPITAL

A GREEK TEMPLE

- Architectural elements of a characteristically **Greek** temple.

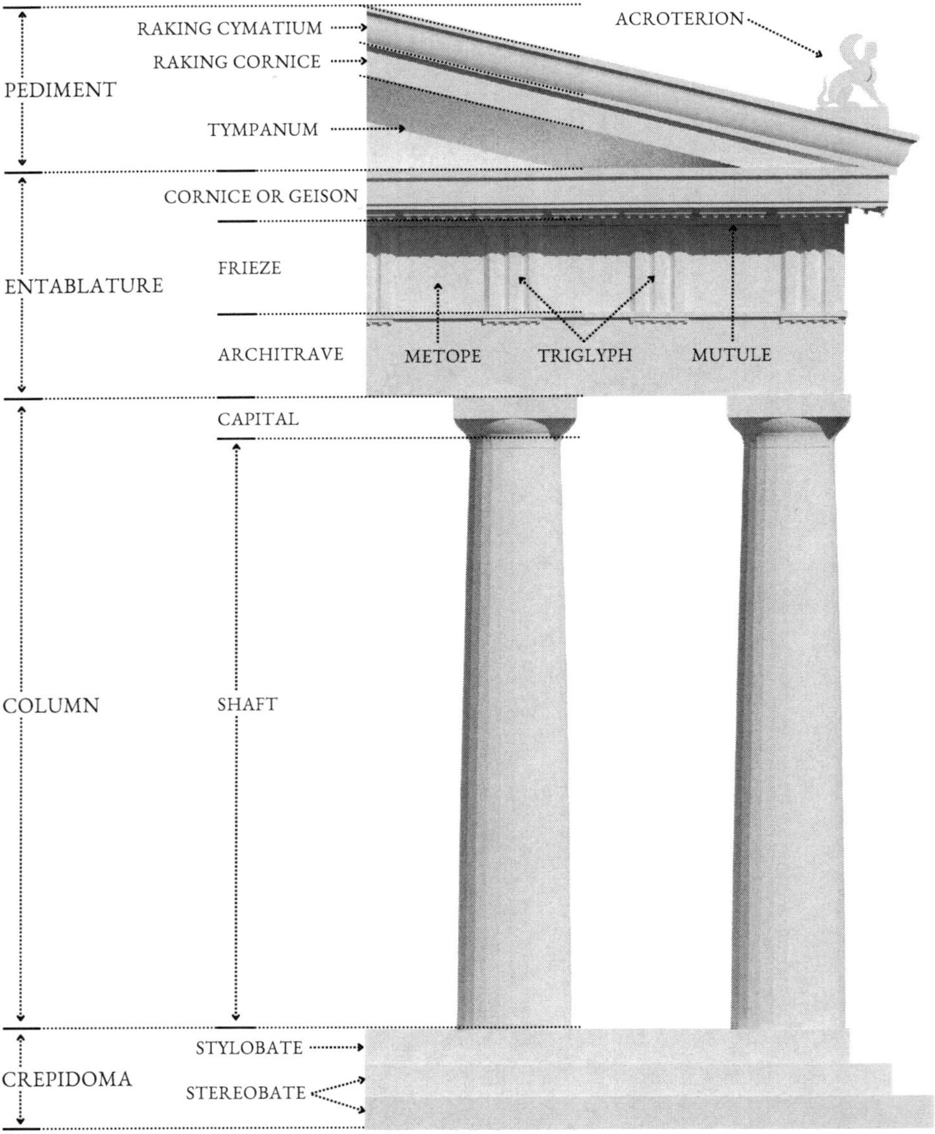

THE TEMPLE OF HEPHAESTUS, ATHENS (~449 BC)

A ROMAN TEMPLE

- Architectural elements of a characteristically **Roman** temple.

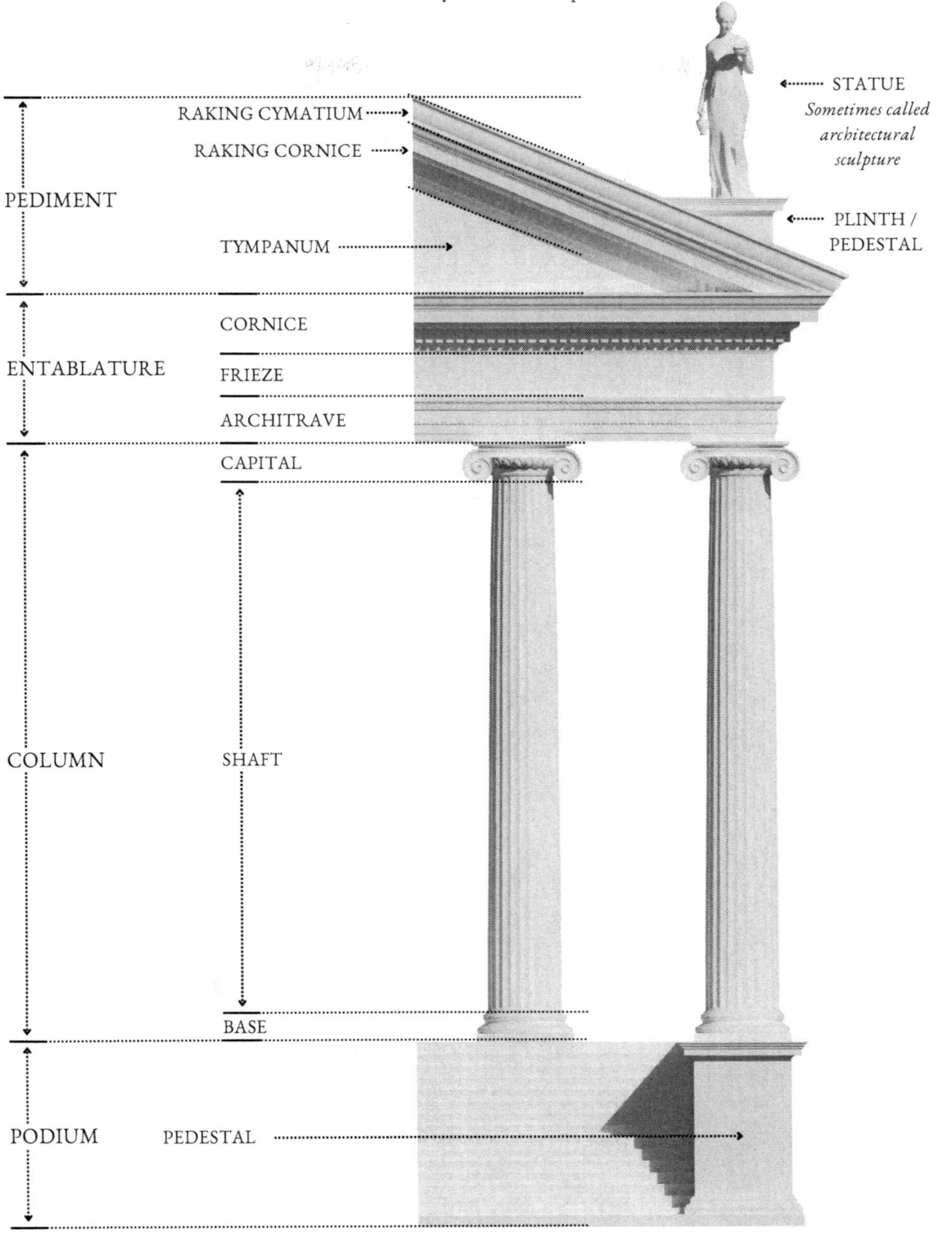

THE TEMPLE OF PORTUNUS, ROME (~80 BC)

CAPITALS

Capitals are the topmost members of columns and pilasters. They are usually the most distinctive feature of each of the five architectural Orders, as their size, style and decoration vary greatly. Capitals widen the upper part of the column to help distribute the weight of the entablature above it and provide a smooth visual transition between the vertical column and the horizontal entablature.

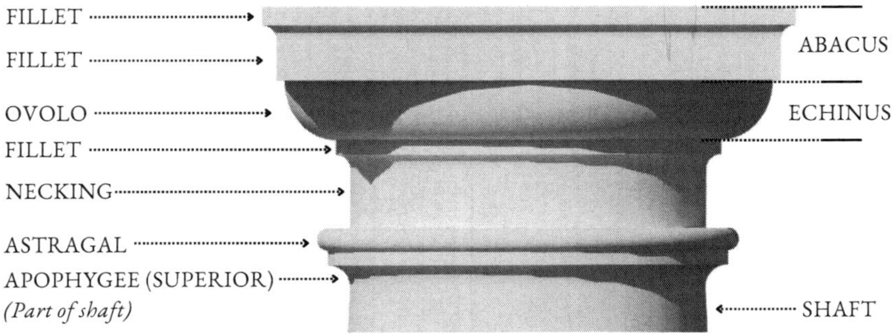

TUSCAN CAPITAL (SIMPLE)

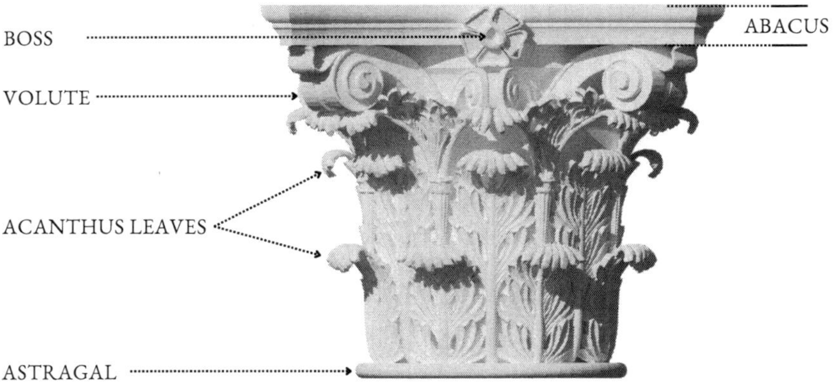

CORINTHIAN CAPITAL (COMPLEX)

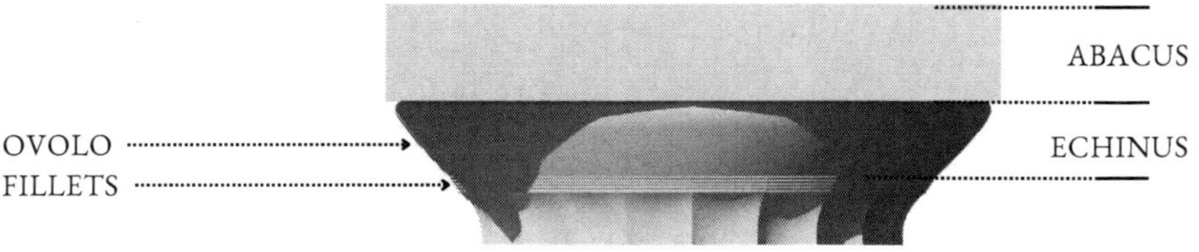

GREEK DORIC CAPITAL

- The word capital is from the Latin *caput* meaning 'head.'
- The square abacus was originally used to prevent rainwater running down the column's shaft.
- Detailed capitals for each of the five Orders are found later on in Part II: The Five Orders.

ENTABLATURE

The **Entablature** is the horizontal structure found above columns, spanning between them. Entablatures consist of the architrave (lowest part, resting on capitals), frieze (middle, often decorative), and cornice (top, projecting). The cornice includes the bed-mould (supporting moulding), corona (flat, projecting surface), and cymatium (topmost moulding, curved). The bed-mould usually has the most differentiation between the Orders.

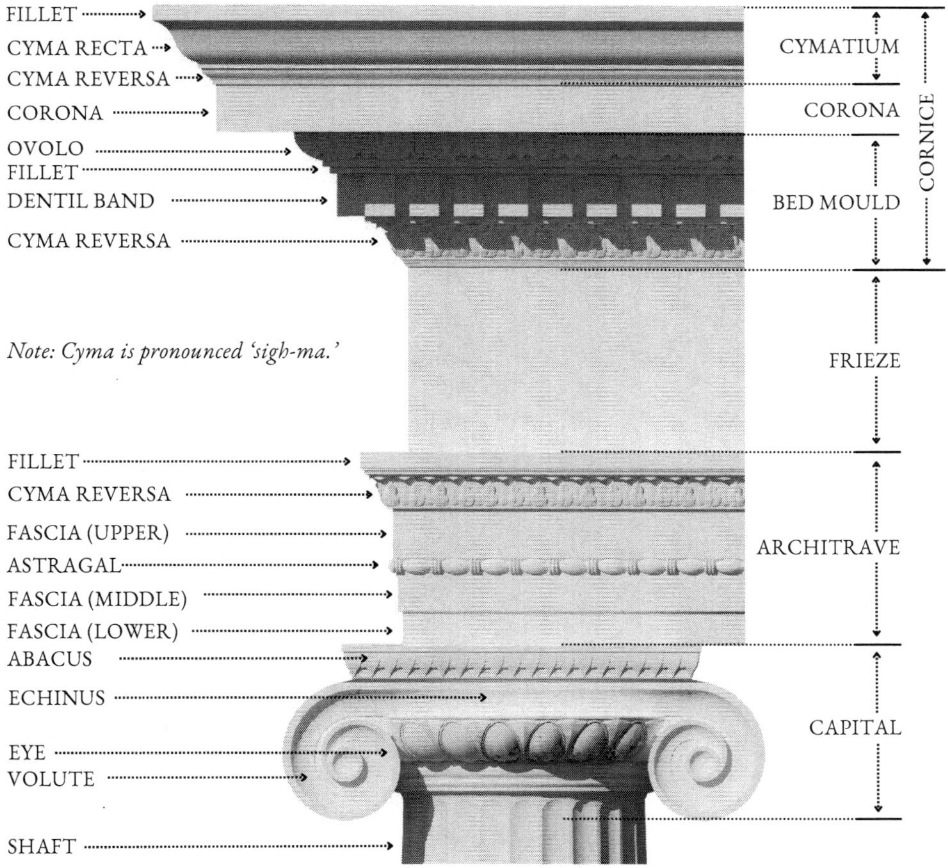

Note: Cyma is pronounced 'sigh-ma.'

THE IONIC ORDER

- The word 'architrave' is from the Greek *arkhos* ('chief') and the Latin *trabs* ('beam'); combined they means 'chief beam,' reflecting its role as the primary support member in an entablature.
- 'Cornice' is from the Latin *corona* ('crown') signifying its crowning role atop structures.
- 'Frieze' comes from the Middle French *frise,* and is probably from the Latin *Phrygium* ('Phrygian work'), a region once famous for making long and highly decorative cloths.
- The underside of both the corona and the architrave is called the soffit. These areas are often richly decorated, particularly in the Corinthian and Composite Orders.

ALIGNMENT OF ENTABLATURE

For the placement of entablature on top of a column, there is a simple rule: the frieze (B) and the lowest part of the architrave (C) should always be directly over, and in line with, the top of the column's shaft (i.e. the thinnest part of the column - E).

- Points A, B, C, D, & E are all in the same vertical plane: A: balustrade or pedestal. B: frieze. C: lowest fascia of architrave. D: necking of column (for Doric & Tuscan). E: top of column's shaft (thinnest part).
- This rule is important, as it aesthetically emphasises the column's support, visually conveying structural strength and providing 'comfort' to the eye.

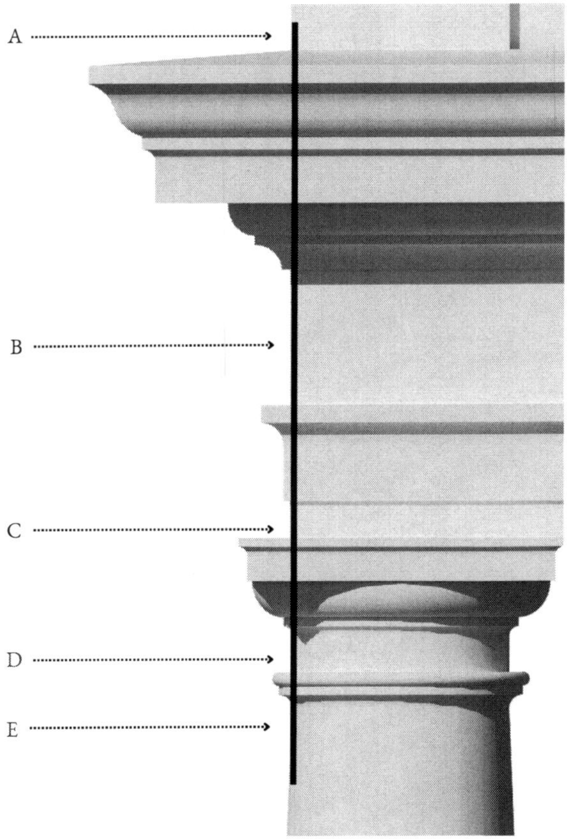

TUSCAN ORDER ALIGNMENT

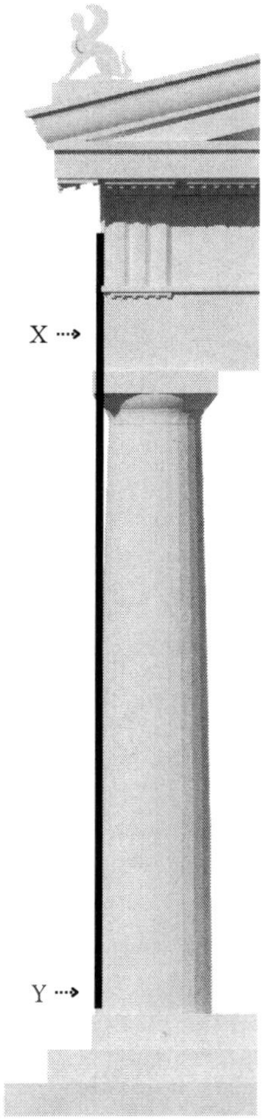

GREEK DORIC ALIGNMENT

- This rule applies to all entablatures except those of Greek Doric, where the edge of the architrave is in the same vertical plane as the base of the column (X and Y).

A COLUMN'S BASE

A **Base** protects the column from weathering, particularly water erosion, which is most likely to occur at the bottom of the column. The curves and projections of bases help both to deflect water and to provide a visually strong, graceful termination to the column.

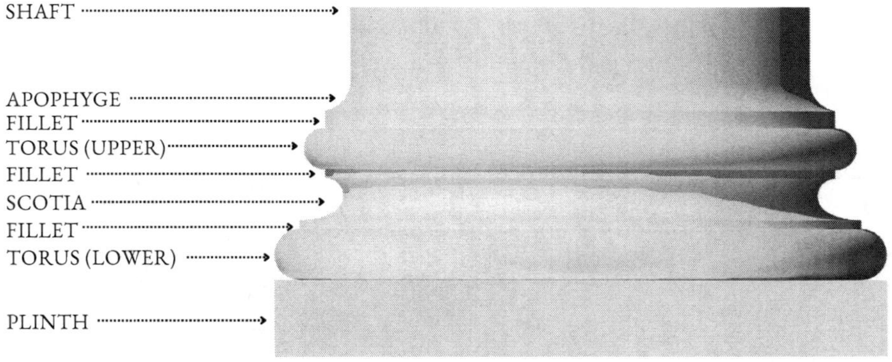

THE ATTIC BASE

The **Attic Base** became the most commonly used base for a column, employed with all of the classical Orders except for the Tuscan Order. Historically, however, it was favoured by the Romans, primarily for the Ionic and Corinthian Orders. It is characterised by two rounded tori separated by a scotia (above).

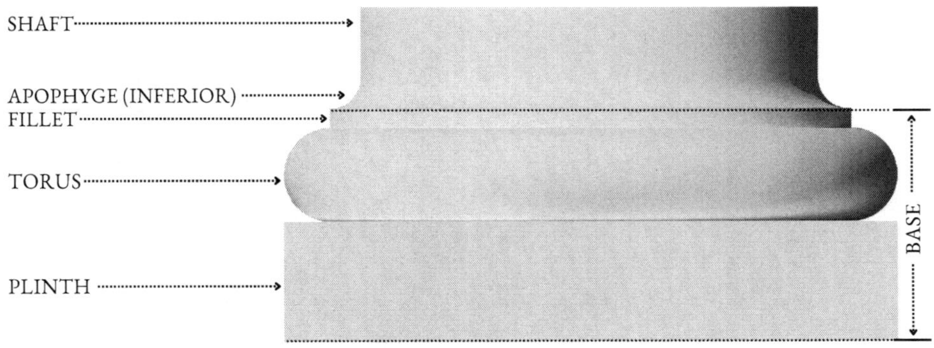

TUSCAN BASE

- All columns have bases, except for Greek Doric columns, which meet the stylobate directly (page 14). This is because historically the Ionic Order was the first to introduce a base.
- The Attic base is named after *Attica*, the region surrounding Athens in antiquity.
- The apophyge inferior is the cavetto curve at the bottom of the column and is part of the shaft, not the base. Likewise, at the top of the shaft, you would find the apophyge superior, which is part of the shaft, not the capital.

PEDESTALS

A **Pedestal** is a supporting base for a column, statue or urn. Comprised of a plinth, die, and cornice, pedestals may enhance the elevation, slenderness and visual prominence of a feature.

- Generally, pedestals that support columns are **1/3** the height of the column (according to G.B Vignola and James Gibbs). However, they vary greatly in size, with later architects typically preferring smaller pedestals, often with dimensions around 3/10 the height of the column.
- The plinth of a column base set on a pedestal should be the same width as the die of the pedestal and should sit directly atop it (B).

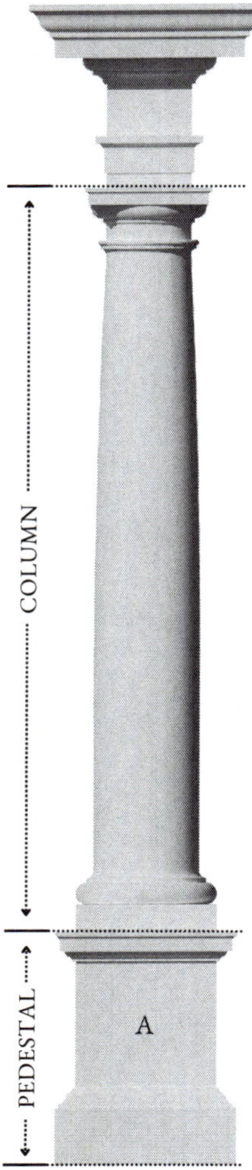

THE TUSCAN ORDER

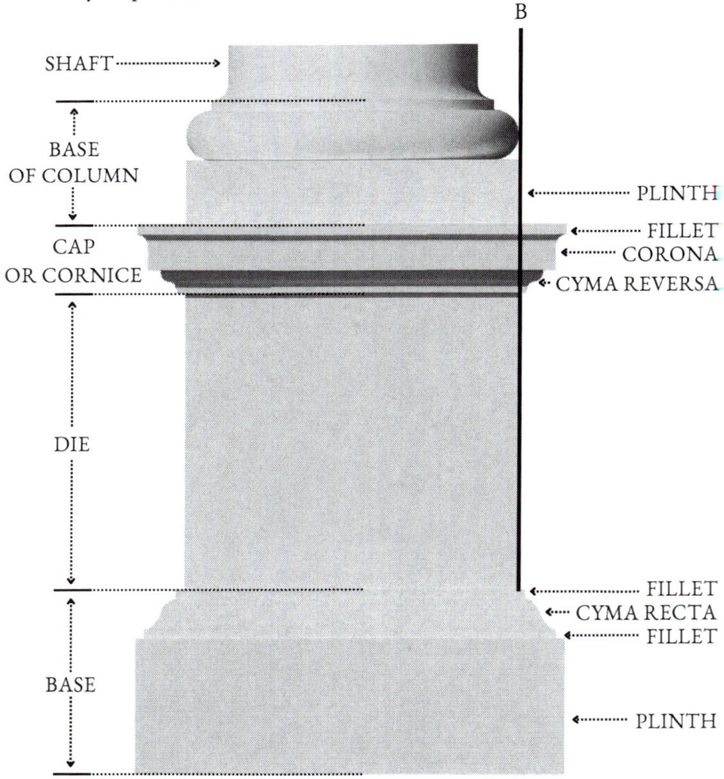

TUSCAN PEDESTAL

- All columns may be set on a pedestal except for Greek Doric columns, which instead always meet the stylobate directly (page 14).
- Some argue that pedestals may compromise the proportions of an Order, often making columns appear too slender. Andrea Palladio, though he often used pedestals, describes them as inadvisable, as they are 'less attractive and less grand.'

ENGAGED COLUMNS & COLUMN VARIATIONS

An **Engaged Column** is a column that is partially attached to a wall and typically projects **3/4** of its diameter, with the remaining 1/4 set into the wall. Sometimes they project as little as 1/2 their diameter or as much as 4/5. Like ordinary columns, engaged columns are load-bearing structures.

An ordinary, free-standing column is sometimes called an 'insulated' column

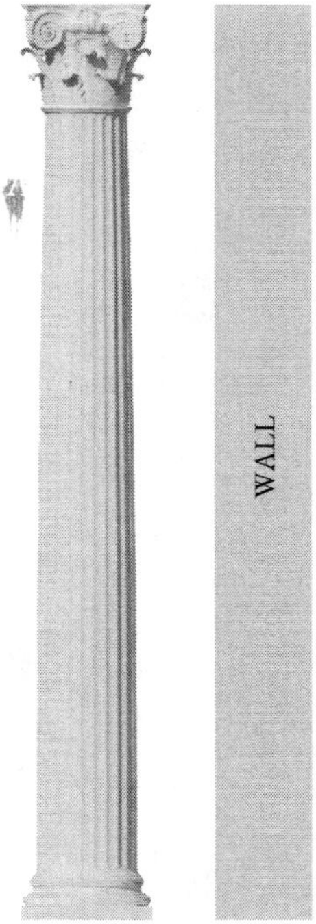

COLUMN

Engaged columns are occasionally called 'detached'

ENGAGED COLUMN

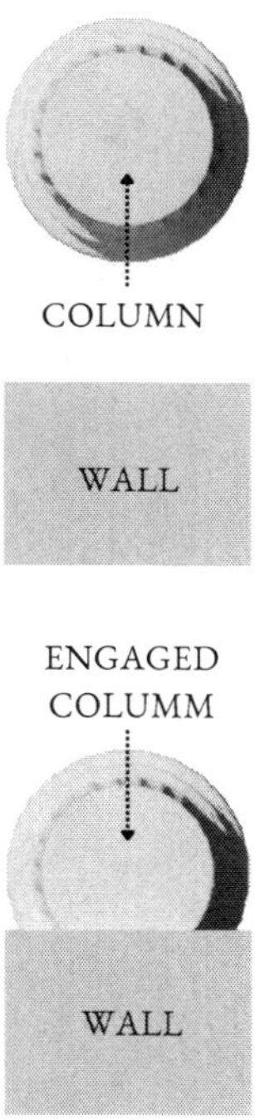

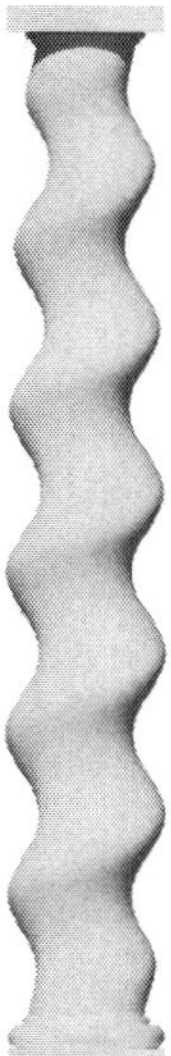

SOLOMONIC COLUMN *(Above)*

A column's shaft may be made from one large carved piece of stone, known as a **Monolithic** shaft, or from several segments stacked on top of each other, called **Drums**.

- Greek architecture often employed columns made of many drums, whereas the Romans favoured monolithic shafts. More often than not, post-Renaissance work features drums (with columns split into three large pieces), as they are easier to work with.
- Similarly, the Greeks did not use engaged columns, but the Romans did frequently.
- The word monolithic comes from the Greek *mono* ('one') and *lithos* ('stone').
- A **Solomonic column** is an ornate Baroque-style column that has a twisted spiral shaft, and is thought to symbolise divine wisdom.

DRUMS

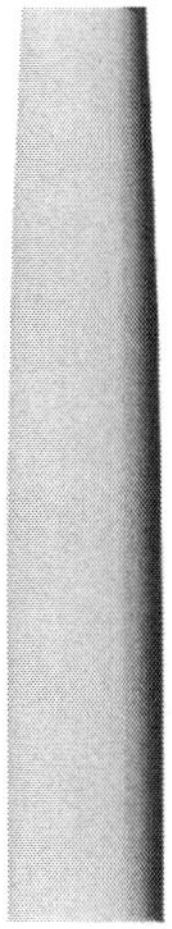

MONOLITHIC

PILASTERS

A **Pilaster** is a sort of rectangular, 'flattened' column that projects only slightly from a wall and mirrors the profiles and proportions of ordinary columns. Sometimes they are referred to as 'square engaged' columns. Pilasters are primarily decorative elements, visually enhancing façades, and unlike columns and engaged columns, they do not bear significant weight loads. Pilasters were originally used by the Romans but became a highly popular feature in Renaissance, Baroque and Neoclassical architecture.

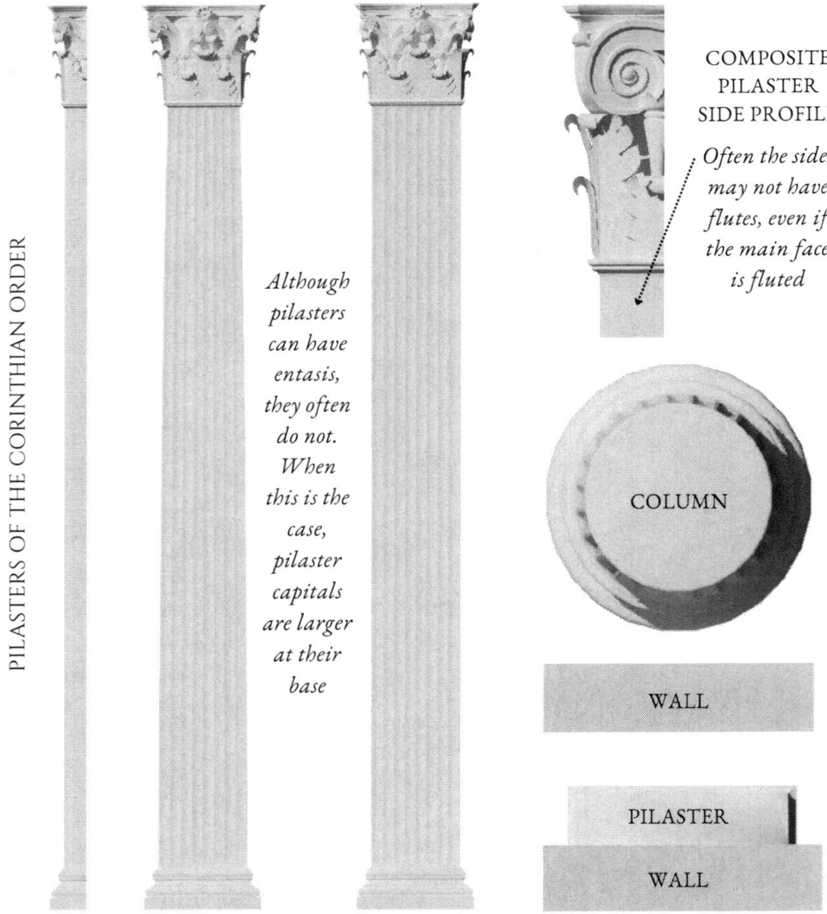

PILASTER *Side Profile* | PILASTER *Entasis* | STRAIGHT PILASTER *No Entasis* | PILASTER AND COLUMN IN PLAN VIEW

- According to Sir William Chambers, when pilasters are used alone (as in a façade that only has pilasters), they should project one-quarter of the shaft's diameter from the wall. Pilasters that are placed behind columns should only project one-eighth of the shaft's diameter from the wall.
- If fluted, they usually have 7 flutes on their front face (although the range is generally 5-9), and either one, two or none on their sides.

ANTA

An **Anta** is a rectangular pier that protrudes slightly from the end of a wall, found in ancient Greek architecture. Antae (plural of anta is antae) are integral parts of the wall's construction that are normally placed at the sides of porticos and doorways, or placed behind a row columns (A). Unlike pilasters, antae are structural, and the profiles of their capitals are usually not the same as the capitals of their neighbouring columns.

- When columns are placed between two antae, the building layout is described as *in antis.*
- Temples that incorporate antae are referred to as anta temples.
- Their 'shafts' are never fluted.

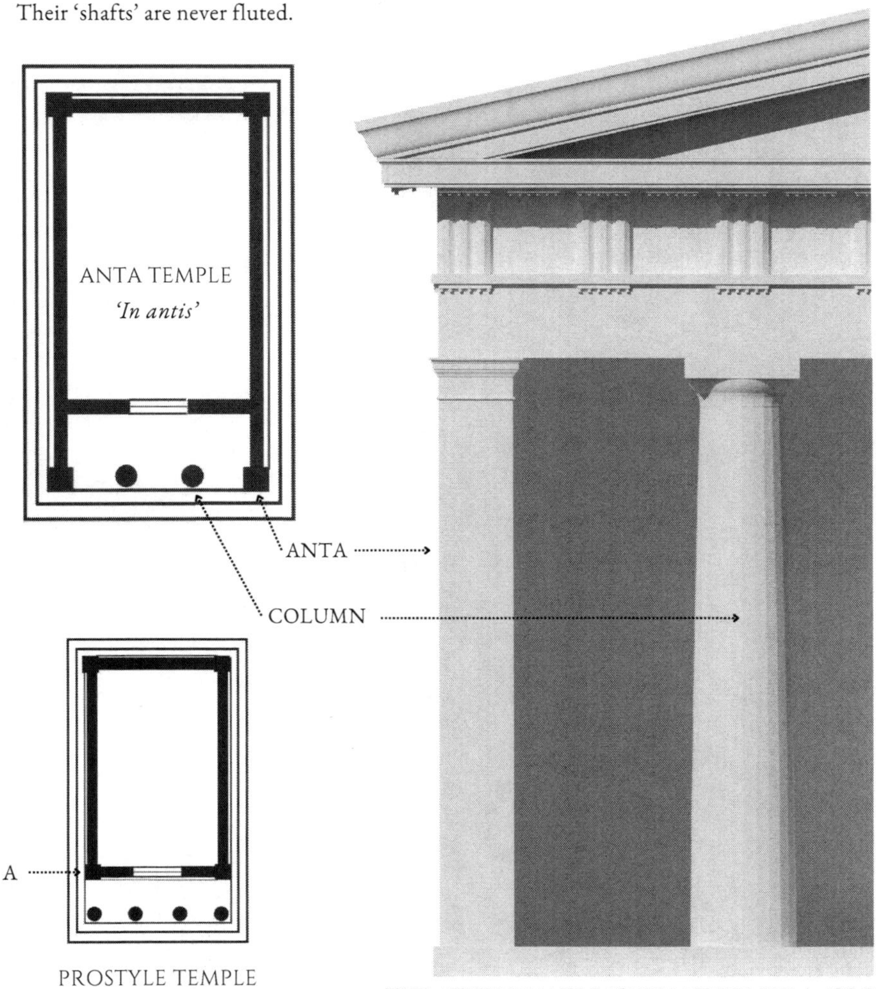

PROSTYLE TEMPLE

THE ATHENIAN TREASURY AT DELPHI (~480 BC)

- Essentially an anta is the ancient Greek equivalent to a pilaster.
- Additional classical temple floorplans and layouts are covered on page 127.

ENTASIS & TAPERING

Entasis, sometimes called diminution, is the slight convex curve in a column's shaft, curving upward. The word entasis is from the Greek *enteino* meaning 'to stretch' or 'to swell.' This is different from a **Taper,** which is a linear (non-curved) reduction in thickness towards one end. Entasis primarily exists to counteract the optical illusion that columns, when viewed from a distance, may appear concave or seem to shrink at their base. This phenomenon arises from the conical structure of the eye's curved lens. Entasis corrects this illusion, providing columns with an appearance of strength and straightness; all columns should have entasis.

- For most column shafts, entasis begins **1/3** of the way up from the base (A). This results in the diameter at the top of the shaft (B) measuring **5/6** that of the shaft's base diameter (C). This style can be called a 'Roman' entasis.
- Alternatively, in Greek Doric columns, entasis extends across the whole height of the shaft (D).

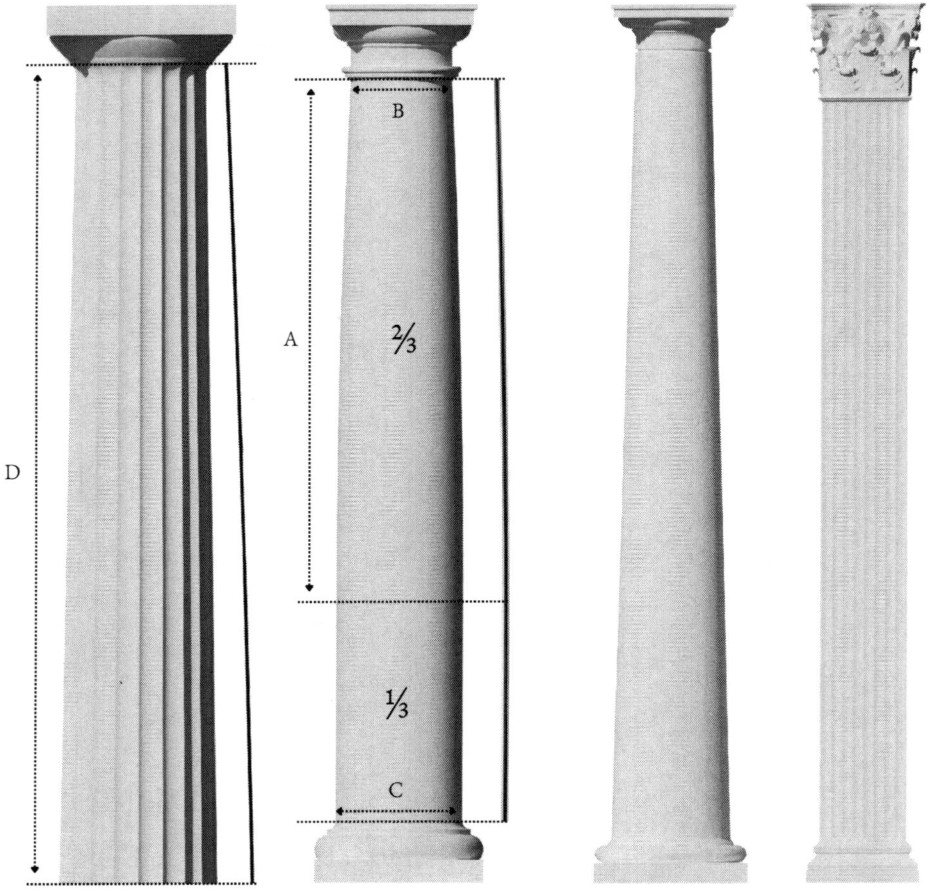

GREEK DORIC ENTASIS | ROMAN TUSCAN ENTASIS | STRAIGHT TAPER *Less elegant* | PILASTER *No entasis*

ENTASIS METHODOLOGY

There are two principle methods for describing Roman entasis: those of Serlio and Palladio, both architects of the Italian Renaissance. However, the two methods are often hardly perceptible from one another.

- **Palladio's** method: entasis begins 1/3 of the way up the shaft from the base, with the shaft's profile curving towards the top from this point. The lower third remains straight.
- **Serlio's** method: the whole column is subject to entasis, being completely curved. The column is widest 1/3 of the way up, curving from the base outward to this point, and then continuing to curve inward from this point to the top of the shaft. The change in diameter is subtle; the thickest point may only be an extra 1/60 of the shaft's diameter wider than it is at its base.
- Note: **Greek** Doric method: entasis begins at the base of the column and is curved all the way up.
- Generally, the diameter of the column's shaft at its top is between 4/5 (James Gibbs) and 5/6 (Sir William Chambers) of its base diameter.

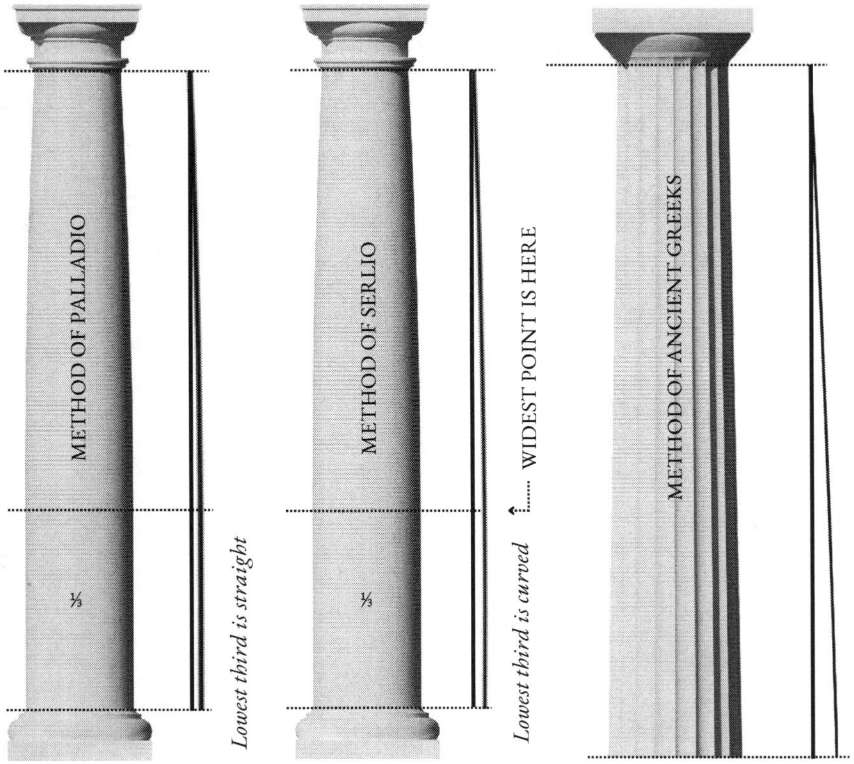

- It is also theorised that the swelling effect of entasis originated to represent the stress placed on the columns due to the weight above them, or that columns are tapered in imitation of trees.
- The entasis of Tuscan and Doric columns appears to be more pronounced because they have shorter proportions yet have the same 5/6 diminution across their height.

FLUTING

A **Flute** is a decorative groove or channel, that is usually semi-circular or semi-elliptical in section. **Fluting** refers to a series of vertical flutes, typically running up the shaft of a column, in contrast to a totally smooth column. Fluting can enhance the effect entasis by capturing shadows along the shaft, while also protecting the column from water damage. There are two types of fluting:

- Firstly, where the flutes' edges meet at a sharp point, called an arris (A). This type is favoured in ancient Greek Doric architecture, where fluting is almost always present.
- Secondly, where the flutes are separated by vertical fillets (B). This variation was favoured by the Romans and has remained the most common type of fluting since. In Roman architecture, fluting was more decorative than structural, a tradition that continued into later classical styles.

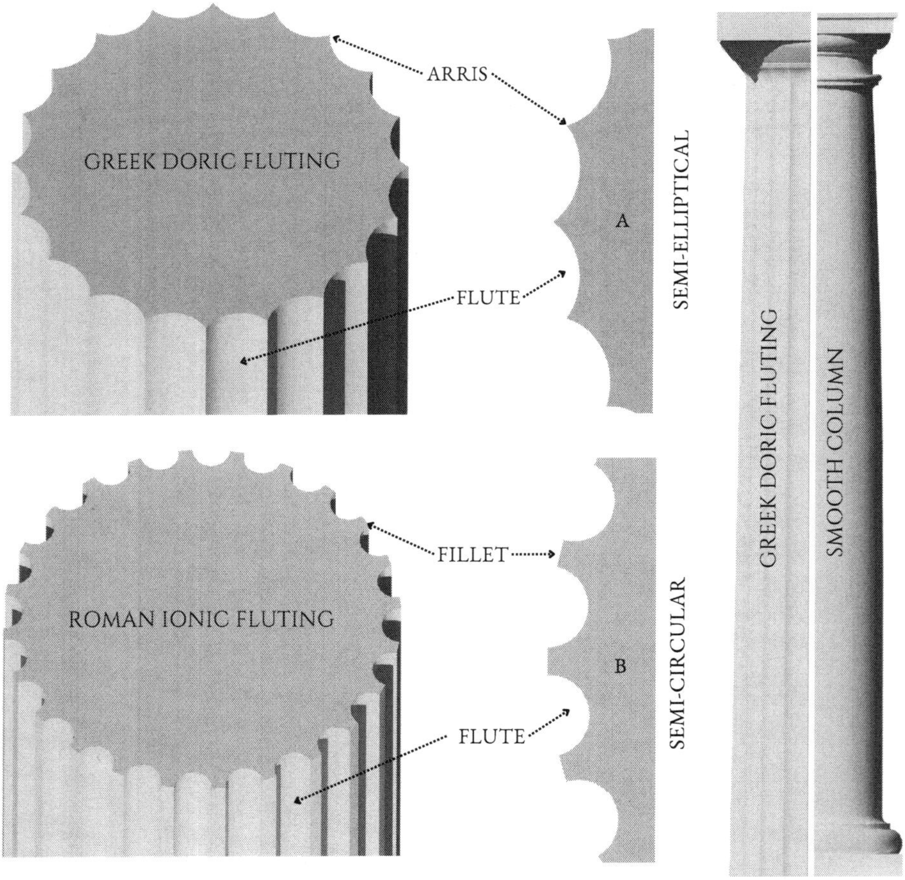

- Columns of the Doric Order have **20** flutes.
- Columns of the Ionic, Corinthian, and Composite Orders have **24** flutes.
- Columns of the Tuscan Order are never fluted.
- Pilasters (except Tuscan) generally have 7 flutes on their face, and 1-2 on their sides.

FLUTING VARIATIONS

Cable Fluting: Cable fluting refers to flutes that are partially re-filled with a moulding, usually cylindrical rods. These rods extend up to 1/3 of the shaft's height, at the same height as the start of the entasis. It is thought that cable fluting may prevent weather damage to the flute's edges at the base of a column.

Stopped Fluting: Fluting that starts 1/3 of the way up the shaft, at the same height as the entasis. The lower section is typically left plain, but rarely, may feature surface decorations.

Spiral Fluting: Helical flutes that twist upward (not to be confused with a Solomonic column).

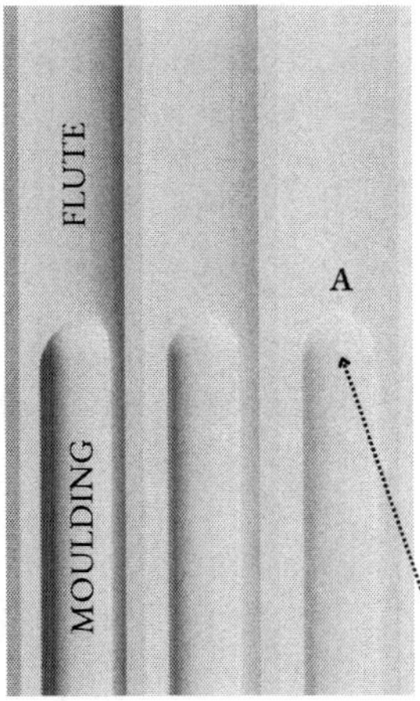

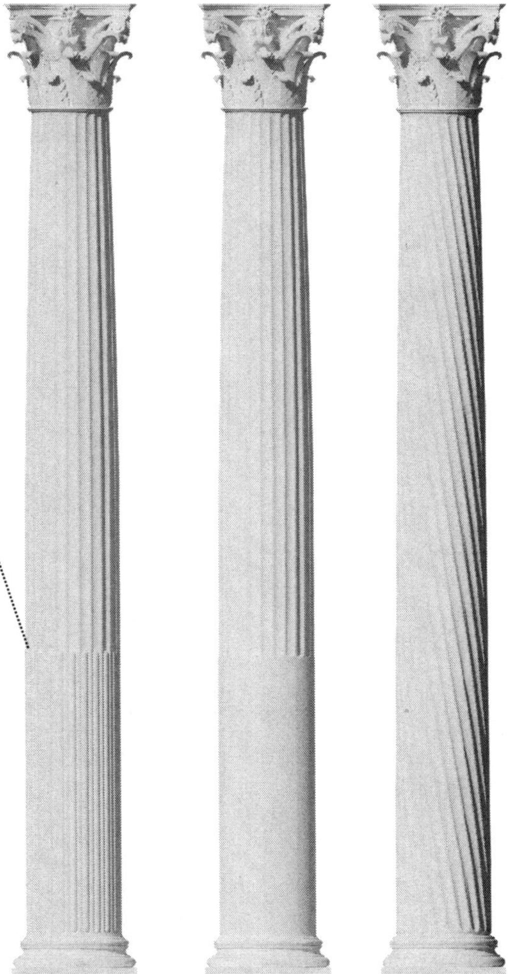

CABLE FLUTING — STOPPED FLUTING — SPIRAL FLUTING

- The Greeks did not use any of these variations, they instead originated with the Romans. Cable fluting and stopped fluting were more typically used from the Renaissance onwards.
- Usually, the rods of cable fluting terminate in hemispheres (A).
- The rods of cable fluting may feature highly ornate decorations, such as flame twist motifs in imitation of candles. Extravagant decorations like these are usually seen in Baroque and Neoclassical designs and are more often used with the Corinthian and Composite Orders.
- Spiral and stopped fluting are relatively rare.

MOULDINGS

A **Moulding** is a shaped strip of material with a distinctive profile, used to articulate or cover transitions between surfaces. In classical architecture, mouldings are often richly decorated and serve both functional and ornamental purposes.

- There are several core profiles (below) which are used to create different shadow patterns. The careful interplay of light and shadow they create is designed to capture the eye, as all our perception of form relies on light and dark.
- Mouldings are the backbone of the five Orders and classical architecture in general. They shape the profiles and forms of almost everything, from cornices and architraves to capitals, corbels, door and window surrounds, ceiling decorations and more.
- The shape of each moulding also reflects its structural role. The thicker ovolo and cyma reversa are better suited to supporting elements above them, whereas the more delicate cavetto and cyma recta are more elegant but weaker, making them suitable for the top of a cornice, for example.
- Mouldings are arranged in certain sequences due to the requirement for certain shadow effects and for constructional and weathering reasons.

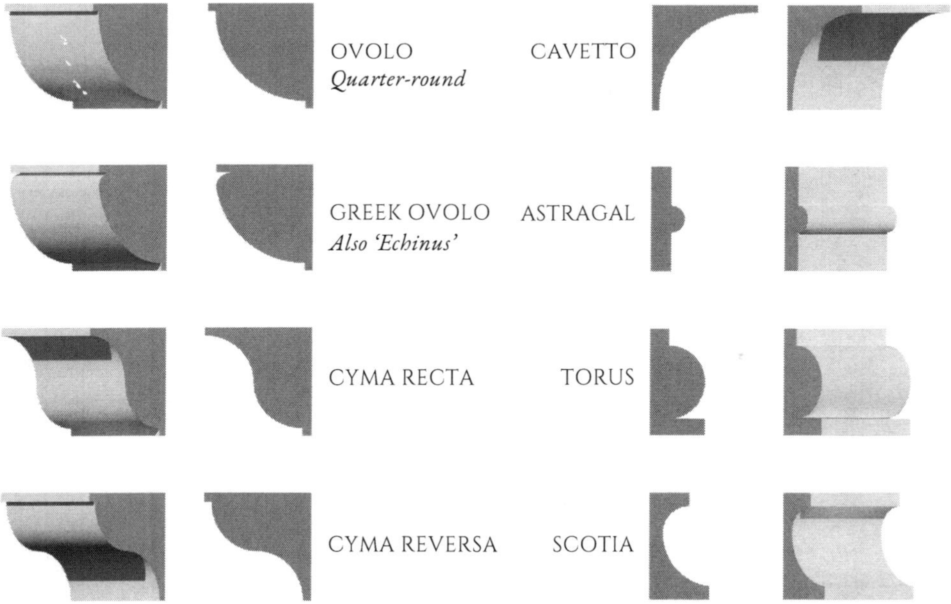

"Whoever does not have, among other branches of knowledge, an understanding of the exceedingly important art of moulding cannot be called an architect."
—Martino Longhi the Younger (1625)

- Broadly speaking, mouldings are divided into curved (above) and flat types (next page). All curved mouldings are derived from various manipulations of a quarter-circle.
- Originally, mouldings may have covered the joints between elements in early wooden structures.

MOULDINGS

Classical buildings are meant to be seen in the natural light of day, with their forms carefully moulded to produce varying contrasts of light and dark. Each moulding profile will cast a unique shadow profile (below), the most important of which are the cavetto (dark at the top) and ovolo (dark at the bottom). Again, this contrast is important as this is generally how our eyes detect form. Note: A cyma recta is simply a cavetto placed atop an ovolo, the cyma reversa is the 'reverse'.

The science or study of shadows and architectural shading is called Sciagraphy (also spelled *sciography or skiagraphy*). This discipline is used to its fullest in classical architecture. For example, even reflections from the top fillet of an architrave and the abacus of a capital may reflect light upwards, illuminating the underside of the corona of a cornice, revealing the rosettes, modillions and bed-mouldings.

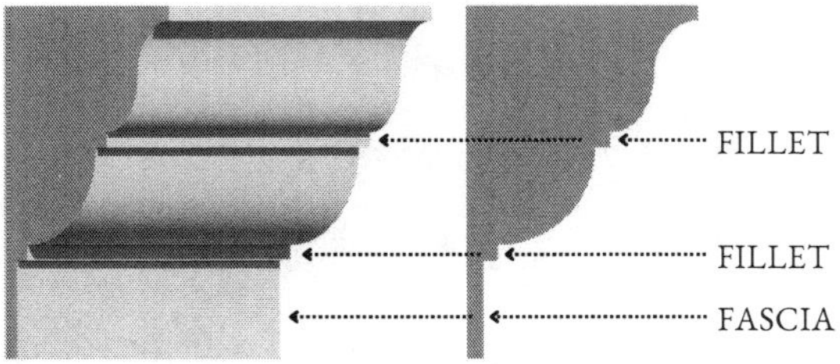

- Fillets and Fascia are flat mouldings, in contrast to the curved mouldings we have already seen.
- **Fillets** are narrow, typically square, flat bands used to distinguish and separate other mouldings like ovolos and cyma rectas (above).
- **Fascia** are much larger, flat, horizontal bands typically found as part of architraves or the corona of a cornice.
- Note: the cyma profiles are often later referred to as 'Ogee.'

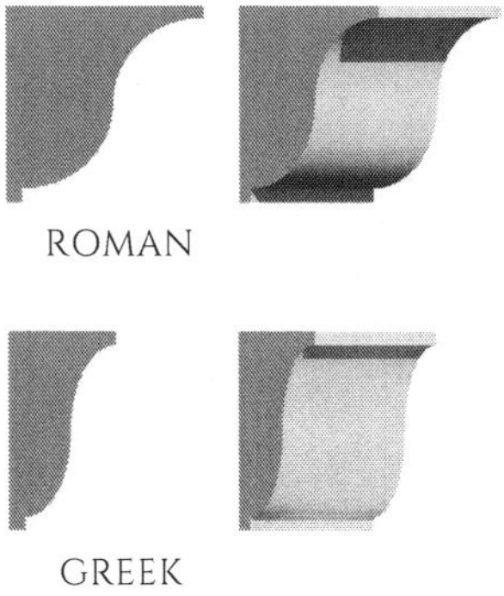

- When comparing Greek and Roman moulding profiles, Greek mouldings are usually shallower. Note: Greek profiles are not used outside of Greek architecture.

DECORATIVE MOULDINGS

Any plain moulding profile may be decorated with ornamental motifs, typically featuring natural forms like acanthus leaves. This is also called an 'enriched' moulding or an 'enrichment.'

- All decorative mouldings are shaped to match the profiles of the mouldings on the previous pages. For example, the Roman leaf pattern (below) fits the cyma reversa profile, maintaining the same shadow profile, whilst now being distinctly decorated.

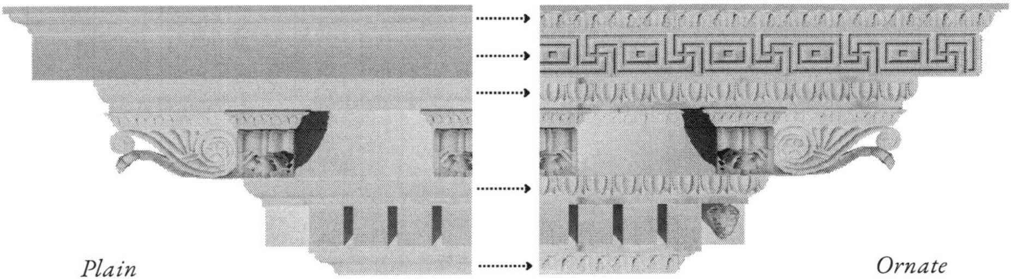

Plain *Ornate*

MOULDINGS OF A CORINTHIAN CORNICE

For many of the decorative mouldings that fit cyma profiles, the same decoration, such as the Roman leaf pattern (below), may be used for both the cyma reversa and a cyma recta. The only difference is that the decoration is inverted and oriented to fit each moulding accordingly.

CYMA RECTA

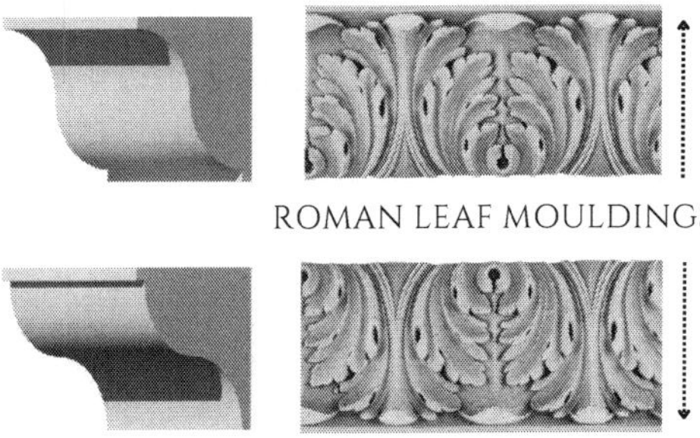

ROMAN LEAF MOULDINGS

CYMA REVERSA

- Acanthus is the most common natural motif found in classical architecture. It is used in mouldings, corbels, modillions and Corinthian capitals, and appears in all architectural styles, from Greek to Neoclassical.
- The acanthus leaf is always highly stylised (right).
- Acanthus symbolises enduring life.

ACANTHUS

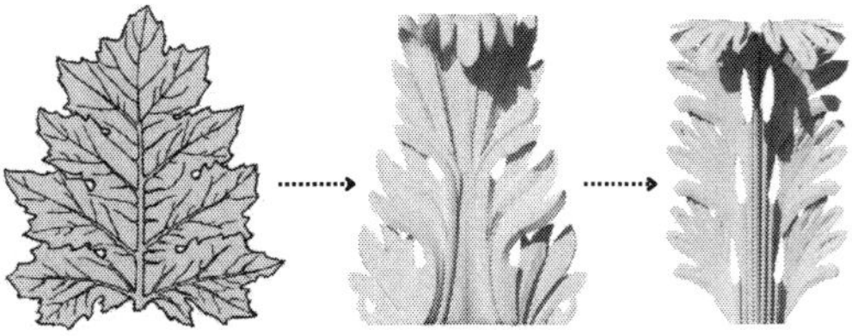

Natural acanthus leaf *Stylised acanthus leaf* *Variation*

DECORATIVE MOULDINGS

There are countless variations of **Decorative Mouldings,** particularly in later architectural styles. Therefore, the focus here will be on the most important, enduring and commonly used mouldings originating from antiquity. Each decorative moulding will note the profile it fits in **bold**; for example, the Egg-and-Dart fits the **Ovolo** profile. First are the decorative mouldings that fit curved profiles, like ovolos, cymas and astragals, followed by several 'running' or flat mouldings.

EGG AND DART

- **Ovolo**
- Thought to represent the opium poppy and its leaves.
- Greek egg-and-dart usually has 'slimmer' eggs.
- The corners of an egg-and-dart moulding are often covered with an acanthus leaf.

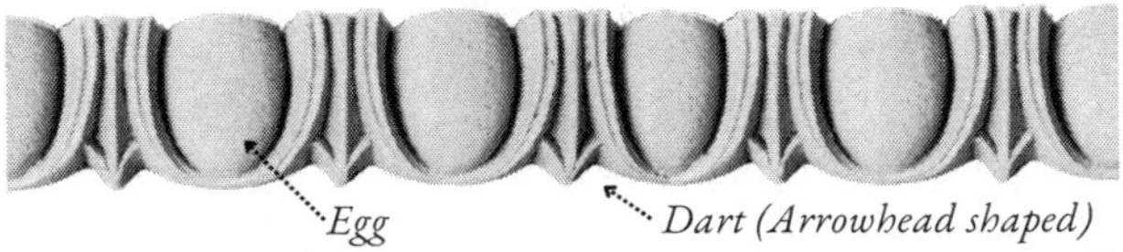

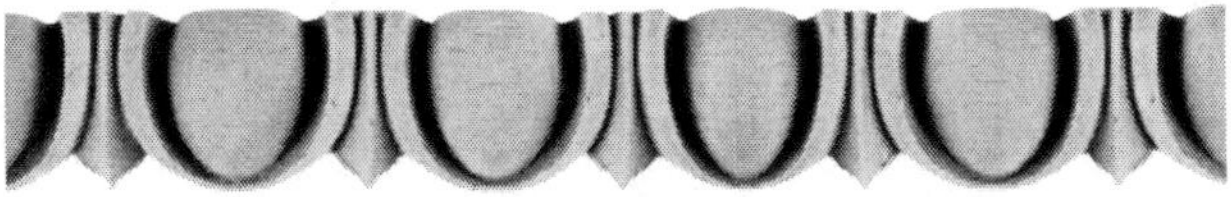

Simple variation

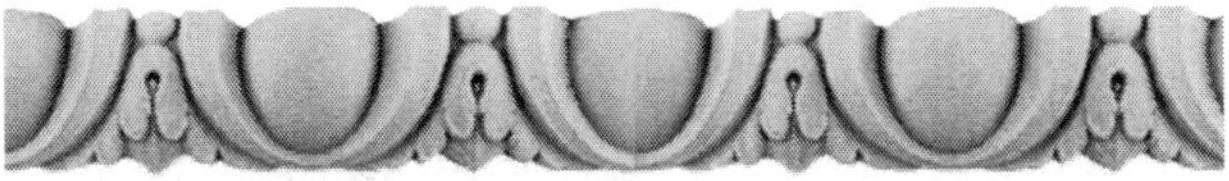

Egg-and-Leaf - ornate variation

ROMAN LEAF

- **Cyma Recta**
- **Cyma Reversa**
- Features acanthus leaf patterns.
- Roman development of the Greek leaf motif.

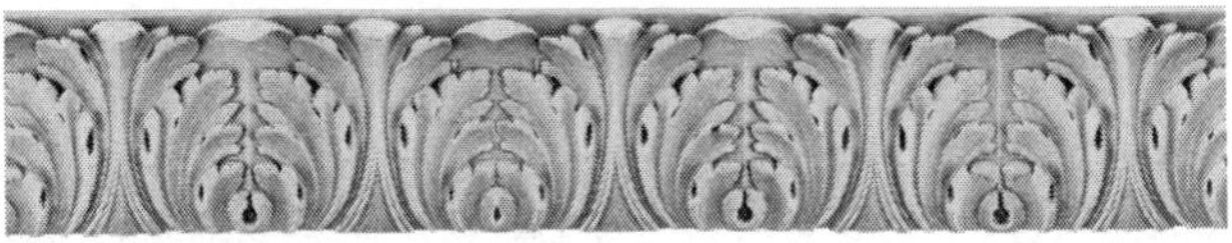

GREEK LEAF

- **Cyma Reversa**
- Thought to be a lotus leaf.
- Sometimes called leaf-and-dart, lambs-tongue, or lesbian leaf (named after the island of Lesbos).

TONGUE

- **Cyma Reversa**
- Tongues are often found in other mouldings.

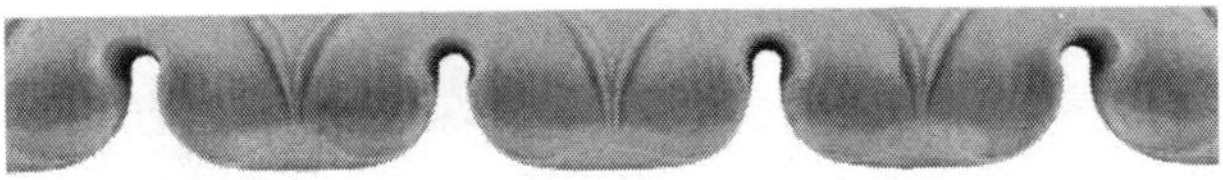

May also derive from a simplified Greek leaf (above)

DECORATIVE MOULDINGS

TOUNGE AND LEAF

- **Cyma Reversa**
- **Cyma Recta**
- Combines acanthus or lotus and tongue.
- Some also call this Roman leaf (Franz Meyer - page 129).

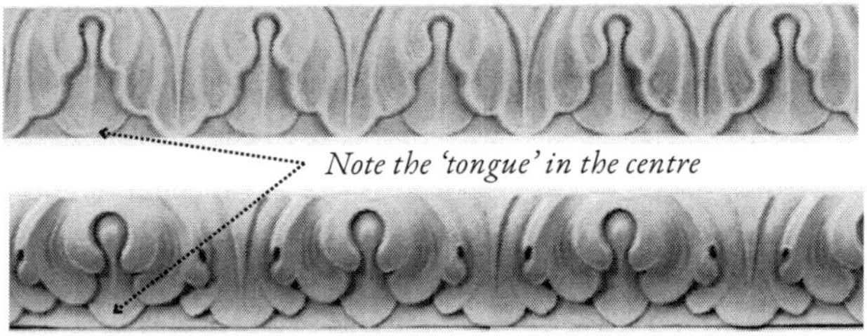

BEAD AND REEL

- **Astragal**
- Repeating chain of beads and spools or reels.
- One of the most common enrichments.
- Symbolises continuity.

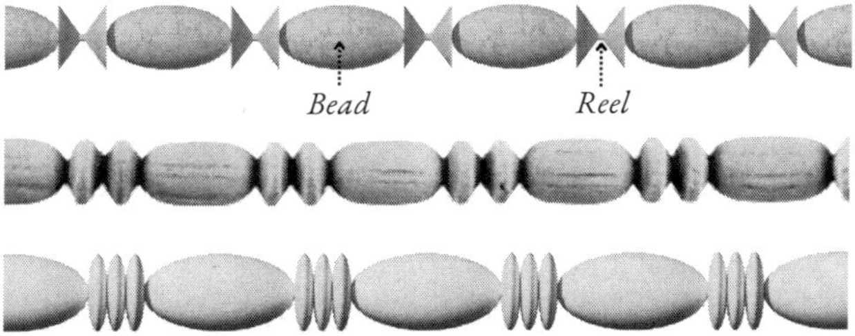

BEADING

- **Astragal/Bead**
- Chain of spherical beads.

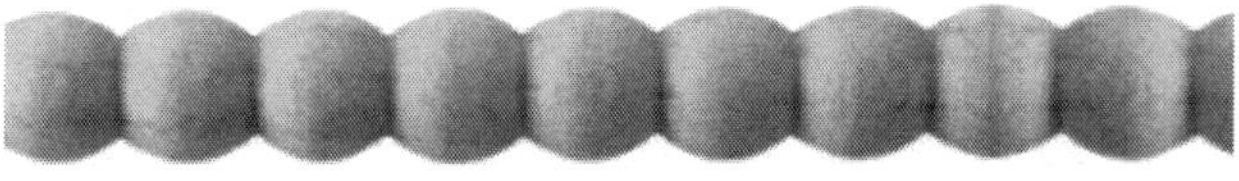

ROPE TWIST

- **Astragal**

LAUREL / BAY LEAF

- **Torus**
- **Pulvinated (curved) frieze**
- Laurel symbolises victory.
- Often, the laurel leaves are strapped or banded together (right-centre).

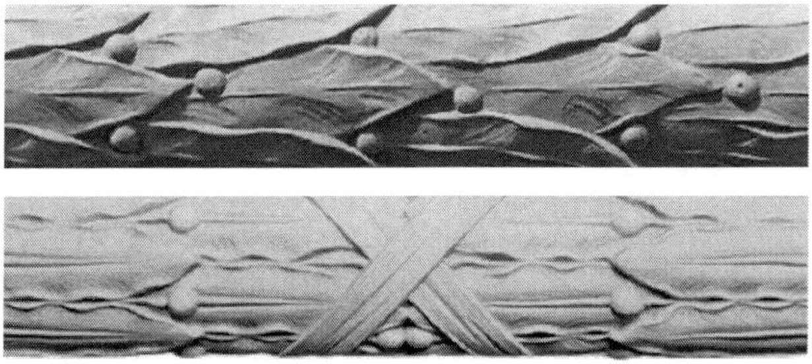

Renaissance and Neoclassical variations (above)

Greek variation

DECORATIVE RUNNING MOULDINGS

A **Running Moulding** is a continuous decorative band featuring interlocking and repeating patterns. They are typically found on flat mouldings, such as the corona, fascia or frieze. Note: some of these mouldings may also fit curved profiles.

GREEK KEY

- **Running**
- Also called a fret, fretwork or a meander pattern.
- One of the only geometric motifs.
- Popular in Greek styles.

Double Greek key

VITRUVIAN SCROLL

- **Running**
- Also called a wave pattern or a Vitruvian Wave - named after Vitruvius.
- Features stylised waves.

Decorated variation

GUILLOCHÉ

- **Running**
- **Torus**
- Interlaced 'ribbons.'
- Occurs in many variations; single, double and triple are most common.
- The single version may also be called a 'coin' pattern.

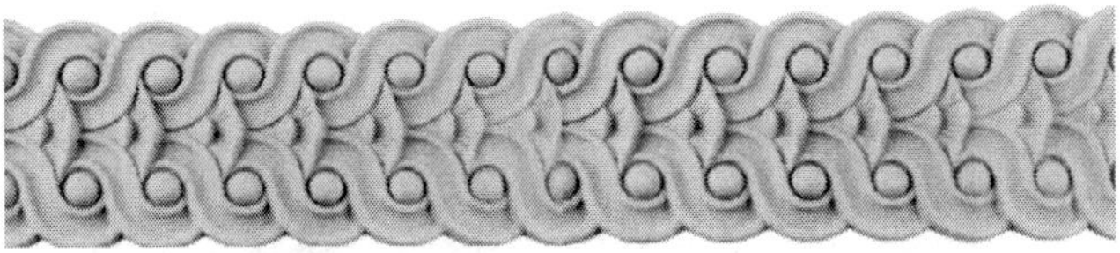

Greek knot pattern

DECORATIVE RUNNING MOULDINGS

ANTHEMION

- **Running**
- **Cyma Recta**
- Also known as the honeysuckle or the lotus palmette motif, as the flowers and plants it depicts are palmette leaves and lotus flowers.
- Also used for acroteria.

Stylised variation

ACANTHUS LEAF

- **Running**
- **Cyma Recta**
- **Cyma Reversa**
- **Ovolo**
- **Cavetto**
- Running acanthus is often called scrollwork.
- Acanthus features in many other mouldings. For example, it is seen in the Roman leaf, the tongue-and-leaf, the corners of an egg-and-dart, leaf-and-dart and as a running scrollwork.
- 'Regal' acanthus is used for taller mouldings.
- An 'Egyptian cavetto' may refer to a large cavetto, or a flat fascia moulding that only has a small cavetto at its top.

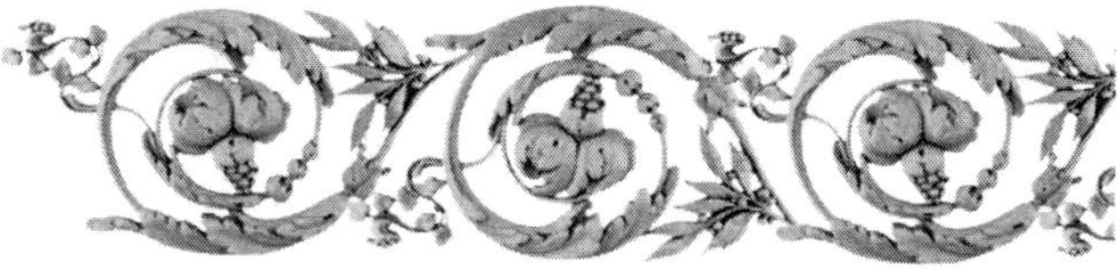

Running variations

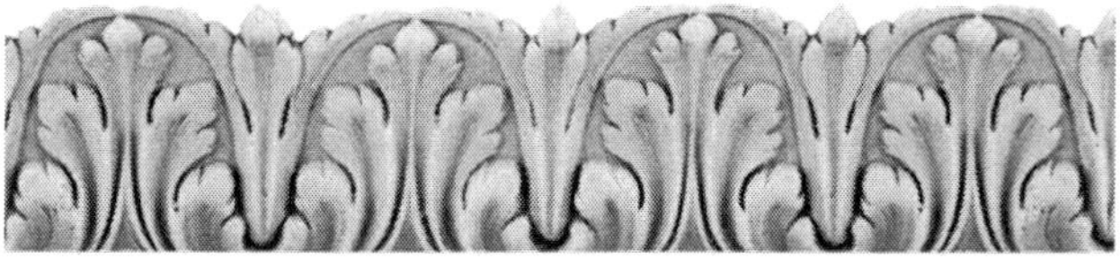

Cyma variation

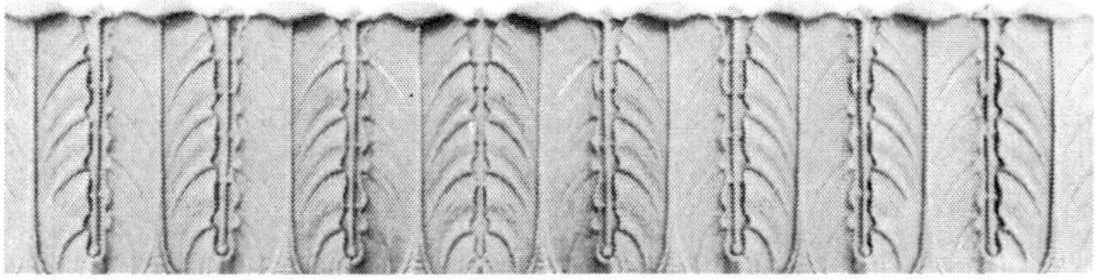

Regal variation

Egyptian cavetto variation

DENTILS & MODILLIONS

Dentil: A small rectangular block used as a repeating ornament in the bed-mould of cornices, particularly those of the Ionic and Corinthian Orders. Dentils resemble teeth, are purely ornamental and do not offer support to members above them.

Modillion: A small cantilevered (supported at only one end) bracket or block found in cornices and placed at regular intervals to support the corona and other elements above them. Modillions, typical of the Corinthian and Composite Orders, are both structural and ornamental, and are often scroll-shaped and ornately decorated.

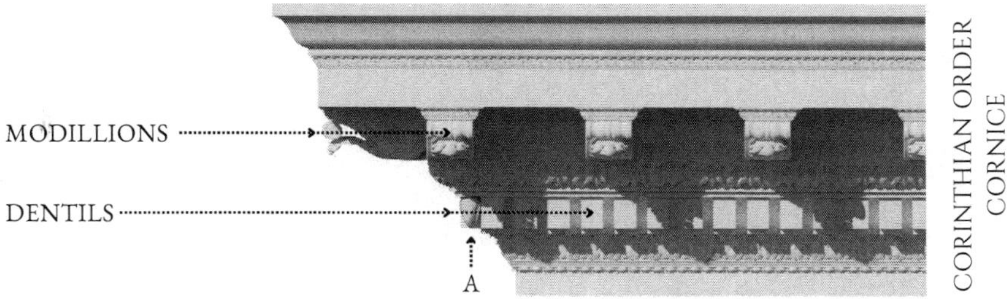

Rules for **Dentils**:

- According to Sir William Chambers, the width of a dentil should be approximately 1/9 of a diameter wide, with their height being 1.5 times their width. They should be spaced 1/18th of a diameter apart, that is, the intervals between them are half their width. *Note: 'diameters' refer to the diameter of the base of the column's shaft and are discussed further on page 42.*
- The projection of a dentil is equal to its width, thus appearing square from underneath.
- There should always be a dentil aligned with the centre line of a column (point B on next page).
- On the corners of ornate cornices, dentils may feature a pinecone ornament for decoration (A) or remain plain in simpler cornices.
- Sometimes, between the dentils, a smaller square of material is inserted, slightly breaking up the gap between the dentils. This is called a dentil-band (B).

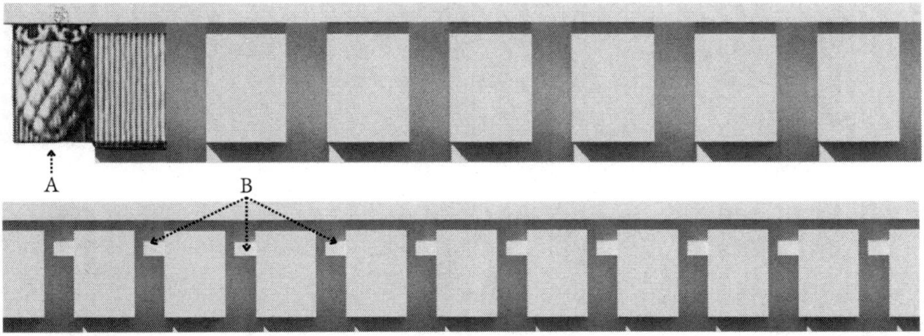

- Dentil is from the Latin *dens,* translated as 'small teeth.'
- Vitruvius states that dentils represent the ends of rafters found in early wooden Ionic structures.

MODILLIONS

Rules for **Modillions:**

- For Corinthian Order cornices, modillions are typically spaced **2/3** of a diameter apart to their centres (A), according to Sir William Chambers and James Gibbs. *Note: 'diameters' refer to the diameter of the base of the column's shaft and are discussed further on page 42.*
- For cornices of the Ionic and Composite Orders, modillions are typically spaced **1/2** a diameter apart to their centres.
- These placements are precise and ensure that modillions remain evenly spaced across a building and align with the spacing of the columns (see page 91 for column spacings).
- Modillions bust be placed directly in line with the centre of a column (B).
- At the corners of a cornice, modillions should meet perfectly (C).
- Between modillions, in the soffit of the corona, there often are coffers and rosettes (D).
- There are several variations of modillions, depending on which of the five Orders they are used with.

SIDE PROFILE

FRONT

UNDERSIDE

CORINTHIAN MODILLION

Usually highly ornate, decorated with palmette and acanthus leaves.

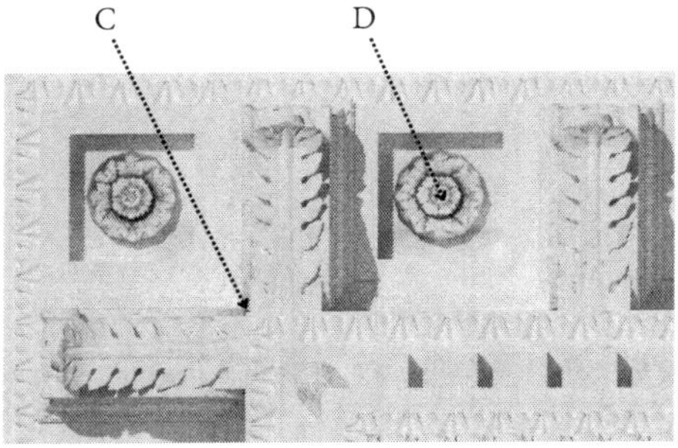

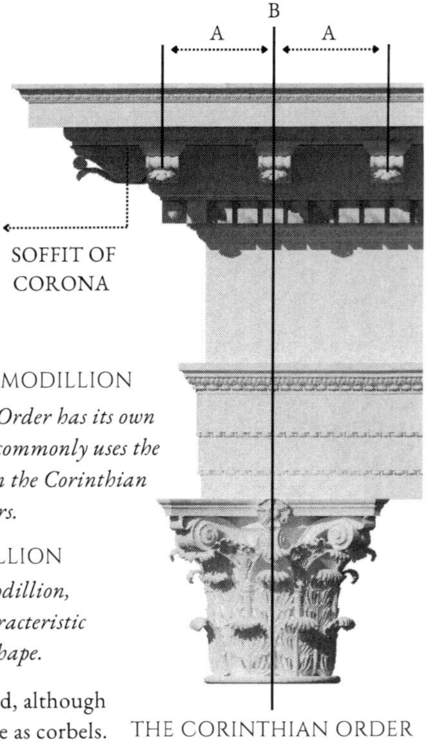

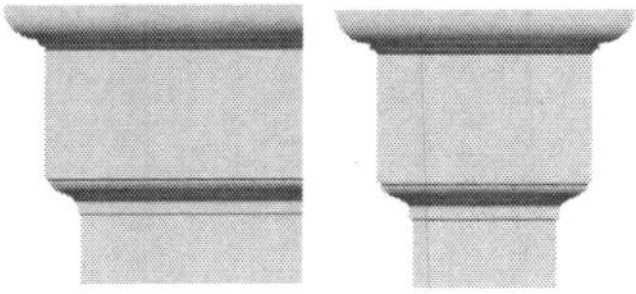

COMPOSITE MODILLION

The Composite Order has its own modillion, but commonly uses the modillions from the Corinthian and Ionic Orders.

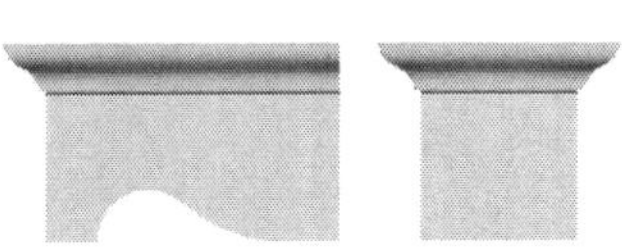

IONIC MODILLION

The simplest modillion, featuring a characteristic curved cut-out shape.

- Modillions are a form of console (page 120) and, although they are support brackets, they are not the same as corbels.

THE CORINTHIAN ORDER

ANGLED MODILLIONS, DENTILS & MUTULES

Dentils and modillions used in the raking cornice of pediments are not simply rotated to follow the angle of the pediment's slope. Instead, they remain vertically aligned, with their sides remaining parallel to the upright face of the building, rather than perpendicular to the angle of the pediment. Mutules, found in the cornices of the Doric Order, also follow this rule, with their sides remaining vertically aligned. Mutules are akin to modillions, both being cantilevered support brackets.

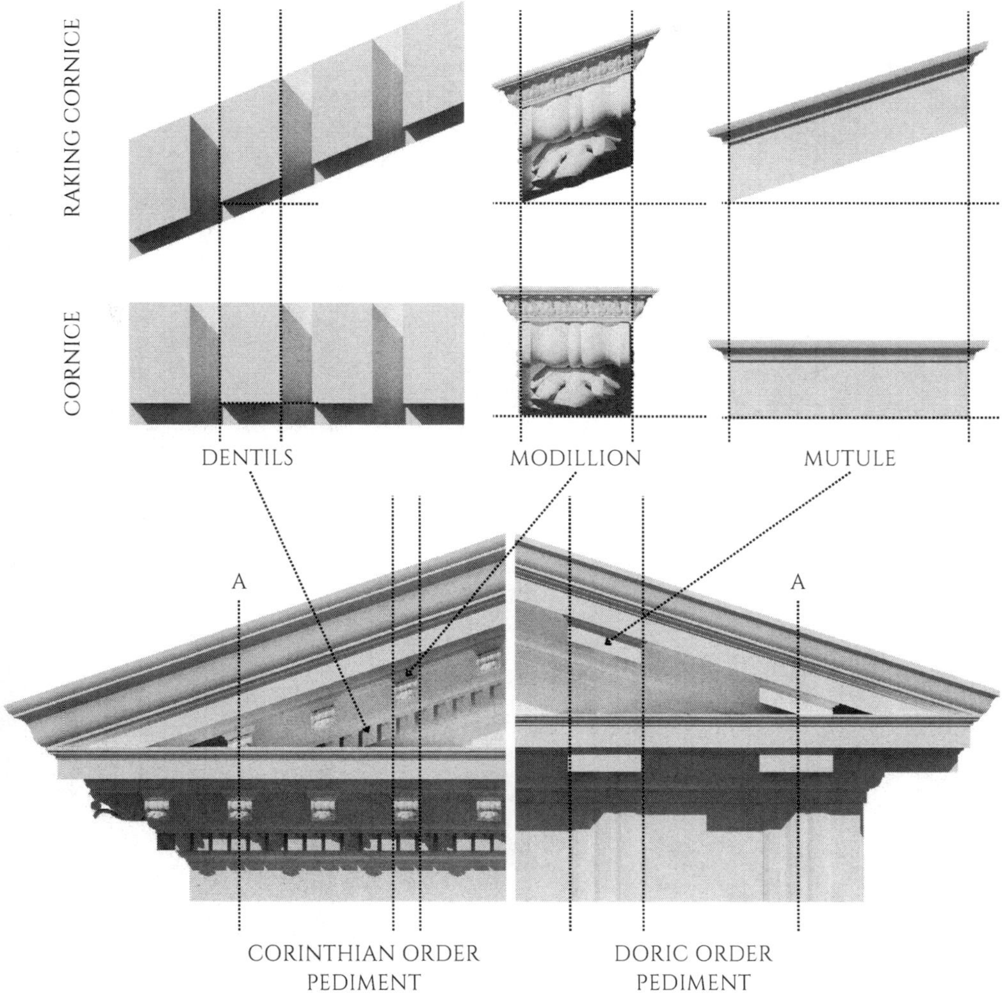

- Raking modillions, dentils and mutules are aligned with those in the horizontal cornice (A).
- Egg-and-dart mouldings usually follow this rule, though not always.
- Most other mouldings, like a Roman Leaf, do not follow this rule; they remain unchanged and simply follow the angle of the pediment.

FUNCTIONS OF CORNICE

The original purpose of a **Cornice** is to keep water from running down the sides of a building and to direct it away. A cornice of this type, inherited from earlier wooden constructions, is sometimes referred to as an 'eave cornice.' Cornice may be used alone or as part of a full entablature.

- At the top of a cornice, between points A and B, there is a downward-sloping section called a 'wash.' This ensures that rainwater runs off the top of the cornice rather than into the building. Note: this feature is often absent from architectural drawings of entablatures but nevertheless is present in actual constructions.
- All cornices should have a 'drip' (C) at the bottom edge of the corona also to direct water away from the building. Water will drip downwards from this point (C) to (D).
- Additionally, cornices may have channels (E) carved into their tops so they can act as gutters, capturing and directing rainwater away from the roof and building.

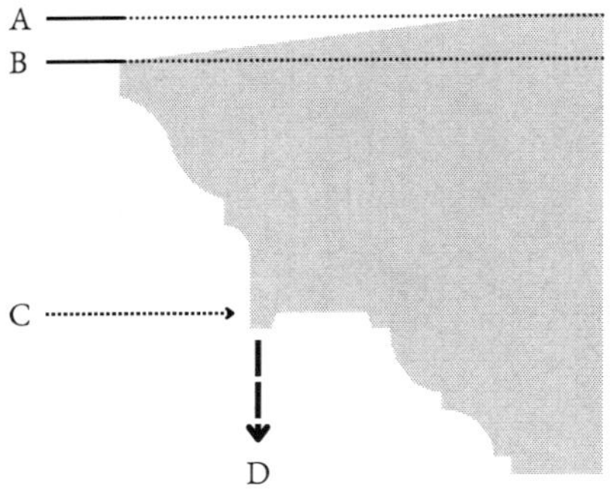

DRIP CROSS SECTION

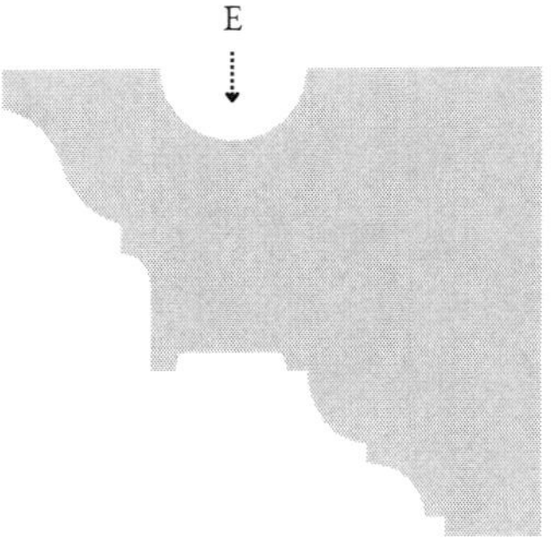

GUTTER CROSS SECTION

Cornices, whilst functional, are also beautiful, primarily due to their proportions and the variety of mouldings from which they are comprised. Historically, many architects and authors have noted that cornices may appear to be so harmonious because they often share the same proportions as the human head or face, creating a familiar, quasi-natural form that the brain instinctively identifies as beautiful.

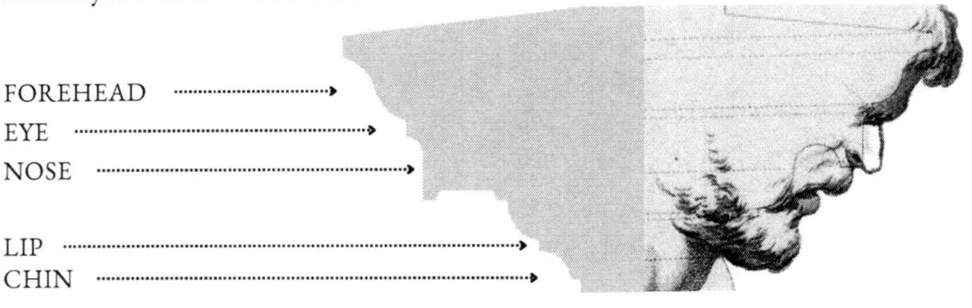

CORNICE FACE PROFILE

According to the French architect Jacques-François Blondel

- A drip or gutter would ordinarily be hidden from view, as seen in the entablature on page 18. The cornice examples on this page are of the Tuscan Order.

PART II
THE FIVE ORDERS

TUSCAN	DORIC	IONIC	CORINTHIAN	COMPOSITE
1:7	1:8	1:9	1:10	1:10

Roman invention (Renaissance canon)

The three classical Greek Orders

Roman invention (Renaissance canon)

THE ORDERS & A BRIEF OVERVIEW

The five Orders of architecture, **Tuscan, Doric, Ionic, Corinthian** and **Composite,** are systems of architectural proportion and design. Originating in ancient Greece, the Orders were heavily developed by the Romans and codified by Vitruvius in the first century BC. The Orders were since further refined by Renaissance architects like Andrea Palladio (b. 1508), defined by proponents of the Baroque movement such as James Gibbs (b. 1682), and perfected by Neoclassical architects such as Sir William Chambers (b. 1723). The Orders are the backbone of classical architecture and form the foundations for much of Western architecture, having guided construction for centuries, from temples to banks, libraries to houses, and monuments to churches, from Rome to London, Paris, New York and beyond.

Each Order has a different history, distinct proportions, details, and decorative elements, especially in their capitals and entablatures. We will examine each each of the five Orders through a brief historical and structural overview, outline precise design details, and explore a selection of variations and examples. There are no surviving Greek texts on their architecture; consequently, we will draw upon textual sources from Roman, Renaissance, Baroque, and Neoclassical architects. All the architects listed below wrote historically significant texts, which also serve as the citations for the rest of this book:

- Vitruvius *(c. 80 - 15 BC)* - Roman
- Giacomo B. Vignola *(1507 - 1573 AD)* - Renaissance
- Andrea Palladio *(1508 - 1580 AD)* - Renaissance - Inspired the later Palladian movement
- **James Gibbs** *(1682 - 1754 AD)* - Baroque
- **Sir William Chambers** *(1723 - 1796 AD)* - Neoclassical

All these authors follow standardised designs, ultimately owing their approach to Vitruvius. However, each has their own individual organisation and proportions for the Orders, shaped by the opinion and taste of each architect. Artistic interpretation often takes precedence over strict rules. Consequently, classical architecture is note necessarily a set of 'rules' set in stone; it is often understood as a series of 'guidelines.' To quote the Renaissance painter, sculptor and architect Michelangelo (1475 -1564): "My eye is my measure." A little artistic creativity is always in order.

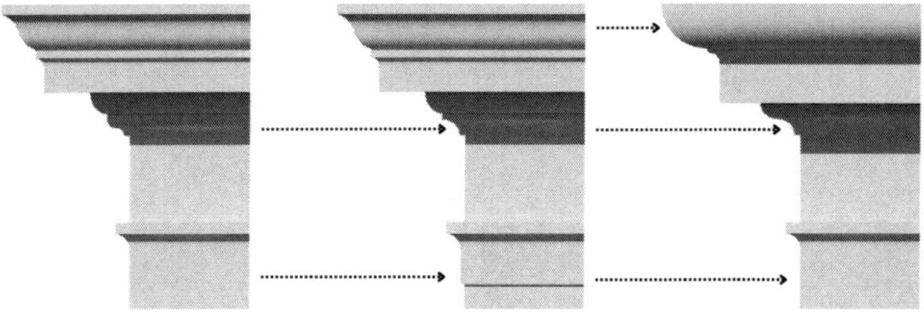

Sir William Chambers *James Gibbs* *G. B. da Vignola*

TUSCAN ENTABLATURE VARIATIONS

- That said, it is also unwise to stray too far from these guidelines. It is very important that the use of the Orders remains proportional, beautiful, and sufficiently strong. Otherwise, one risks creating unrefined, less attractive and weaker structures, that lack historical continuity.

THE ORDERS & PROPORTION

The five Orders are often represented, as on page 39, with the Tuscan Order appearing 'short' and the Corinthian Order 'tall.' Below is an alternative, more sensible approach: using columns of equal height, as they are typically employed in actual buildings. It becomes clear that, with the graduation of the Orders, columns get slimmer and not necessarily taller, as is often depicted. This comparison better illustrates the thickness and strength of the Tuscan and Doric Orders, and the elegant and refined character of the Ionic, Corinthian and Composite Orders.

- These are idealised layouts, most like those of Baroque and Neoclassical architecture.
- Regardless of the Order, the entablature is usually 1/4 of the height of the column.
- The pedestal is usually 3/10 of the height of the column.
- Ratios below refer to proportion of the shaft's base diameter to the total column height.

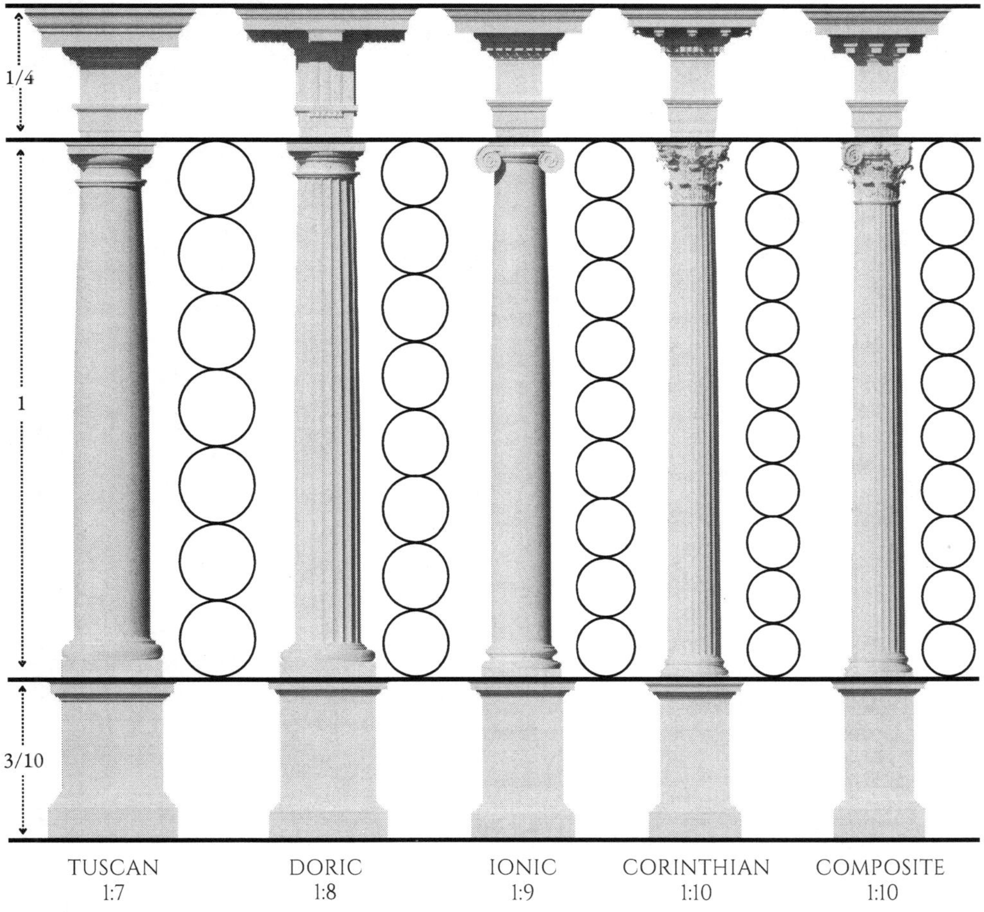

- Note: Vitruvius used slightly thicker base-diameter to column-height ratios: Tuscan 1:6, Doric 1:7, Ionic 1:8, and Corinthian and Composite 1:9.

PROPORTION: DIAMETERS & MINUTES

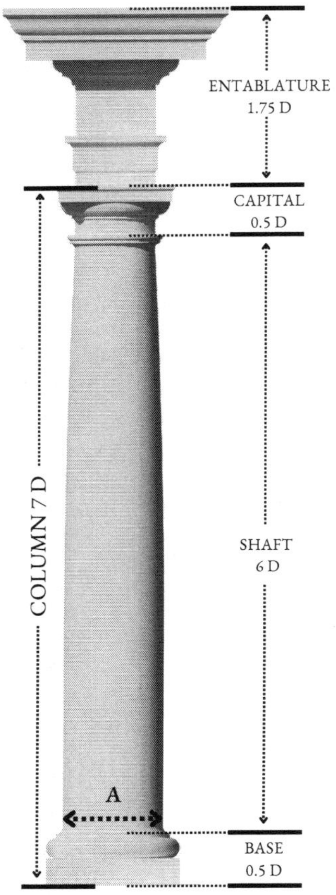

THE TUSCAN ORDER

Diameters

The **Diameter**, sometimes called a module, refers to the width of a column's shaft at its base (point A). Diameters are used to define the proportions of the rest of the Order, such as the height of the capital and entablature, and even the rest of the building, including column spacings and door sizes. This system ensures the whole structure remains proportional to itself.

Minutes

A **Minute** is a simple fraction, equal to 1/60th of a diameter. For example, 45 minutes equals 0.75 diameters. Historically, this unit has helped architects proportion finer details, such as the sizes of mouldings in entablatures or column bases. Throughout this book:

- **1 Diameter always refers to 60 minutes.**
- **Abbreviations are used: D = Diameter, M = Minutes.**

Examples

1) In the Tuscan Order to the left, let us assume it used around a porch that is 3.15 meters tall. Adding the 7-diameter column height to the 1.75-diameter entablature height, gives a total of 8.75 diameters for the total porch height. Dividing the 3.15m by 8.75 results in a base diameter of 36cm.

2) This also means that each minute in the Tuscan cornice below equals 0.6cm (36 divided by 60 = 0.6). As the cyma recta (point B) is 11.25 minutes tall, using our calculated value of 0.6cm per minute, we know the cyma recta is therefore 6.75cm tall. Naturally, the same logic applies when using feet and inches, and for the other Orders.

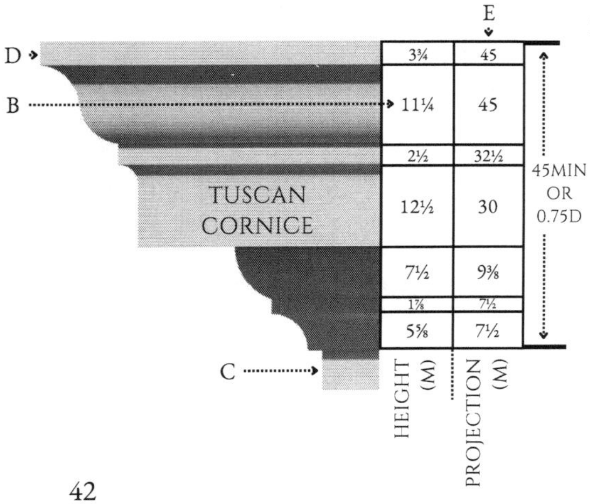

Height & Projection

- The diagram to the left is how the Orders are proportioned throughout this book.
- The **Heights** indicate how tall each individual moulding is. This are *non-cumulative* - point B represents only the height of the cyma recta.
- **Projections** show how far each element extends outward from the edge of the frieze (point C). These measurements are *cumulative* - point D projects a total of 45 minutes outward from point C, as noted at point E.

THE TUSCAN ORDER

TUSCAN ENTABLATURE
According to James Gibbs

THE TUSCAN ORDER

The **Tuscan Order** is the simplest and least decorated of all the Orders. Developed by the Romans, it is likely a simplification of the Doric Order, though some argue it is derived from early Etruscan architecture (Tuscany, Italy). Being the bulkiest and most 'solid' Order, it is used to convey strength and simplicity, and is ideal for civic, rustic and utilitarian buildings.

The Tuscan Order is distinguished by:

- 1:7 shaft-diameter to column-height ratio
- Plain entablature
- Plain capital with astragal
- No dentils, modillions or coffers in the cornice
- Unfluted column
- All mouldings are devoid of ornamentation

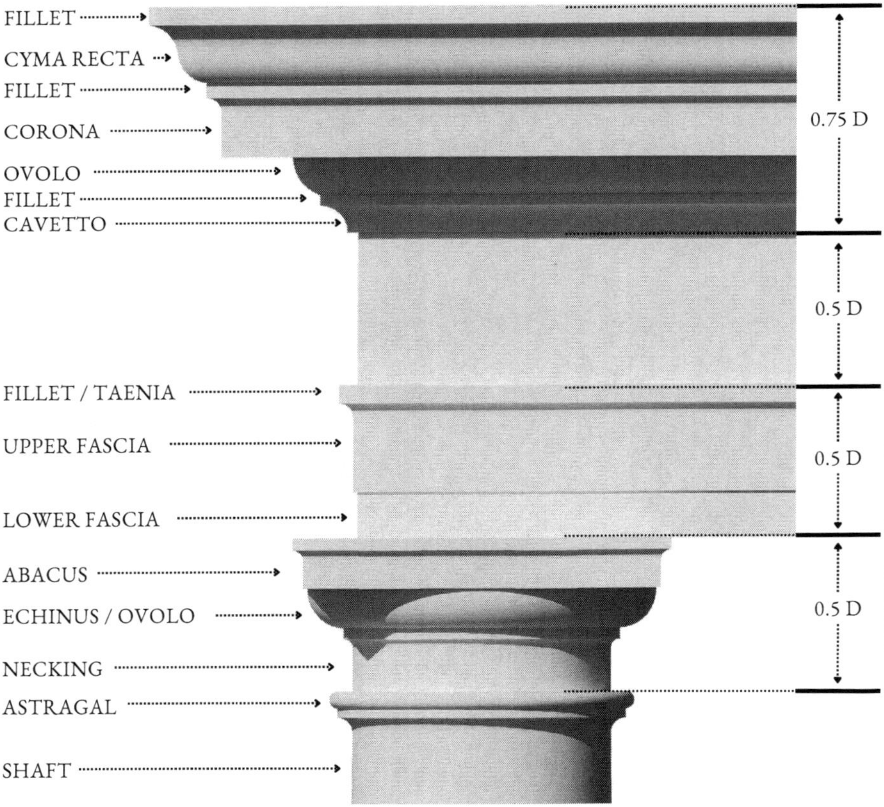

TUSCAN ENTABLATURE
According to James Gibbs

- The Tuscan Order was popularised by architects of the Italian Renaissance and was commonly used from the Renaissance onwards.
- Compared to the other Orders, the Tuscan Order is more frequently rusticated (page 103-4).

ASPECTS OF THE TUSCAN ORDER

Note: Changes of scale

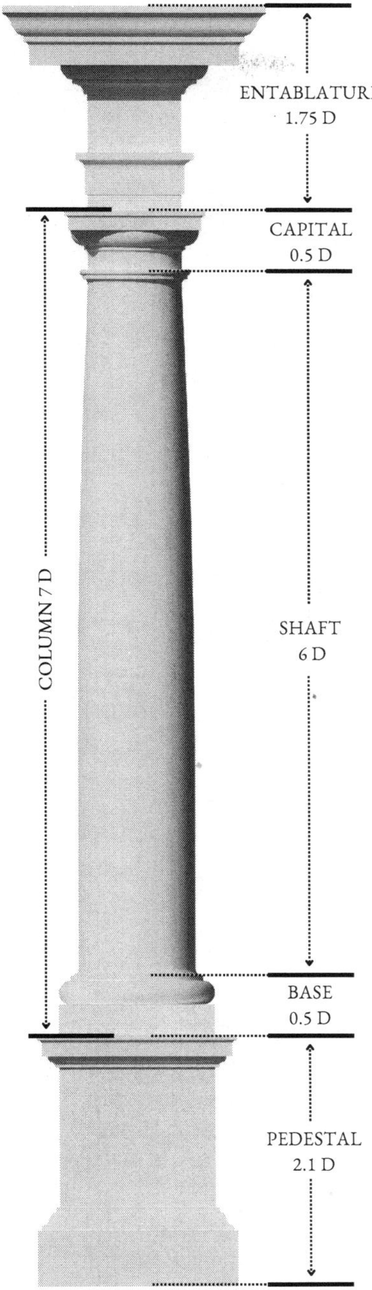

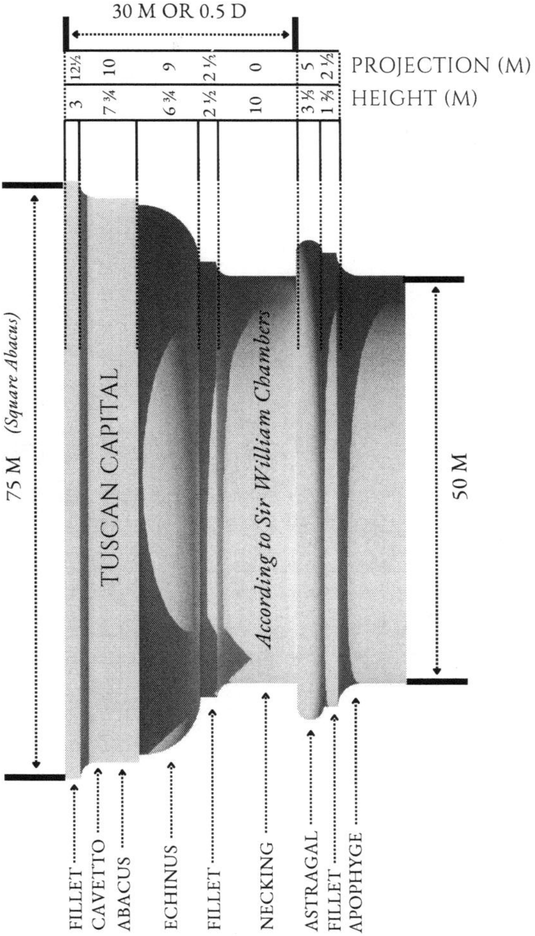

ASPECTS OF THE TUSCAN ORDER

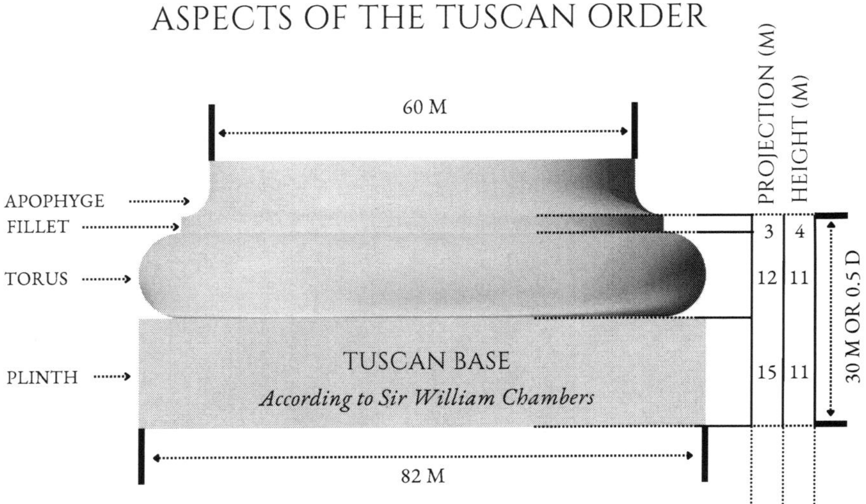

Note: Changes of scale

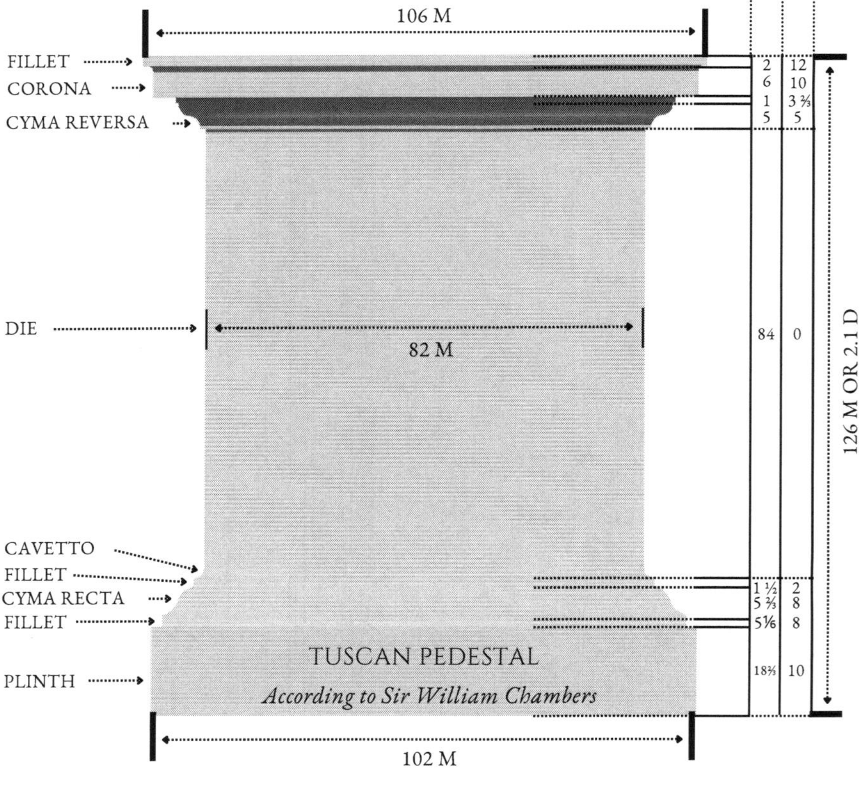

TUSCAN ENTABLATURE IN DETAIL

ENTABLATURE

	HEIGHT (MINUTES)	PROJECTION (MINUTES)
45M OR 0.75D	3¾	45
	11¼	45
	2½	32½
	12½	30
	7½	13⅛
	1⅞	7½
	5⅝	7½
30M OR 0.5D	30	0
30M OR 0.5D	5	5
	17	1⅓
	8	0

SOFFIT OF CORNICE

	PROJECTION (MINUTES)
45M OR 0.75D	1⅞
	5⅝
	5⅝
	16⅞
	2½
	12½

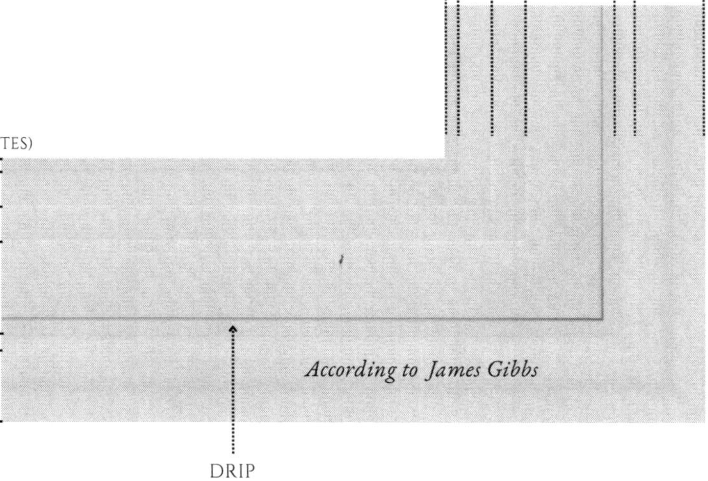

- Note that James Gibbs, in his literary works, does not use minutes, but instead a system of direct proportionality. Herein, his proportions have been translated into minutes.

VARIATIONS OF THE TUSCAN ORDER

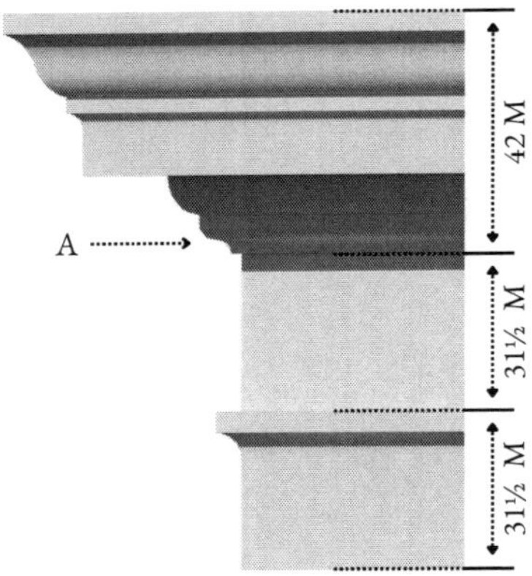

Sir William Chambers

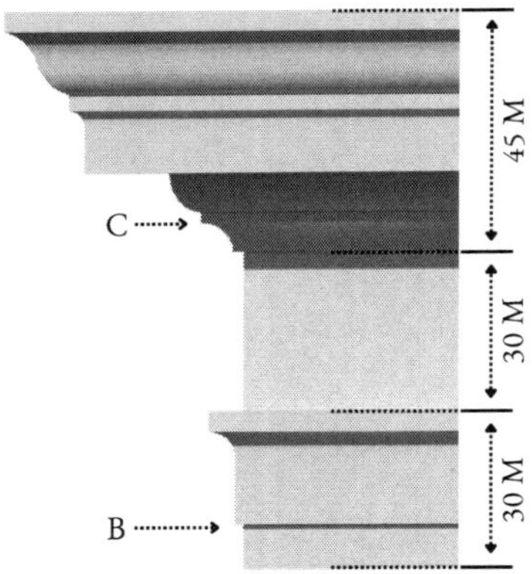

James Gibbs

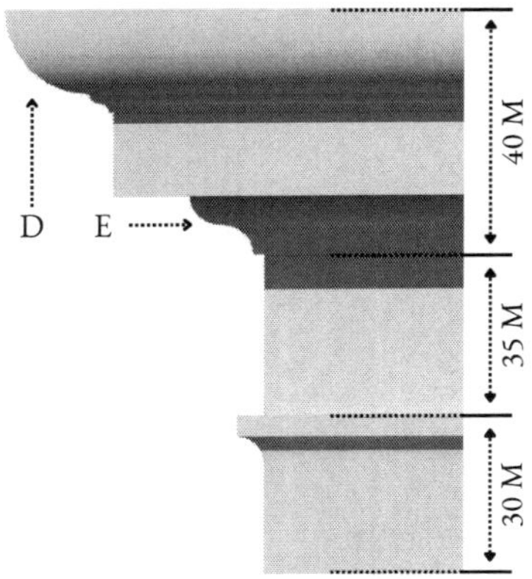

G. B. Vignola

The variations within the Tuscan Order are minimal, due to its lack of ornamentation and fewer mouldings. This simplicity has been consistently observed by all historical architects.

- Vitruvius and Serlio used a shorter diameter-to-height ratio of 1:6.
- Andrea Palladio and Sir William Chambers noted that the Tuscan Order may use a taller column ratio of 1:7.5, typically for door porticos where additional height is desired.
- Again, the Tuscan Order is favoured for civic, rustic and vernacular architecture.
- Chambers uses a cyma reversa in the bed-mould instead of a cavetto (A), based on his theory that lower mouldings should provide suitable support.
- Gibbs uses an architrave that is split into two fasciae (B), and a more traditional cavetto-fillet-ovolo bed-mould (C).
- Vignola unusually ends the top of the cornice with an ovolo instead of a fillet (D), and omits the fillet in the bed-mould (E).
- Though almost never decorated, the Tuscan Order of the colonnade at St Peter's Square, Rome, has a dentil-band in the bed-mould of its cornice.

Note: It can be difficult to differentiate between Tuscan and Doric columns. One distinguishing feature is that the Doric capital usually has a cyma reversa at the top instead of a cavetto (F). More definitively, the entablature above the capital should provide the clearest distinction: Doric entablatures should always include triglyphs and metopes in their friezes (see page 52).

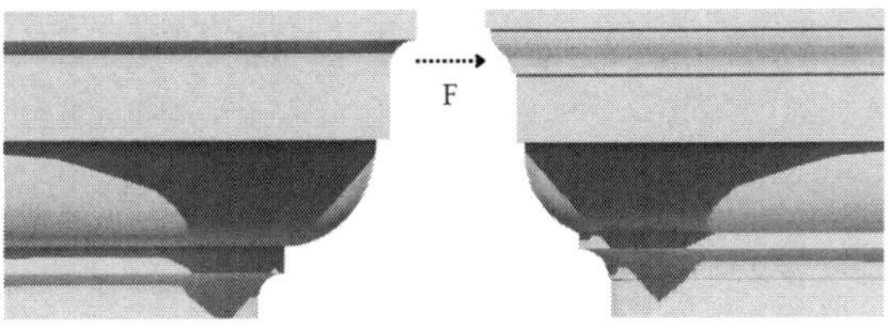

TUSCAN CAPITAL DORIC CAPITAL

Famous examples: *Bernini's Colonnade - St Peter's Square, Rome; Amphitheatre of Verona; Palazzo Massimo alle Colonne - Rome; Christ Church, Spitalfields, London.*

EXAMPLE OF THE TUSCAN ORDER

BERNINI'S COLONNADE, ST PETER'S SQUARE, THE VATICAN CITY (~1667 AD)

Bernini's colonnade is a grand Baroque ensemble forming an elliptical piazza, created by a series of Tuscan columns that are organised into rows of four. Built between 1656 and 1667, it is one of the most famous, and more decorated variations of the Tuscan Order.

THE DORIC ORDER

DORIC ENTABLATURE
According to William R. Ware

THE DORIC ORDER

The **Doric Order** is the oldest (seventh century BC), simplest and thickest of the three Orders of classical Greek architecture (page 39). Next to the Tuscan Order, the Doric is the second bulkiest Order and is traditionally regarded as the most 'masculine.' It is often used for civic and militaristic architecture, as it is thought to symbolise strength, order, permanence, and moral integrity.

The Doric Order is distinguished by:

- 1:8 shaft-diameter to column-height ratio
- Frieze of alternating triglyphs and metopes
- Bed-mould that features mutules, (mutules are similar to modillions)
- Plain architrave
- Any other curved mouldings may be enriched with ornamentation
- Often fluted; if so, with 20 flutes

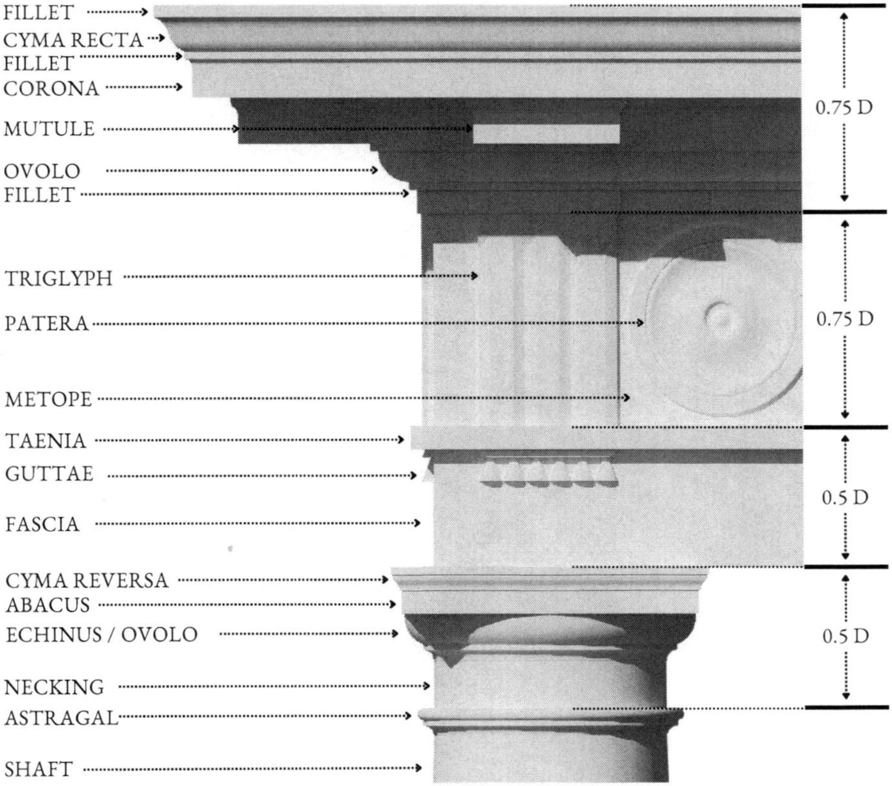

MUTULARY DORIC ENTABLATURE

According to James Gibbs

- A key distinctive feature of the Doric Order is the triglyphs, metopes and mutules that decorate the entablature. Doric entablatures with mutules are referred to as 'mutulary' Doric (above).

DORIC ORDER DECORATIONS: TRIGLYPHS & MUTULES

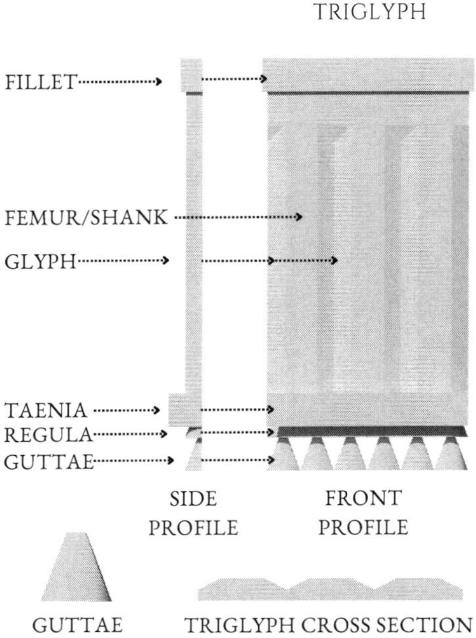

- **Triglyphs** are vertical rectangular panels that appear in repeating rows between metopes (see next page) along the friezes of Doric entablatures.
- Each triglyph has three complete triangular channels, called glyphs - two full glyphs in the middle and two half-glyphs on the sides, which together form the third glyph of the *tri*-glyph. The remaining flat parts between them are called femurs or shanks.
- Triglyphs imitate the ends of wooden beams from earlier wooden temples. At their base, there are normally six guttae - conical or pyramidal representations of pegs that may have secured the beams in place.
- The taenia is a large fillet; this term is only used for Doric architraves.
- Triglyphs are 1/2 a diameter wide, 3/4 of a diameter tall and project ~ 1/24 of a diameter from the frieze.

- **Mutules** are a type of cantilevered support bracket that help support the very wide Doric corona. They occur in repeating rows called a mutulary band.
- The undersides of mutules, like triglyphs, are decorated with guttae. These are usually arranged in a 6x6 square grid.
- Triglyphs and mutules are always in line with each other (A, B) and are always directly above the centreline of a column (A on page 54).
- Both triglyphs and mutules are spaced 1 ¼ diameters apart, centre to centre.

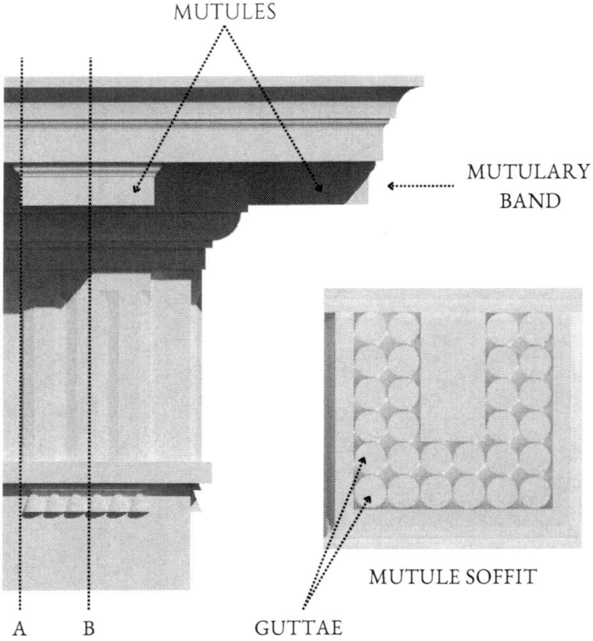

DORIC ORDER DECORATIONS: METOPES

A **Metope** is the square or rectangular space between two triglyphs in Doric friezes. Metopes may be left plain or often decorated with relief sculpture. Below are the two most common sculptural variations:

PATERAE

- A shallow, circular ornamental dish originally used in ancient rituals and sacrificial ceremonies.

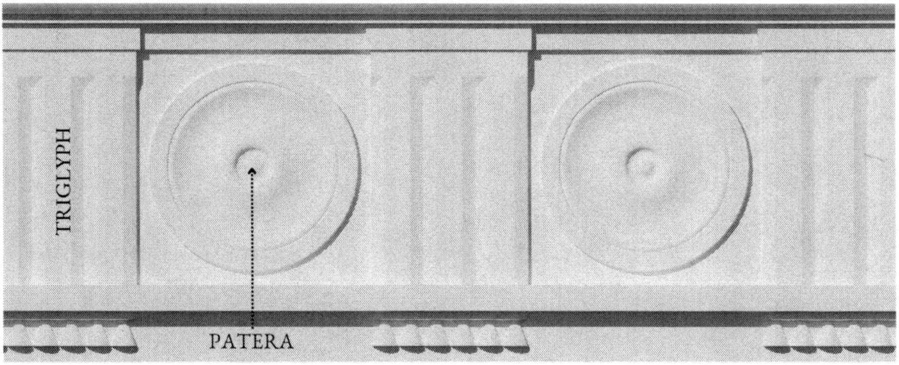

BUCRANIA

- A bucranium represents the skull of an ox and is associated with sacrifice. They often adorned with floral garlands or scrollwork. *Bucrania* is the plural; *bucranium* is the singular form.

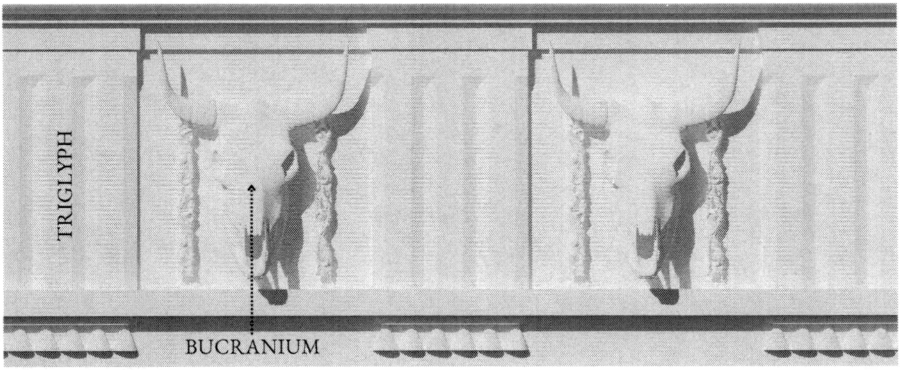

- Metopes are usually **3/4** of a diameter in height and width.
- Although bucrania and paterae are by far the most common decorations, metopes may also include figures such as people, gods, mythical creatures or other ornaments like urns, tools or flowers. Often, a combination of different decorations may be used together.
- Metope decorations may also denote a building's function. For example, a library built in the Doric Order might feature sculptural depictions of books as its metope decorations.

ASPECTS OF THE DORIC ORDER

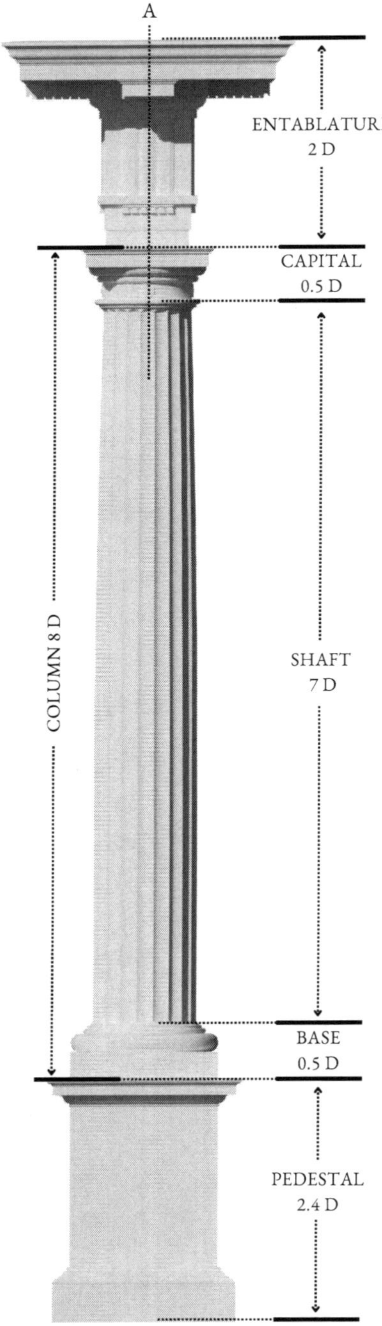

Note: Changes of scale

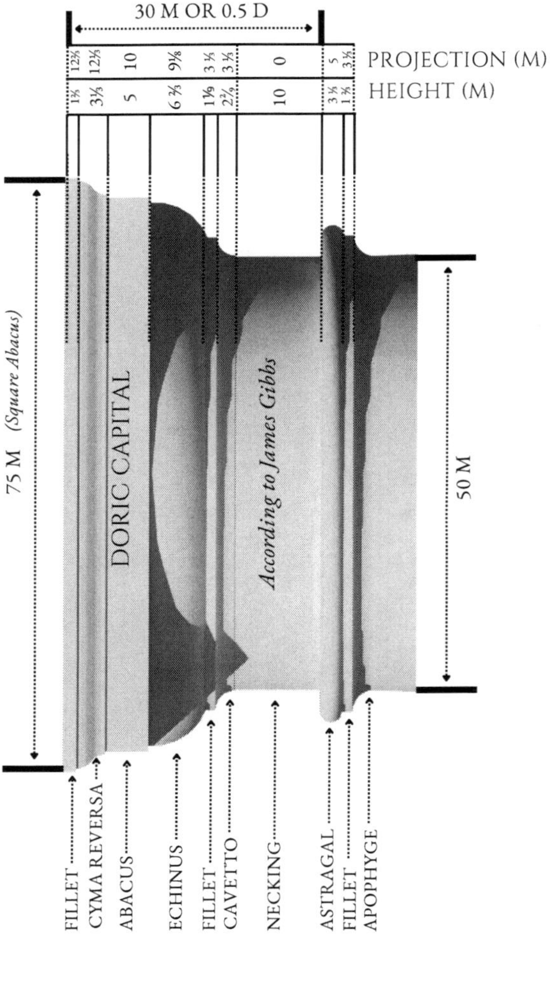

ASPECTS OF THE DORIC ORDER

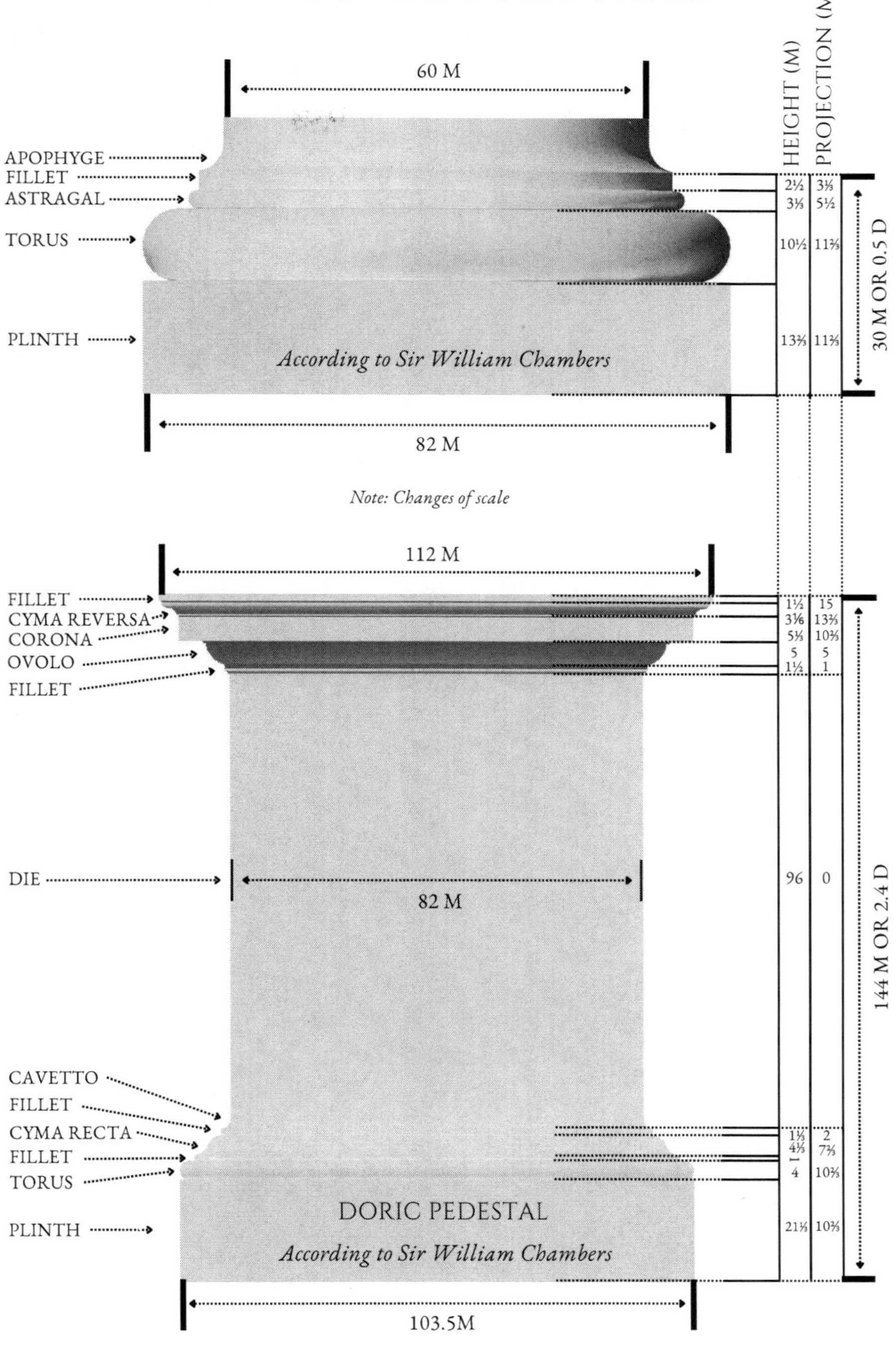

DORIC ENTABLATURE IN DETAIL

ENTABLATURE

	HEIGHT (MINUTES)	PROJECTION (MINUTES)
45M OR 0.75D	2½	57
	7	50
	1¼	49
	2¾	48¼
	8¾	45
	2¾	43¼
	7½	40
	1	10
	5¼	9
	1¼	4
	5	3½
45M OR 0.75D	45	0
30M OR 0.5D	5	3½
	1½	2¼
	4	3½
	15½	0

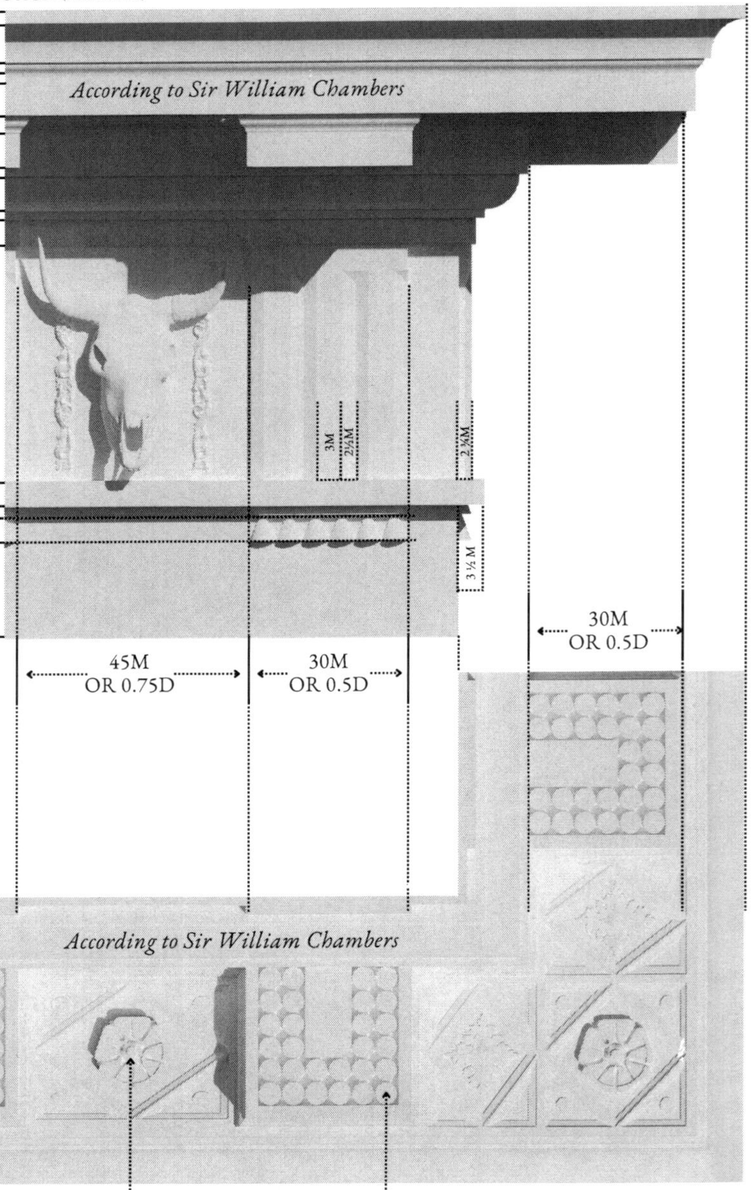

SOFFIT OF CORNICE

	PROJECTION (MINUTES)
57M OR 0.95D	3½
	½
	5
	1
	30
	3¼
	1¾
	[illegible]
	8

ORIGINS: THE ANCIENT GREEK DORIC ORDER

The **Greek Doric Order** was developed in the lands occupied by the Dorians, one of the four principal peoples of classical Greece, probably in the late seventh century BC. Originally, the Doric Order was used in wooden structures. The first stone Doric temples replaced these earlier wooden versions and were built in the same style, retaining many of their features, such as triglyphs, mutules and guttae. This retention of the wooden forms in stone is known as a *skeuomorph*. Although the ancient Greek Doric Order is the 'original' version, it was used far less frequently from the Roman period onward, as the Romans adapted it significantly. There are notable proportional and ornamental differences between classical Greek Doric and the more 'modern' Roman Doric already covered on the previous pages:

- Much thicker shaft-diameter to column-height ratio, often between 1:5 and 1:6.
- Columns have no bases or pedestals; instead, they meet the stylobate directly.
- Fluting is always required for Greek Doric columns, with the flutes normally meeting at an arris not a fillet.
- Entasis begins at the bottom of the shaft, with the shaft gradually diminishing across its full height. The degree of entasis is more variable, sometimes it is exaggerated whilst at other times it is nearly imperceptible.
- The architrave is much taller, usually the same size as the frieze, and is always of one fascia.
- Greek Doric architecture is from where we get the frieze of alternating metopes and triglyphs (with guttae), which are the stylised memories of the crossbeams and retaining pegs from the wooden structures that preceded those in stone.
- Triglyphs used at the corners of the frieze are not placed directly over a column, but are instead pushed to the edge (see next page), resulting in a rectangular metope beside them, and a slightly reduced column spacing for the corner columns.
- Metopes are typically decorated with bucrania and paterae, as well as figures and other ornaments.
- Cornices have much simpler, squarer and reduced profiles.
- Mutules are angled downward in line with the angle of the pediment, and are arranged in a 6x3 grid rather than a 6x6 square.
- Mutules occur above both the triglyphs and the metopes, instead of only above the triglyphs as seen in the Roman style.
- Pediments are much shallower, typically ranging from 12 to 16 degrees, and are usually decorated with statuary and sculpture.
- Anthemion acroteria are nearly always present.
- Mutules are never used in the raking cornice. In Greek architectural theory, they would not have appeared in the pediment of a wooden structure, as the were once crossbeams and not part of the roof.

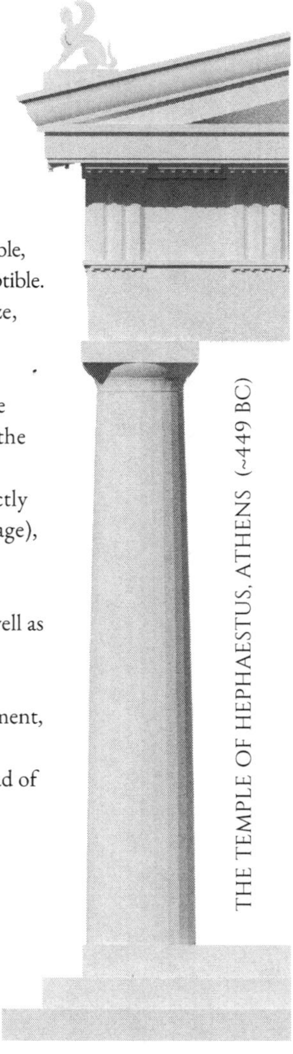

THE TEMPLE OF HEPHAESTUS, ATHENS (~449 BC)

THE GREEK DORIC ORDER

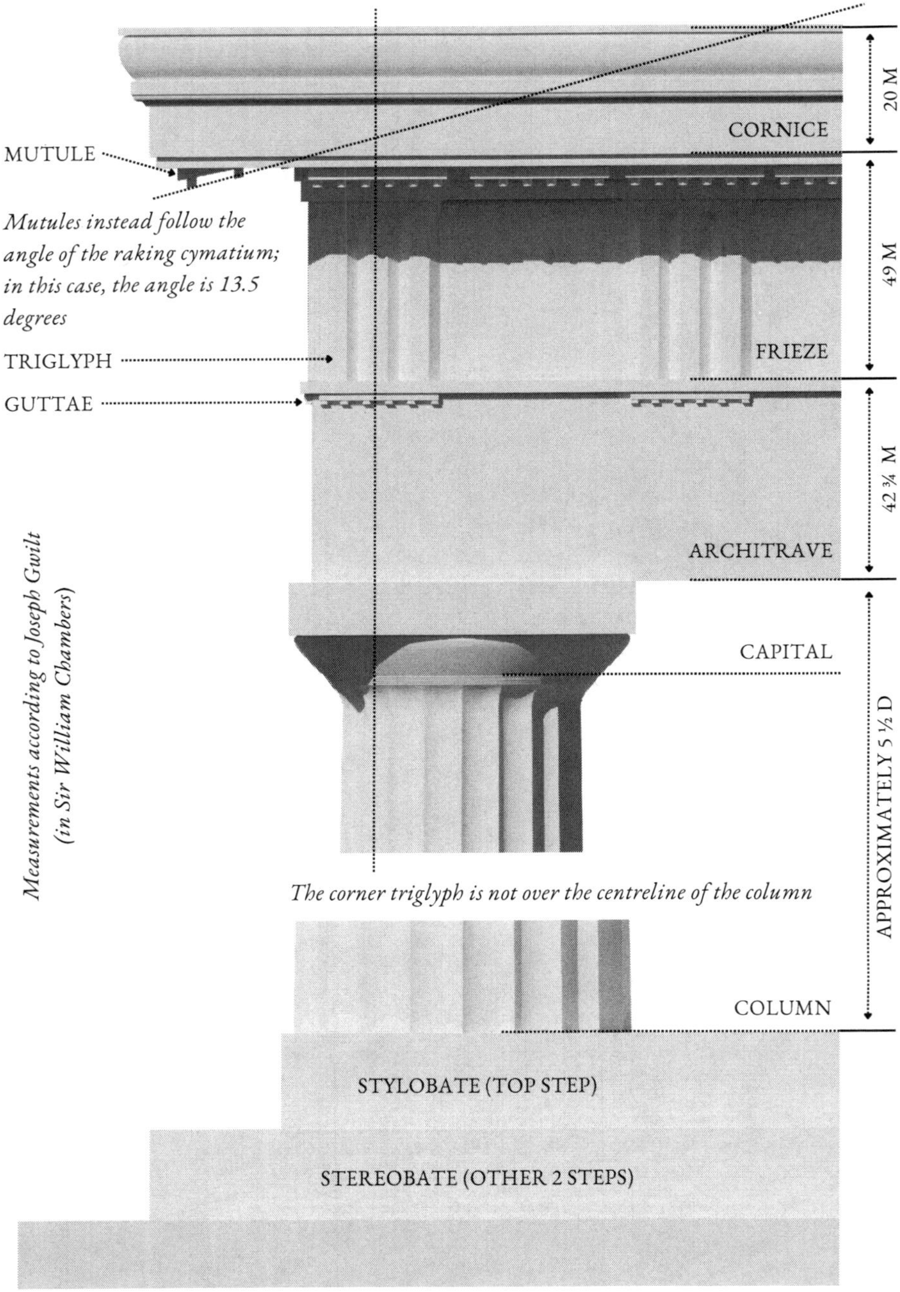

ENTABLATURE OF THE PARTHENON, ATHENS (~438 BC)

DORIC ORDER VARIATIONS

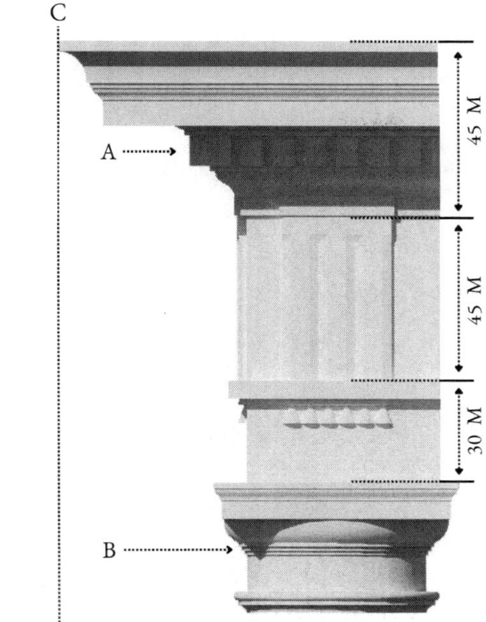

DENTICULATAR DORIC CAPITAL
AND ENTABLATURE
According to G.B. Vignola

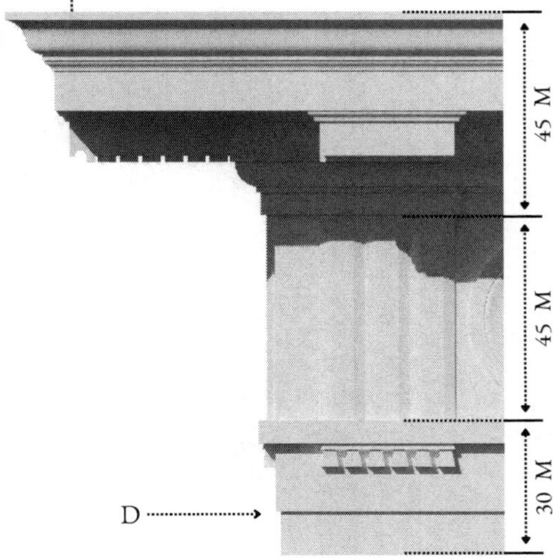

MUTULARY DORIC ENTABLATURE
According to James Gibbs

The Roman Doric Order may vary in the following ways:

- Occasionally the mutules in the cornice are either omitted completely or replaced with diminished 'half' mutules in the soffit only. The bed-mould (A) also has dentils where the mutules would be. Doric entablatures with dentils are so called 'Denticular.'
- Denticular capitals also differ, having three bands of fillets instead of a cavetto under the echinus (B).
- Denticular cornices do not project as much as they do in mutulary ones (C).
- Doric architrave may have one fascia, or sometimes two fasciae (D).
- Particularly after the Renaissance, Doric columns often employed the Attic base (pages 19 & 66).
- The Doric Order, like the Tuscan Order, is commonly used for porches and door porticos, particularly when the rest of a building does not have a full entablature. In these situations, Doric columns are often made taller to accommodate the height of doors. For doorways and porticos, instead of a 1:8 column ratio, they may be enlarged to ratios between 1:8.25 and1:8.5. This is a practice observed from Vitruvius onwards.

Famous examples: *The Parthenon, Athens; The Casino at Marino, Dublin; Temple of Hephaestus, Athens; Brandenburg Gate, Berlin; Lincoln Memorial, Washington.*

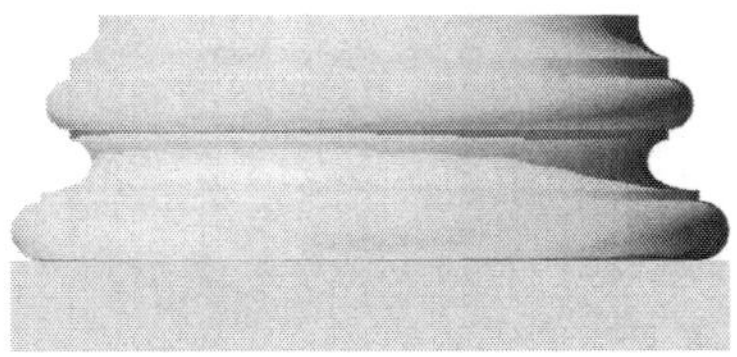

ATTIC BASE

DORIC ORDER VARIATIONS

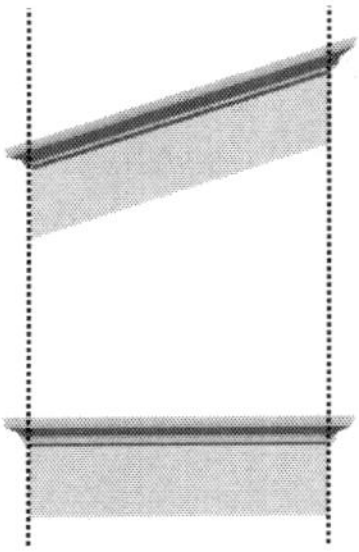

MUTULE

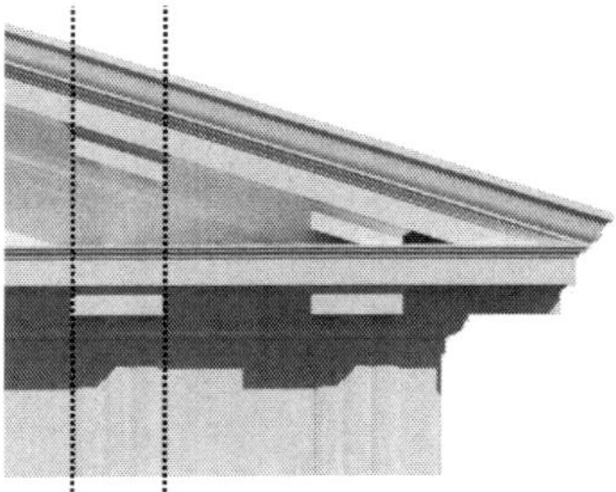

DORIC PEDIMENT

- Mutules used in the raking cornice of Doric pediments do not follow the angle of the slope. Instead, they remain vertically aligned, with their sides remaining parallel to the upright faces of the building (as on page 37). They also align with the mutules of the entablature.

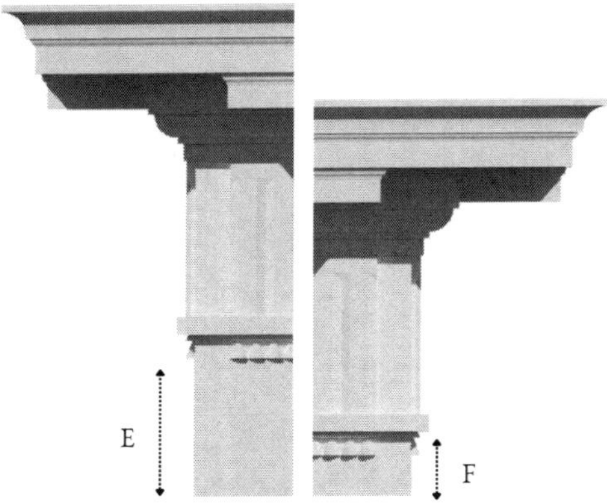

ENTABLATURES

- There are examples of Doric Order architraves varying greatly in height. Sometimes they may be very large, authentic to the ancient Greek Doric (E), whilst at other times they are much shorter (F). Both of these are rare.
- All mouldings profiles (such as those of the capital, base and cornice) may be enriched with decorative mouldings, such as the egg-and-dart echinus and bead and reel astragal below.
- It is common for four rosette flowers to feature in the necking of a Doric capital, with one at every 90 degrees, aligned with the faces of the building.

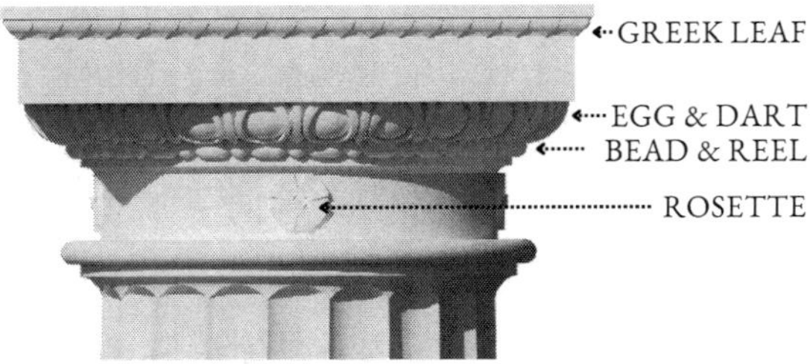

DECORATED CAPITAL

- Metopes may feature alternating decorations of different motifs, in this case (below), a repeating pattern of paterae and bucrania. They also may alternate between decorated and undecorated metopes, or be left plain entirely.

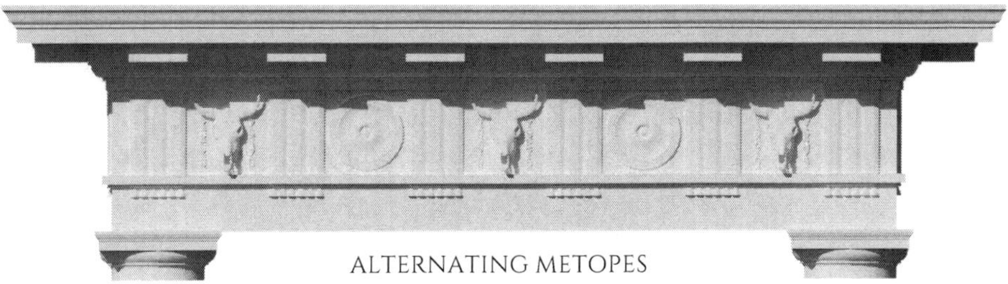

ALTERNATING METOPES

EXAMPLE OF THE DORIC ORDER

THE PARTHENON, ATHENS (~438 BC)

The Parthenon is the most famous Greek temple, renowned for its marvellous architectural engineering and permanence, and is a preeminent example of the Greek Doric Order. Designed by Kallikrates, it was built between 447 and 432 BC on the Acropolis of Athens and was dedicated to the goddess Athena Parthenos - hence its name.

THE IONIC ORDER

THE IONIC ORDER
The Temple of Portunus, Rome

THE IONIC ORDER

The **Ionic Order,** one of the three classical Greek Orders, was developed in the mid-sixth century BC in Ionia, a Greek city-state in Anatolia (modern-day Türkiye). It is primarily identified by the large volutes (spirals) of its capital, and is more slender and richly decorated than the Doric and Tuscan Orders. Particularly suited to civic spaces and temples, it is often associated with the feminine; for instance, all Roman temples dedicated to female deities, like Diana, were Ionic.

The Ionic Order is distinguished by:

- 1:9 shaft-diameter to column-height ratio
- Capital with either four (pulvinar), or eight (Scamozzi) large volutes
- All mouldings may be richly decorated
- Cornice usually has dentils, or may have Ionic modillions
- May have a pulvinated (curved) frieze
- Architrave of two or three fasciae
- When fluted, columns have 24 flutes

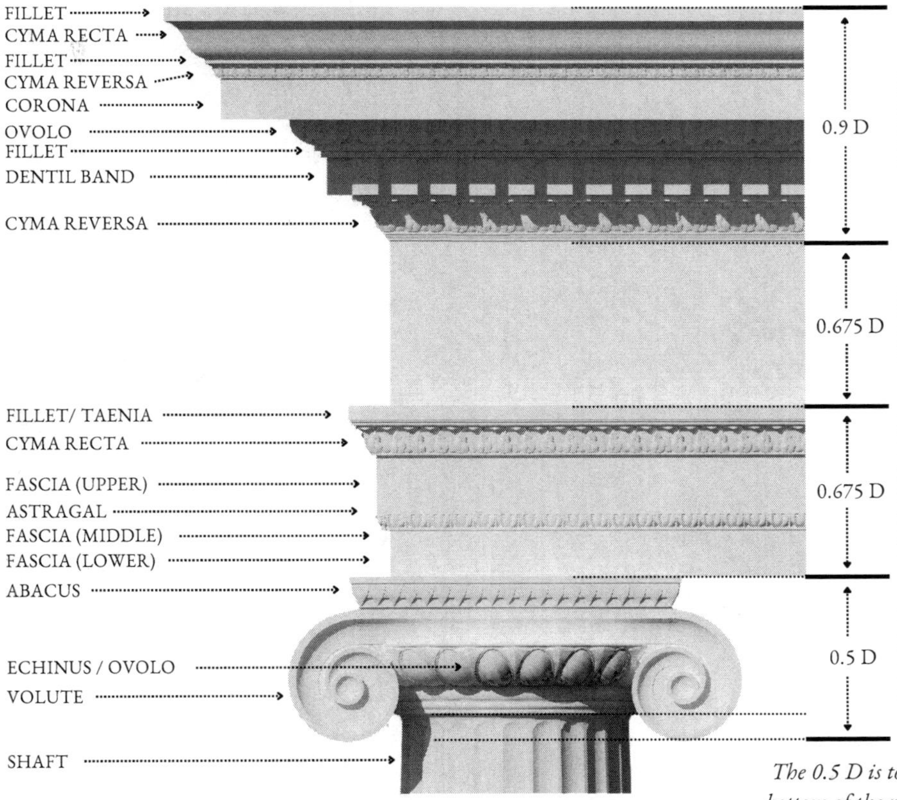

The 0.5 D is to the bottom of the volute

IONIC ENTABLATURE
According to Sir William Chambers

- Volutes may have been inspired by either the shape of certain seashells or ram's horns.

IONIC CAPITALS

There are two main types of **Ionic Capital**: the Pulvinar and the Scamozzi:

- The **Pulvinar** capital has four volutes whose faces are parallel to the front-facing side of the abacus. The volutes on both sides of the abacus are linked with a cushion-like bolster (below). This style was most commonly used in ancient Greek and Roman architecture.
- The **Scamozzi,** or angular, capital has four pairs of volutes that are set at 45 degrees to the abacus. All four faces of the Scamozzi Ionic capital are identical, making it more versatile architecturally, as it can be viewed equally from all angles. The Scamozzi capital became the preferred Ionic form from the Renaissance onwards. It is named after the Renaissance architect Vincenzo Scamozzi, who claimed to have invented it, though examples of this style can be found in Roman architecture.

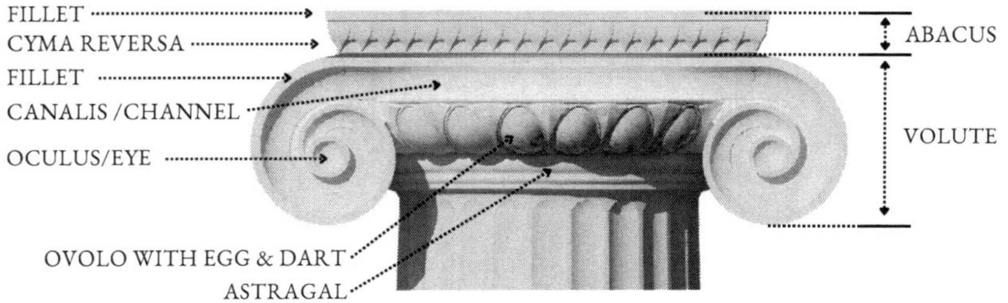

PULVINAR CAPITAL

SCAMOZZI OR ANGULAR CAPITAL

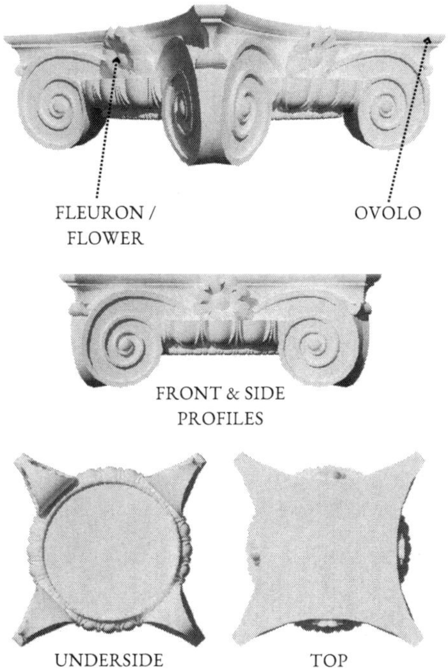

PULVINAR CAPITAL

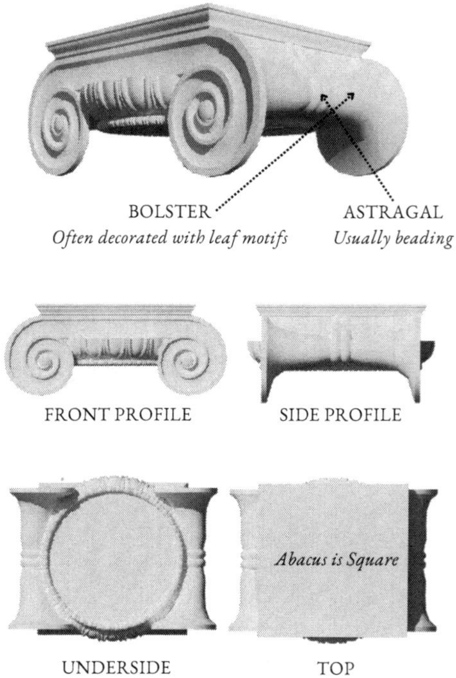

ASPECTS OF THE IONIC ORDER

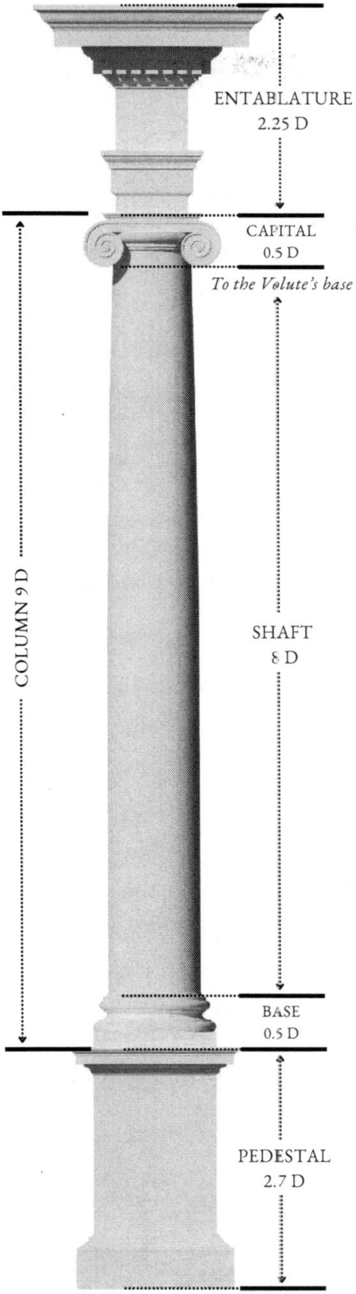

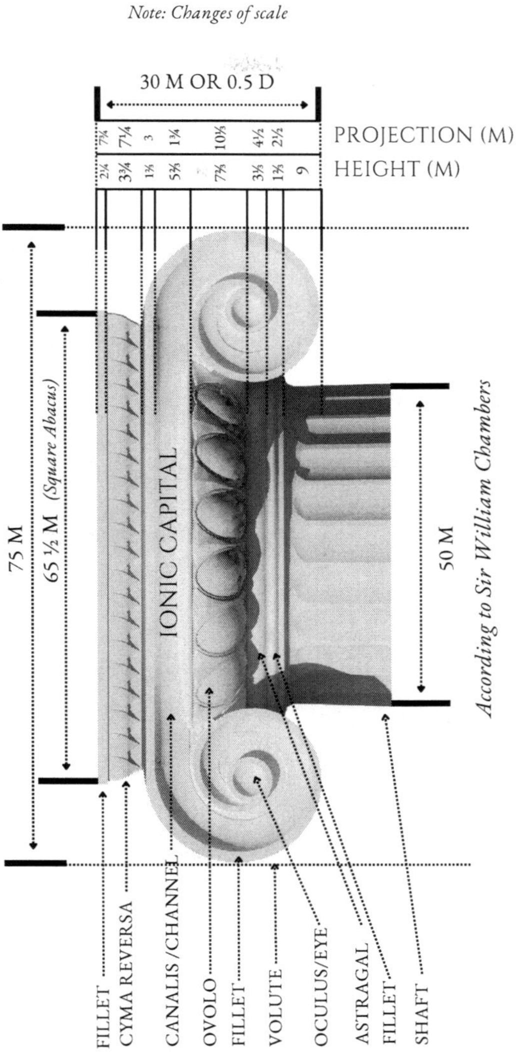

- William Chambers writes that the base of the volute is not the base of the capital, but that the fillet just above the shaft is. This renders the capitals' body only 21 minutes tall. Consequently, he adjusts the shaft's height to 8 Diameters and 9 Minutes tall. Herein, the additional 9 minutes are illustrated at the end of the volute instead.

ASPECTS OF THE IONIC ORDER

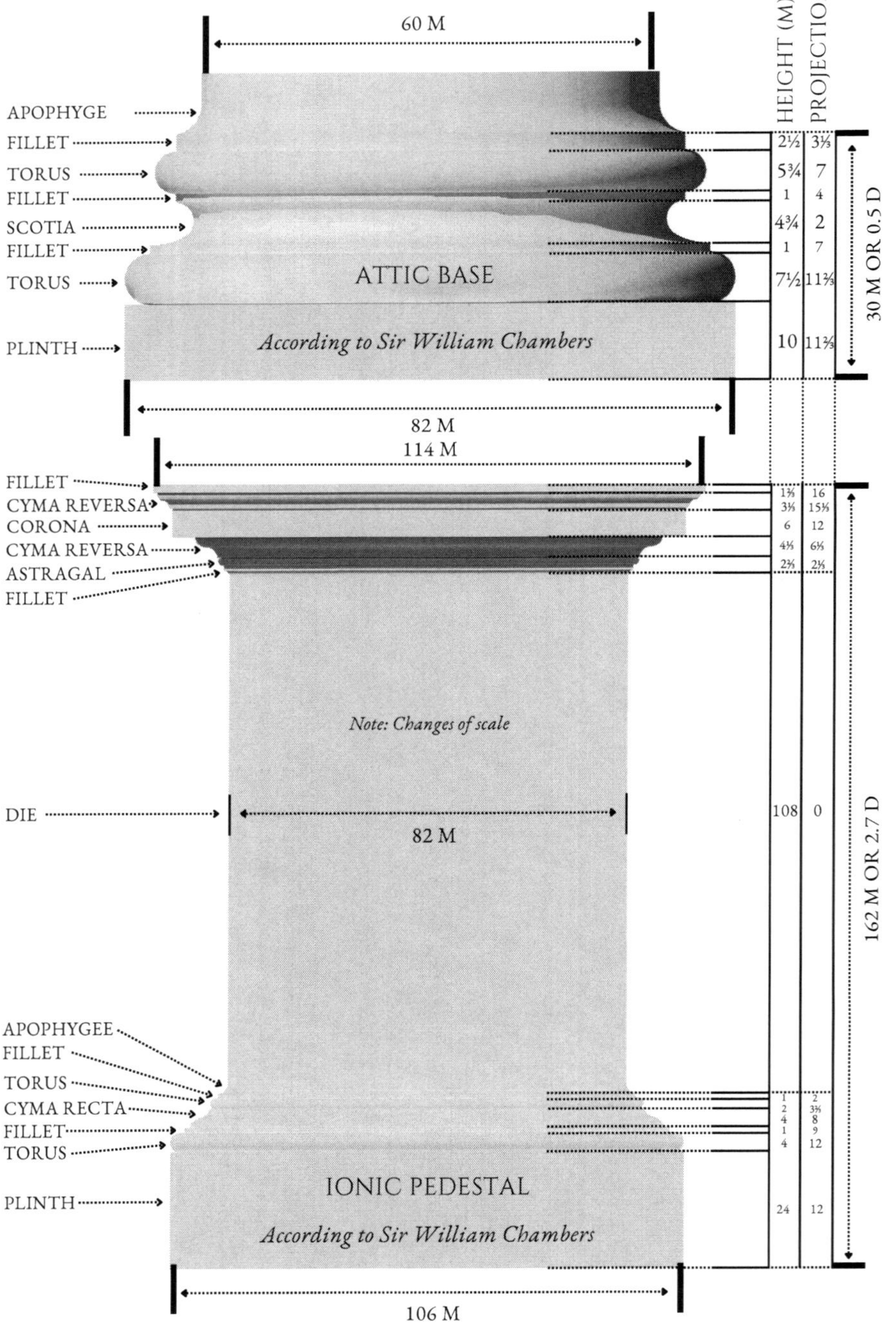

IONIC ENTABLATURE IN DETAIL

ENTABLATURE

	HEIGHT (MINUTES)	PROJECTION (MINUTES)
54M OR 0.9D	2⅔	54
	8⅓ (1)	54 (45)
	3	44½
	11	51
	6¾ (2)	23 (17)
	10½ (1)	15 (15⅗)
	6¾ (1)	7⅔ (8⅓)
40½M OR 0.675D	40½	0
40½M OR 0.675D	2½	8⅔
	6½	8
	15½	3⅓
	2¾	2⅔
	12 (1¼)	0 (⅔)

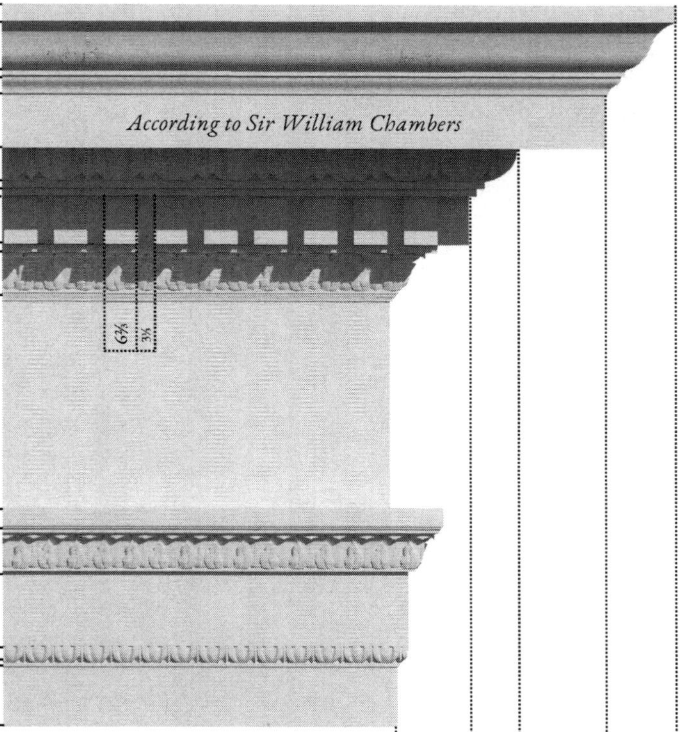

SOFFIT OF CORNICE

	PROJECTION (MINUTES)
45M OR 0.75D	7⅔ (⅔)
	6⅔ (⅔)
	6 (1⅓)
	18 (3½)
	9 (½)

IONIC ORDER VARIATIONS

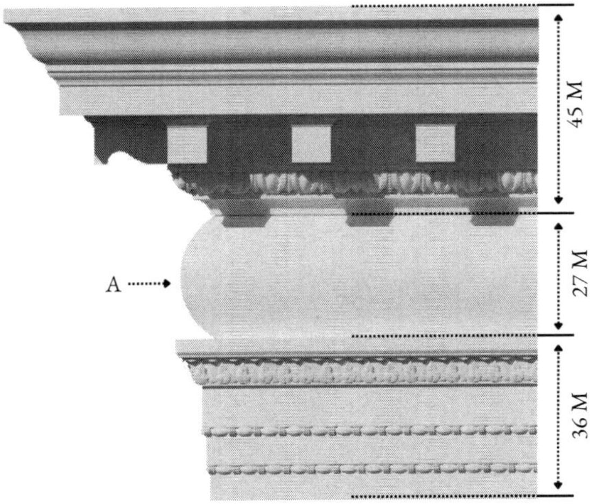

PALLADIO'S IONIC ENTABLATURE
Villa la Rotunda, Vicenza (~1592 AD)

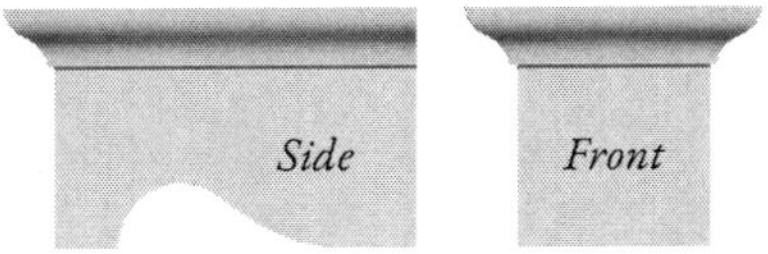

IONIC MODILLION

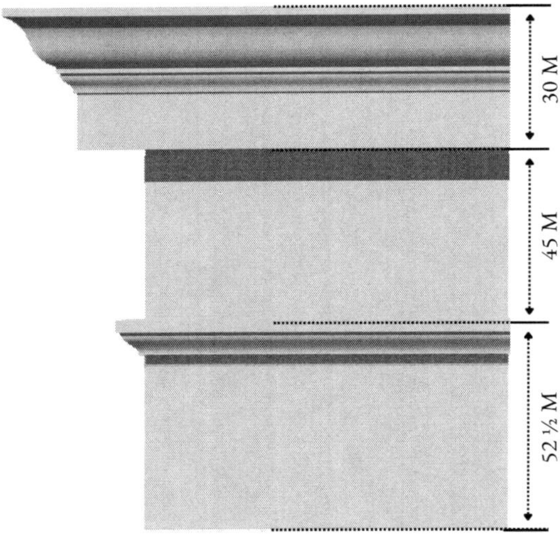

GREEK IONIC ENTABLATURE VARIATION
Temple of Ilissus, Athens (~430 BC)

- Entablatures may have many differing proportions; the example here (top left) has a much shorter frieze.
- The Ionic Order is commonly seen with a pulvinated frieze, characterised by its convex shape (A). The term 'pulvinated' shares the same etymology as the 'pulvinar' capital, both derived from the Latin *pulvinus,* meaning 'cushion shaped.' It is thought that pulvination either mirrors the profile of the volutes in the capital or represents the frieze's compression under the weight of the cornice and pediment above. Pulvinated friezes may also be used with the Corinthian and Composite Orders.
- Architraves may have two or three fasciae.
- Some Ionic cornices feature modillions instead of dentils. Ionic modillions are the simplest compared to the other Orders and typically follow the format shown on the left. Ionic modillions are placed 1/2 a diameter apart, centre to centre.
- Greek Ionic (bottom left) entablatures are much simpler than Roman ones. Their architraves are akin to Doric architraves, being much taller and of one fascia, and their cornices are also much plainer and blockier.
- The Ionic Order was the first to use a true base. The Greek Ionic base (below) is characterised by (top to bottom) a large torus, scotia, astragals and a second scotia, with no large torus at the base.
- From the Renaissance onwards, the Ionic Order always uses the Attic base (page 66).

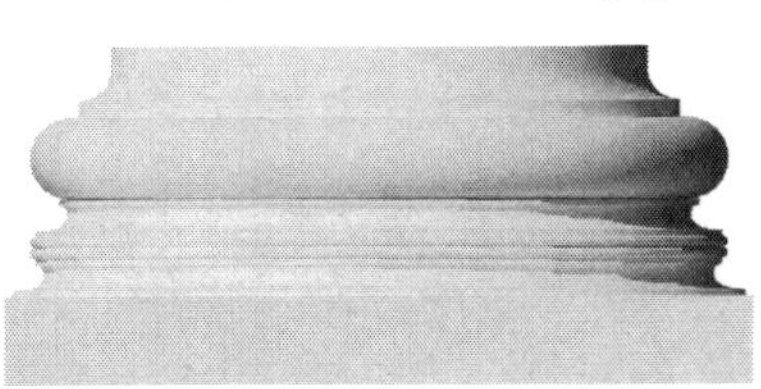

THE GREEK IONIC BASE

IONIC ORDER VARIATIONS

PLAIN (DENTICULAR) ENTABLATURE
With dimensions according to Vignola

PLAIN CAPITAL WITH ASTRAGAL

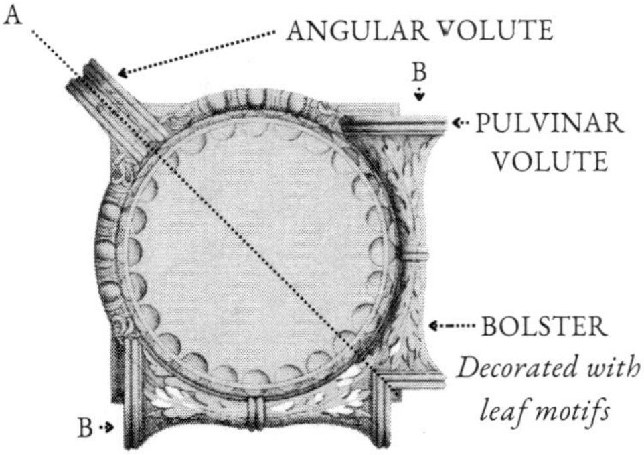

ANGULATED / CORNER CAPITAL
From Palladio's 'Four Books on Architecture'

- Whilst traditionally Ionic entablatures are is highly decorated, they may also be very plain (left). Typically Roman Ionic Orders are very ornate, whereas Neoclassical Ionic Orders may be more restrained.
- Ionic dentils are typically 1/9 of a diameter wide and 1/18 of diameter apart.
- An Ionic cornice with dentils is called a denticular cornice; one with modillions is called a modillion cornice.
- Ionic columns are often unfluted, particularly in Roman and Neoclassical structures. However, when fluted, they always have 24 flutes.
- Occasionally, an astragal may be placed beneath an Ionic capital, as is the case for Tuscan and Doric capitals.
- Vitruvius used a column shaft-to-height ratio of 1:8 instead of 1:9.

Famous examples: *Temple of Athena Nike, Athens; The Erechtheion, Athens; Temple of Portunus, Rome; Chatsworth House, Derbyshire; Villa La Rotunda, Vicenza; The British Museum, London.*

- The remaining Ionic capital variation is the 'angulated' or 'corner' capital (left). It combines two pairs of pulvinar volutes (B), set at 90 degrees to each other, with one angular volute set at 45 degrees (A) to both of these pulvinar volutes. This capital type was used at the corners of ancient pulvinar Ionic structures in Greek and Roman architecture, such as at the Temples of Athena Nike, Ilissus and Portunus.
- It is rarely, if ever, used from the Renaissance onwards, as the Scamozzi Ionic capital became the preferred corner solution, but may be used in Greek revival designs.
- The exact method for laying out volutes is complex; detailed instructions may be found in the works of James Gibbs, Batty Langley, Sir William Chambers, and others (see page 129).

IONIC CAPITAL VARIATIONS

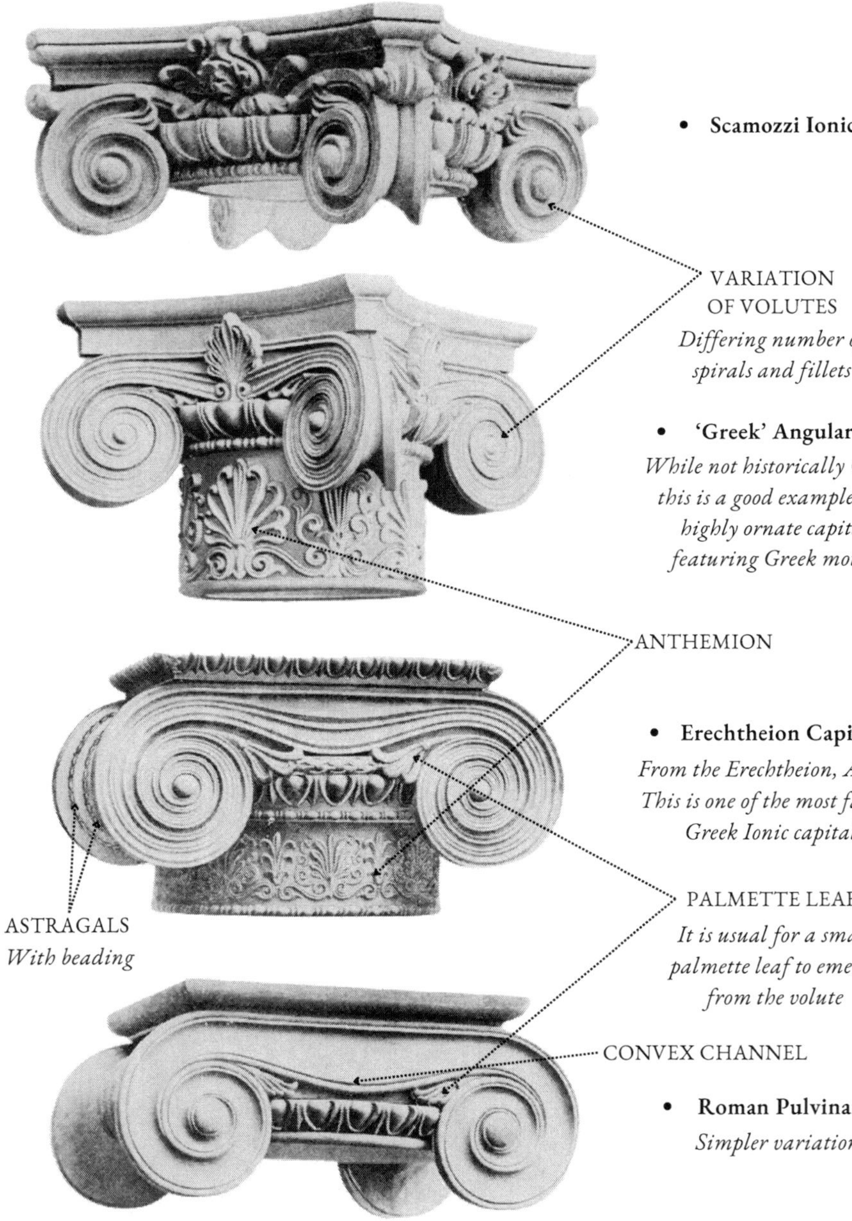

- **Scamozzi Ionic**
- **'Greek' Angular**
  While not historically Greek, this is a good example of a highly ornate capital featuring Greek motifs
- **Erechtheion Capital**
  From the Erechtheion, Athens. This is one of the most famous Greek Ionic capitals
- **Roman Pulvinar**
  Simpler variation

- Ionic capitals from *G.E. Walters 'Catalog of Capitals, brackets and compo ornament for exterior and interior decoration' (1900).*

EXAMPLE OF THE IONIC ORDER

THE TEMPLE OF PORTUNUS, ROME (~80 BC)

The Temple of Portunus was constructed sometime between 120 and 80 BC. It is one of the best-preserved tetrastyle Roman temples, and a fantastic example of the Roman Ionic Order, featuring an ornate entablature, pulvinar capitals and fluted columns. It was dedicated to Portunus, the god of ports, keys, doors and livestock, and stood adjacent to Rome's oldest river port, the Portus Tiberinus. The current Ionic structure, a replacement for an earlier temple.

THE CORINTHIAN ORDER

CORINTHIAN ENTABLATURE

THE CORINTHIAN ORDER

The **Corinthian Order** is regarded as the most ornate and elegant of the Orders. It is distinguished by its slender column, the large acanthus leaves of its capital and a highly decorated cornice. According to Sir William Chambers, it possesses the most 'perfect proportions.' With its opulence, the Corinthian Order is ideally suited to monumental, religious and grand civic structures, like temples, cathedrals and banks.

The Corinthian Order is distinguished by:

- 1:10 shaft-diameter to column-height ratio
- Large, ornate capital with acanthus leaves
- Usually fluted shaft; if so, always with 24 flutes
- Cornice always has modillions and dentils
- All mouldings are usually richly decorated
- Frieze may be richly decorated

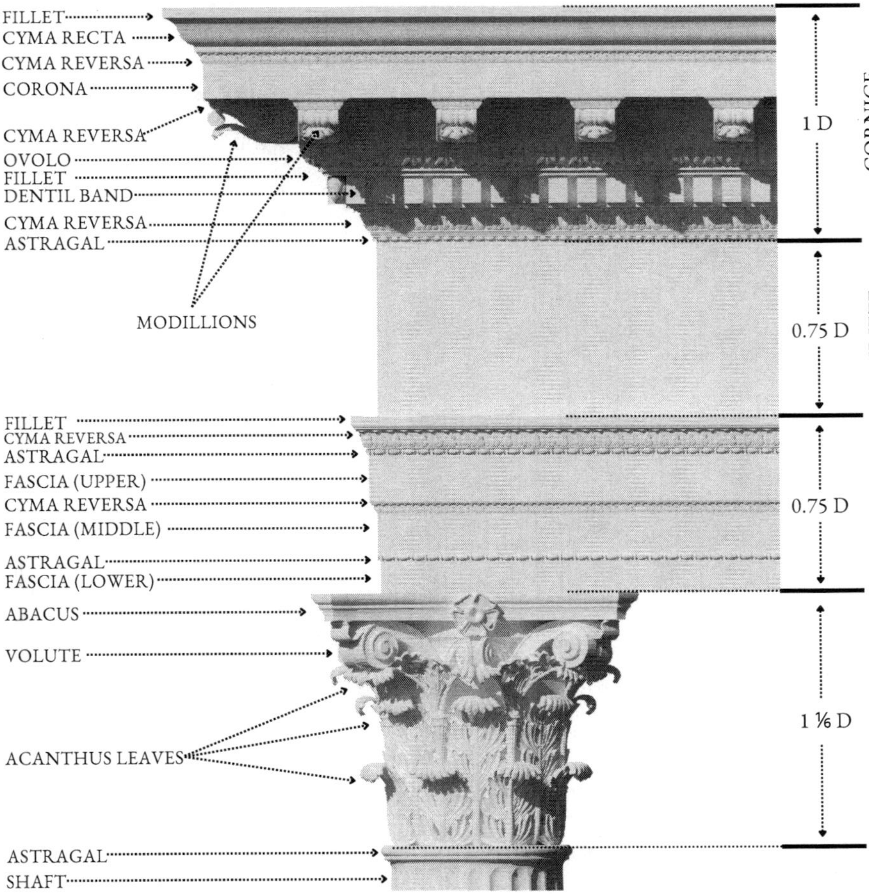

CORINTHIAN ENTABLATURE
According to Sir William Chambers

- The Corinthian Order is one of the three classical Greek Orders, alongside the Doric and Ionic.

THE CORINTHIAN CAPITAL

Corinthian Capitals are easily identifiable: firstly, by the three rows of stylised acanthus leaves; and secondly, by their greater height compared to other capitals, usually measuring 1⅙ diameters tall.

- The name 'Corinthian' is derived from the Greek city of Corinth. However, it is generally thought to have been developed in Athens sometime during the late fifth century BC. Although of Greek origin, the Order was seldom used in Greek architecture. It was instead embraced and championed by the Romans, and remained popular ever since.

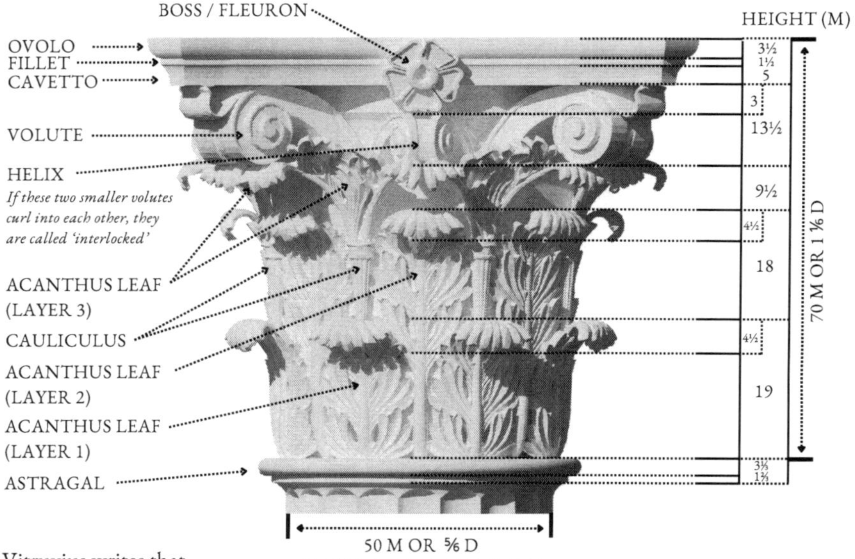

CORINTHIAN CAPITAL

Dimensions according to Sir William Chambers

- Vitruvius writes that the Corinthian capital was invented by Callimachus, a Greek architect and sculptor. Allegedly, his inspiration came from the sight of a woven votive funeral basket that had been left outside, and had become overgrown and intertwined with the leaves of an acanthus plant, forming the spiral volutes and basic structure of the capital.

Sir William Chambers' interpretation of Vitruvius's description

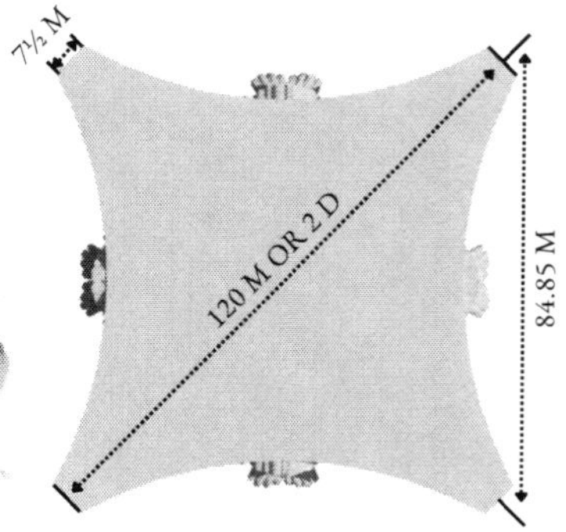

Plan view of the Abacus

THE CORINTHIAN CAPITAL

OBLIQUE ANGLE OF A CORINTHIAN CAPITAL

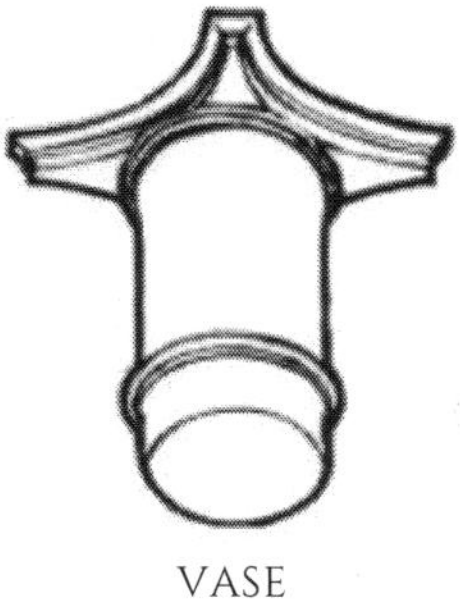

VASE
Blank capital

- Owing to the complexity of the capital (volutes, helices, and acanthus leaves) decorative elements are carved layer by layer on top of the body of the capital. The body to which the acanthus leaves and volutes are attached is called a 'vase.'

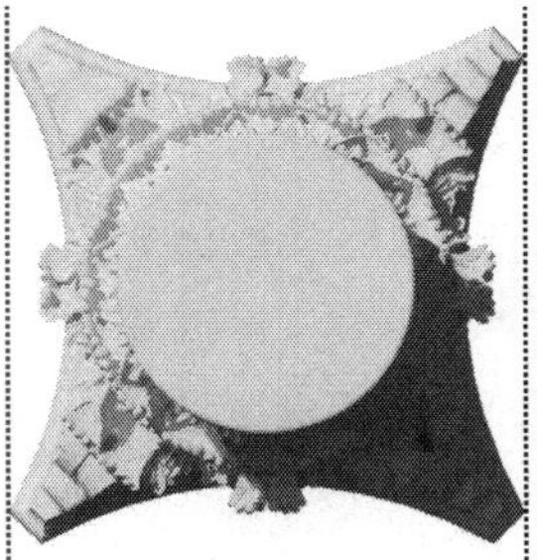

UNDERSIDE

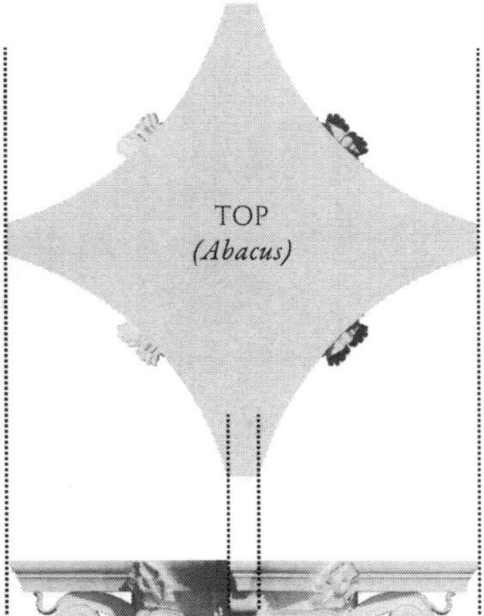

TOP
(Abacus)

FRONT
Viewed at 0 degrees

SIDE
Viewed at 45 degrees

- The Corinthian Capital is larger about its diagonal (see measurements on the previous page). Thus when it is viewed from an oblique angle or directly from the side, it appears much larger.

- The acanthus leaves may vary in their complexity (left below).
- The fleurons may have different flower types (below), and the mouldings at the top of the capital may be enriched, for example, with an egg-and-dart.

LEAF VARIATIONS
Varying complexity and form

FLEURON VARIATION
Variety of flowers and acanthine motifs

ASPECTS OF THE CORINTHIAN ORDER

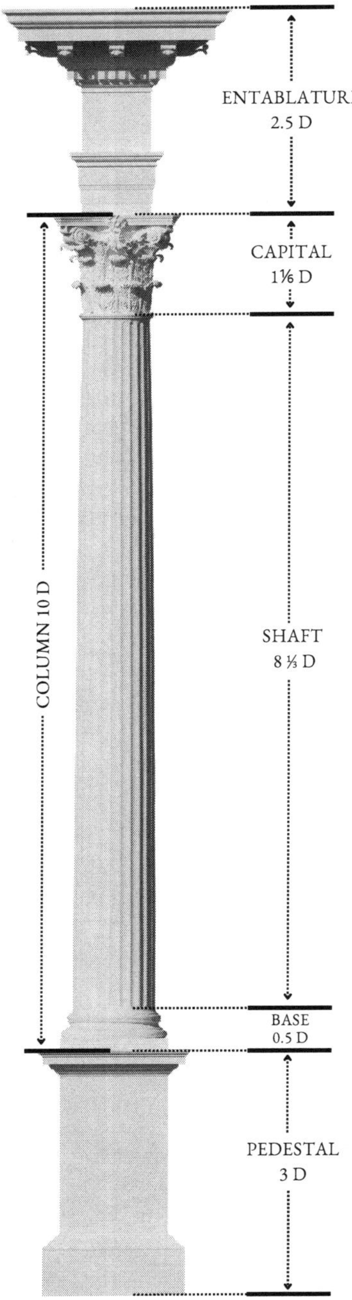

Note: Changes of scale

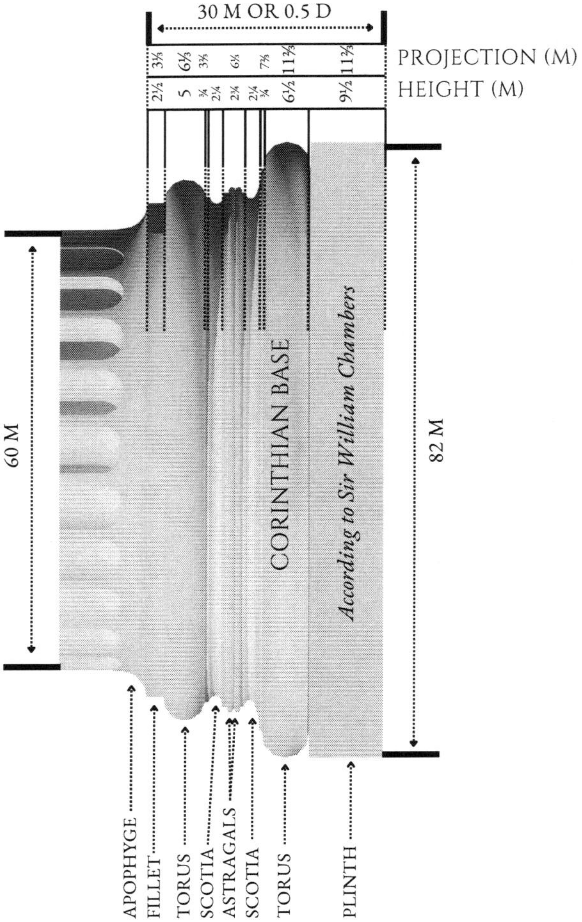

Each of the scotias and astragals are also surrounded by fillets

- Sometimes the Corinthian base is called the 'double astragal base,' given it has a pair of astragals at its centre, between the two scotias.

ASPECTS OF THE CORINTHIAN ORDER

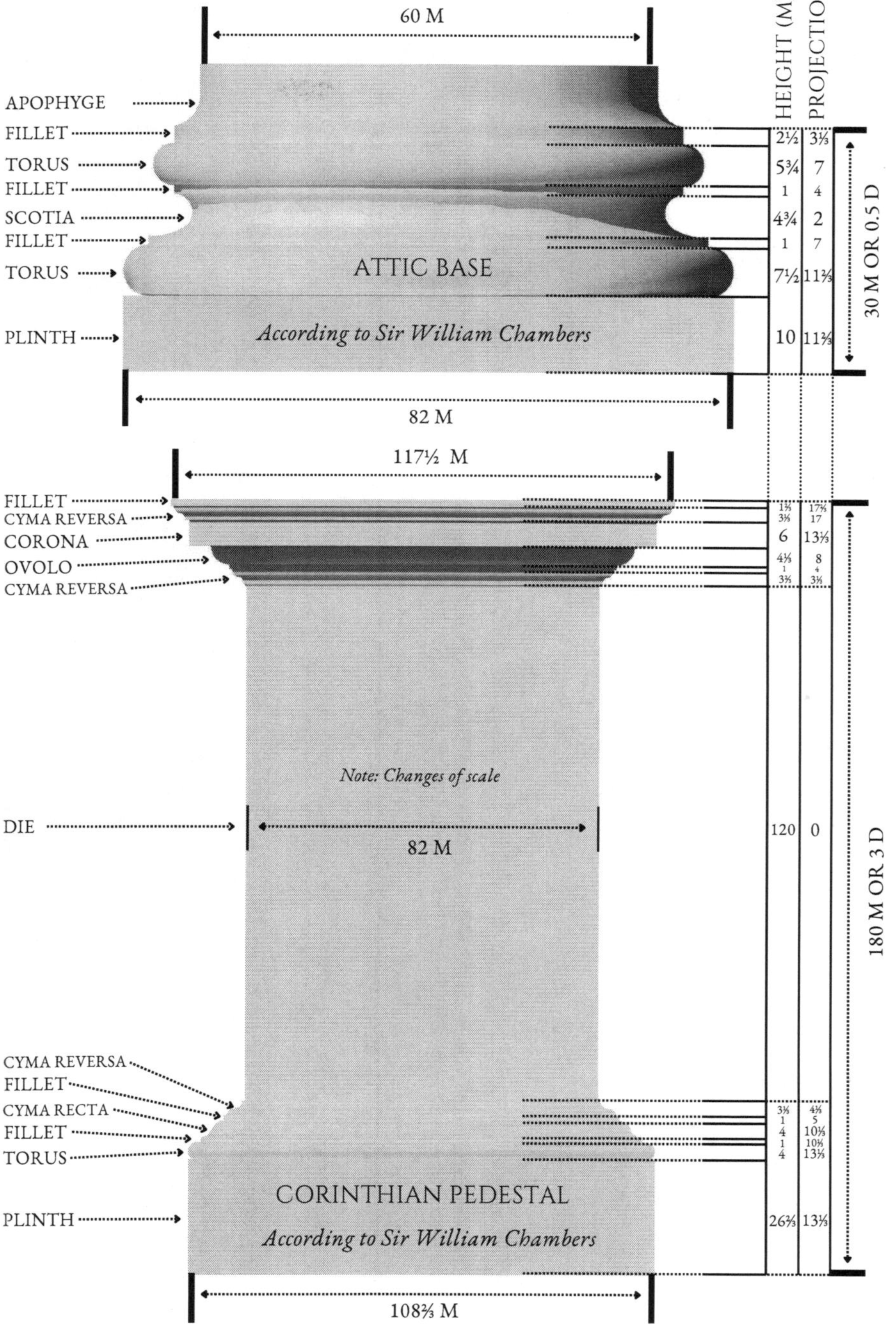

CORINTHIAN ENTABLATURE IN DETAIL

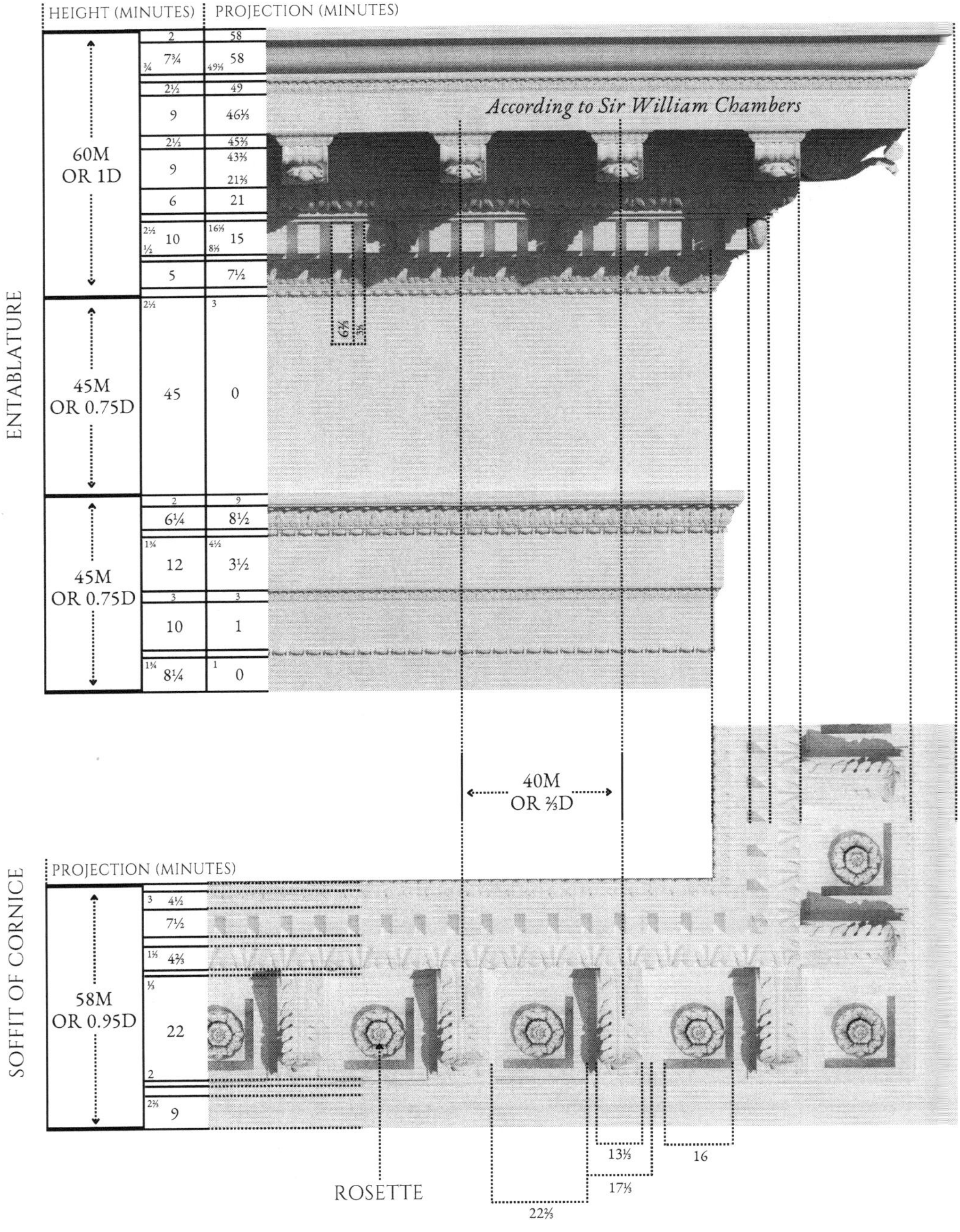

CORINTHIAN ORDER VARIATIONS

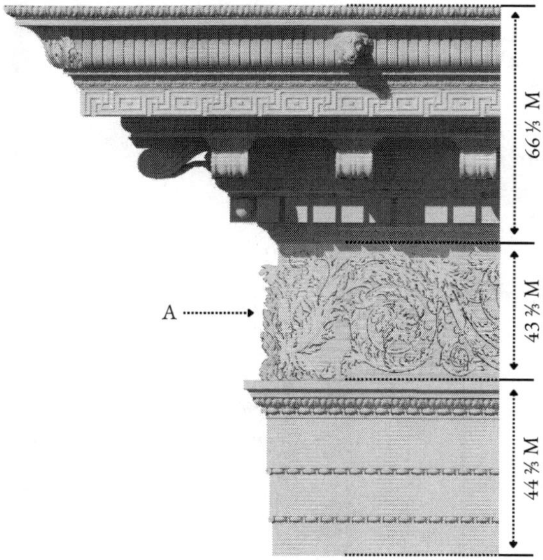

ENTABLATURE OF MAISON CARRÉE

Roman. Nimes, France (~2-7 AD)
Approximate minutes given (see Palladio)

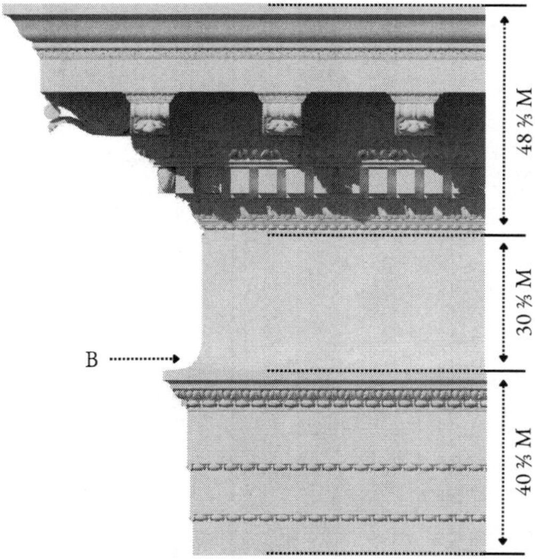

PALLADIO'S CORINTHIAN ENTABLATURE

Approximate minutes given (see Palladio)

- Every moulding of the Order may be enriched. Roman and Baroque versions of the Order are usually the most ornate.
- The Roman Corinthian Order at the Maison Carrée (left) is a highly decorated example. The entablature of Maison Carrée measures approximately 2.5D, with its architrave, frieze and cornice approximately in a 2:2:3 ratio. Additionally, Maison Carrée's modillions are unusually reversed; this is neither advisable nor seen elsewhere.
- The entablature proportions may differ. For example, Palladio's Corinthian entablature (bottom left) is diminished, measuring only 2 diameters tall. In more recent styles, entablatures of 2D and 2.25D are not often seen. They are longer typically used as, according to later architects, they are less grand.
- The frieze (top left) features running acanthus scrollwork (A). Other decorations may include figures, sculpture or carved text indicating the building's dedication or function.
- Mediating the joint between the architrave and the frieze, there may be a cavetto curve (B) to help dispel rainwater away from the top of the architrave.
- Palladio also uses a smaller frieze (bottom left), as he does with his Ionic Order.
- Although a unique Corinthian base exists, the Attic base most commonly used.

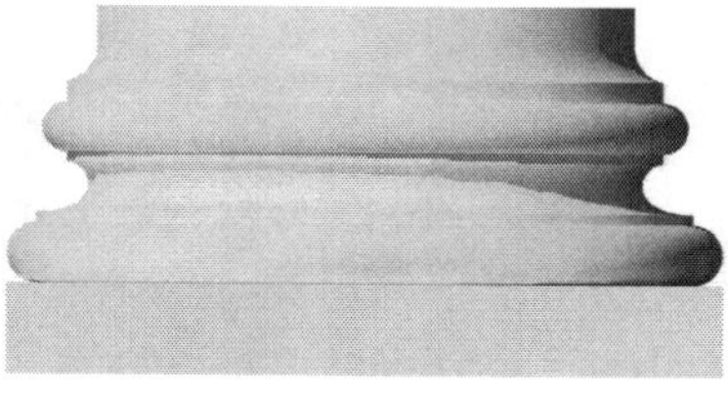

THE ATTIC BASE

CORINTHIAN ORDER VARIATIONS

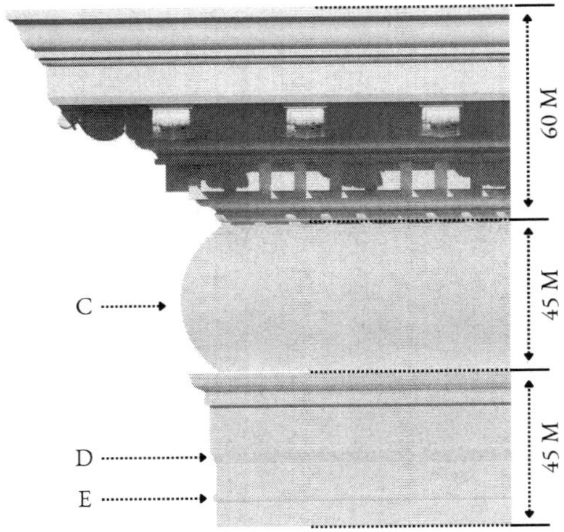

ENTABLATURE WITH PULVINATED FRIEZE

CAPITAL WITH SIMPLIFIED LEAVES
With a profile according to Vignola

MODILLIONS AND COFFERS OF CORNICE

- Occasionally, Corinthian friezes are pulvinated (convex) (C).
- Although canonically ornate, Corinthian entablatures (top left) and capitals (centre left) may be left plain, and shafts are sometimes unfluted; this is more often seen in Renaissance and Neoclassical work.
- The Corinthian cornice almost always includes dentils and modillions. These modillions are usually decorated with acanthus leaves and palmette (below).
- Corinthian modillions are spaced 2/3 of a diameter apart, centre to centre.
- Corinthian dentils are typically 1/9 D wide and spaced 1/18 D apart.
- In the soffit of the corona, in between the modillions, are coffers typically decorated with rosettes (G).
- Capitals have a large variety of leaf styles (F, also page 75) and volute thicknesses, though these volutes are never large.
- Architraves are nearly always composed of three fasciae, separated either by two astragals (previous page), or an astragal (D) and a cyma reversa (E). Occasionally, there are only two fasciae.

Famous examples: *The Pantheon, Rome; Maison Carrée, Nimes; Temple of Bacchus, Lebanon; U.S. Capitol, Washington D.C.; St Paul's Cathedral, London; Castle Howard, North Yorkshire; St Peter's Basilica, Vatican City; New York Stock Exchange, New York; French Panthéon, Paris.*

SIDE PROFILE

FRONT

UNDERSIDE

THE CORINTHIAN MODILLION

EXAMPLE OF THE CORINTHIAN ORDER

MAISON CARRÉE. NIMES, FRANCE (~ 2-7 AD)

Maison Carrée is one of the best-preserved Roman temples in the world. Architecturally, it characterises a Roman temple, with its engaged columns and podium base, and exemplifies the Roman Corinthian Order, with its richly ornamented entablature and complex acanthus capitals. It has since inspired many architects, from the Renaissance architect Andrea Palladio to the designers of numerous Neoclassical structures, such as the Église de la Madeleine and the Virginia State Capitol.

THE COMPOSITE ORDER

THE COMPOSITE ORDER

THE COMPOSITE ORDER

The **Composite Order** is characteristically a combination of the Corinthian and Ionic Orders. It shares the slender column proportions and capital height of the Corinthian Order, and its capital combines the large angular volutes of a Scamozzi Ionic capital with two rows of acanthus leaves. The richness and grandeur of the Composite Order make it ideal for monumental architecture where opulence is required, such as basilicas, mansions and triumphal arches. It is often called the Roman Order, as the Romans invented it, and it was later refined and widely used in Renaissance and Baroque architecture.

The Composite Order is distinguished by:

- 1:10 shaft-diameter to column-height ratio
- Large ornate capital with a Scamozzi Ionic volutes and two layers of acanthus leaves
- Usually fluted shaft; if so, always with 24 flutes
- Cornice always features modillions, either Composite, Ionic or Corinthian
- All mouldings are typically richly decorated
- Friezes may be decorated or pulvinated

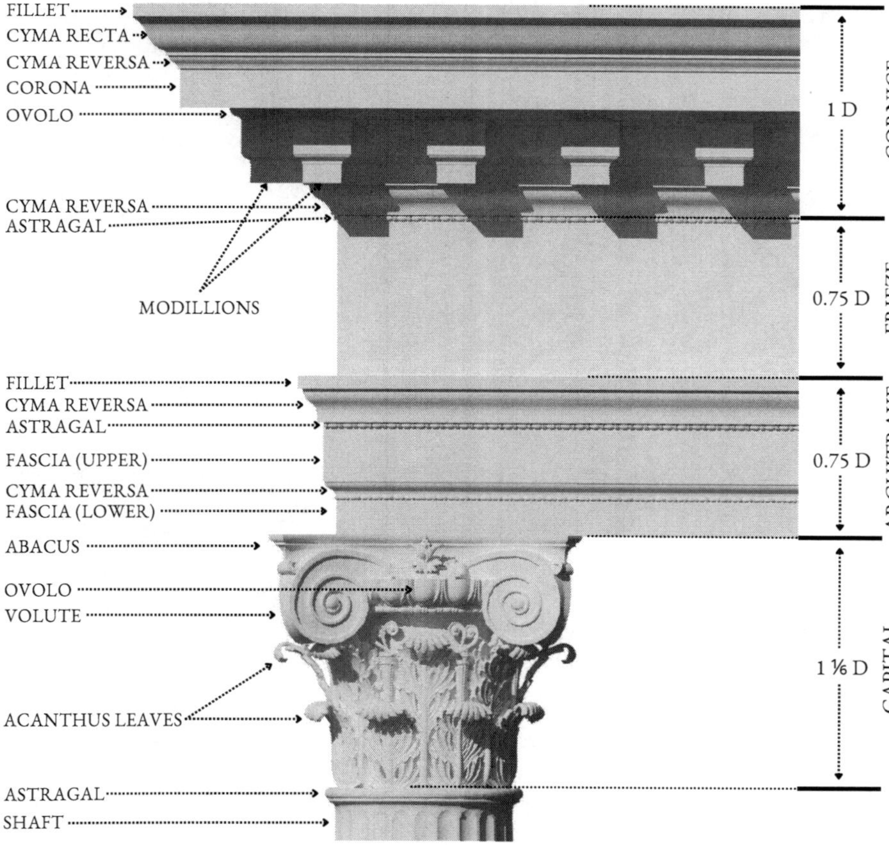

COMPOSITE ENTABLATURE
Inspired by James Gibbs

THE COMPOSITE CAPITAL

The volutes at the top of the **Composite Capital** are always those of the Scamozzi Ionic capital (page 64). Below this are two rows of stylised acanthus leaves, compared to Corinthian capitals, which have three rows. Like Corinthian capitals, Composite capitals are tall, usually measuring 1⅙ diameters in height.

- The volutes may vary in their number of spirals and fillets. As with Corinthian capitals, the acanthus leaves may differ in complexity (page 75), the fleurons may feature various flower types and the mouldings at the top of the capital may be enriched, such as with an egg-and-dart.

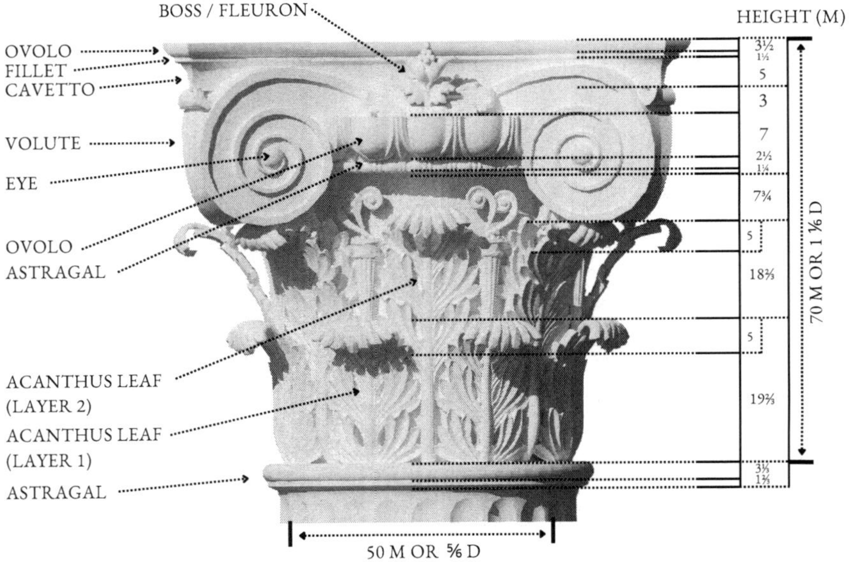

COMPOSITE CAPITAL

Dimensions (only) according to Sir William Chambers

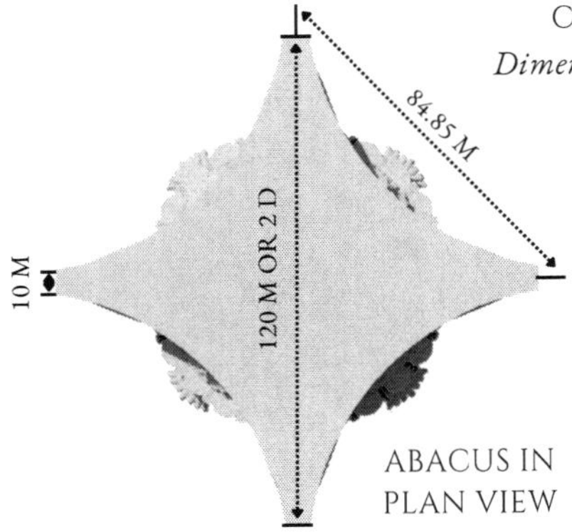

ABACUS IN PLAN VIEW

See page 75 for the variations of acanthus leaves and fleurons which the Composite capital may use.

OBLIQUE ANGLE OF A COMPOSITE CAPITAL

- The Composite Order was not considered its own Order by Vitruvius; instead, it was viewed as a variation of the Corinthian Order. It was later distinguished as its own Order during the Renaissance, popularised by Italian architects like Andrea Palladio and Vincenzo Scamozzi.
- Some of the earliest Roman Composite capitals can be seen on the Arch of Titus (~81 AD).

ASPECTS OF THE COMPOSITE ORDER

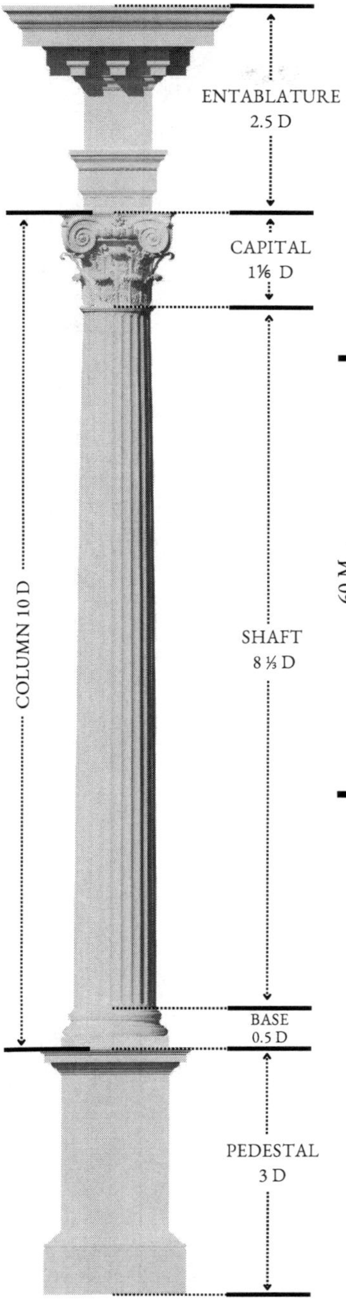

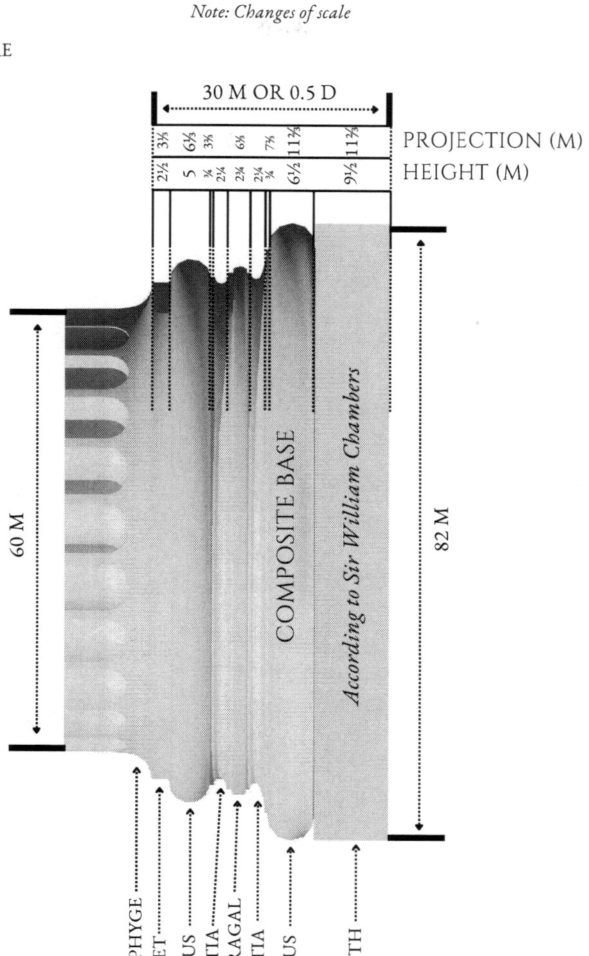

Each of the scotias and astragals are also surrounded by fillets

- Compared to the double-astragal base of the Corinthian Order, the Composite base only has one astragal in between the two scotias.

ASPECTS OF THE COMPOSITE ORDER

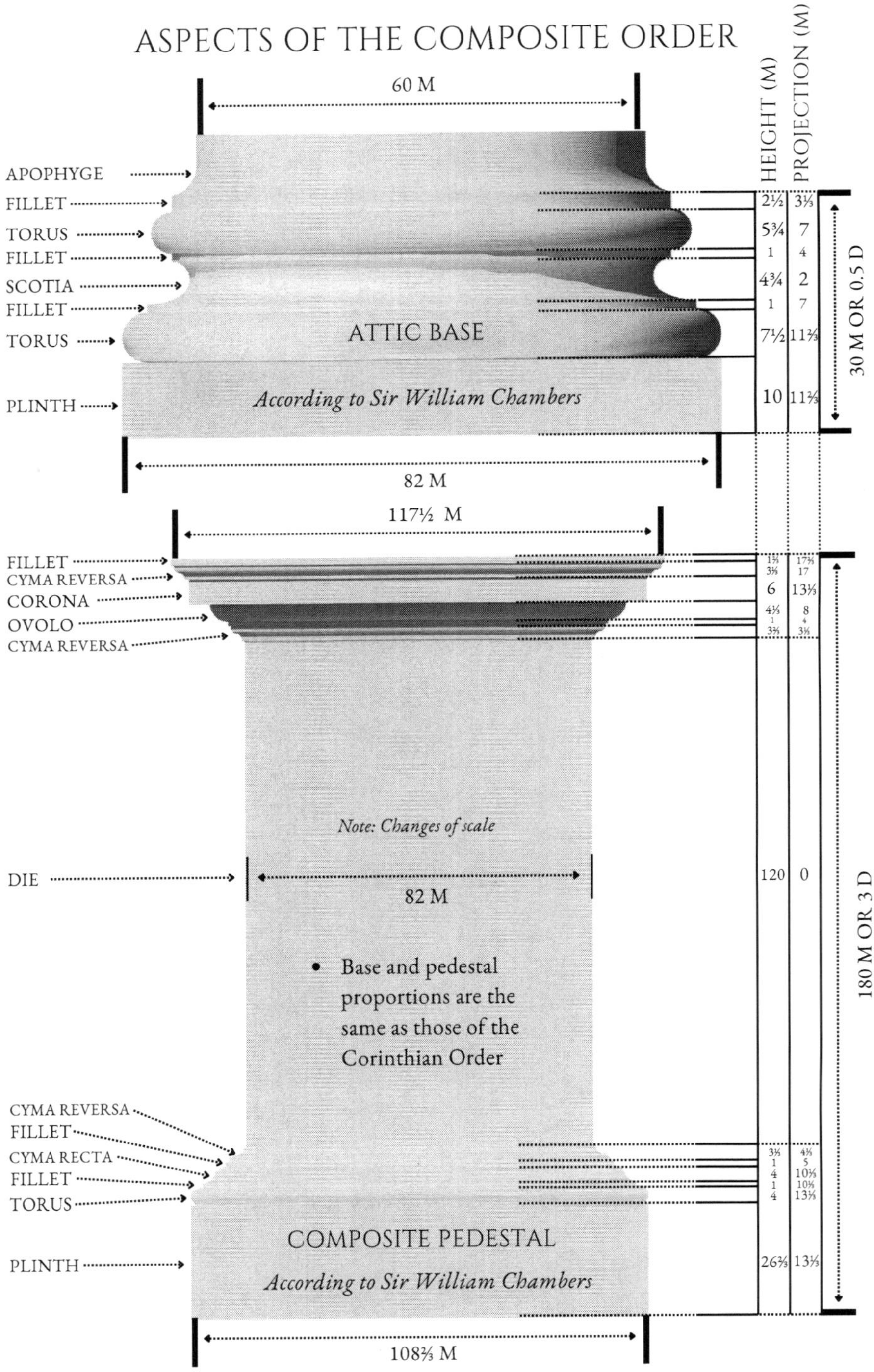

COMPOSITE ENTABLATURE IN DETAIL

ENTABLATURE

	HEIGHT (MINUTES)		PROJECTION (MINUTES)
60M OR 1D	3¾		60
	9	1¼	60 (50)
	3¾		48¾
	11¼		45
	2½		31¼
	9	1¼	28 (28¾)
	2½		27½
	5⅝		26¼
	7½	1⅞	9 (11¼)
45M OR 0.75D	43⅛	1⅞	0 (3¾)
45M OR 0.75D	3¾		11¼
	7½		11¼
	16⅞	1⅞	3¾ (1⅞)
	2½		3¾
	11¼	1¼	0 (1¼)

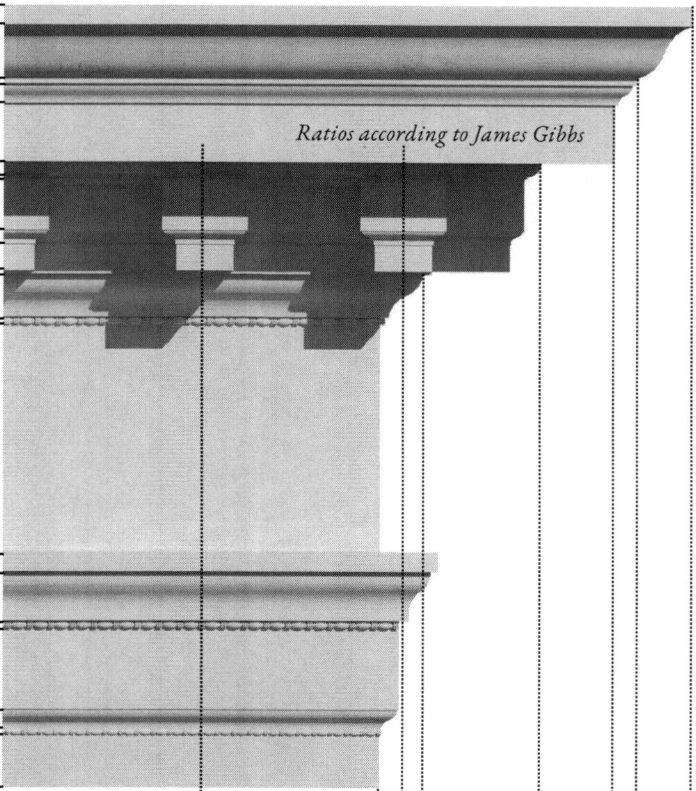

SOFFIT OF CORNICE

	PROJECTION (MINUTES)	
60M OR 1D	5¼	3¾
	15	2¼
	1¼	
	½ ¾	
	13¾	2½
	¾	
	10	1¼

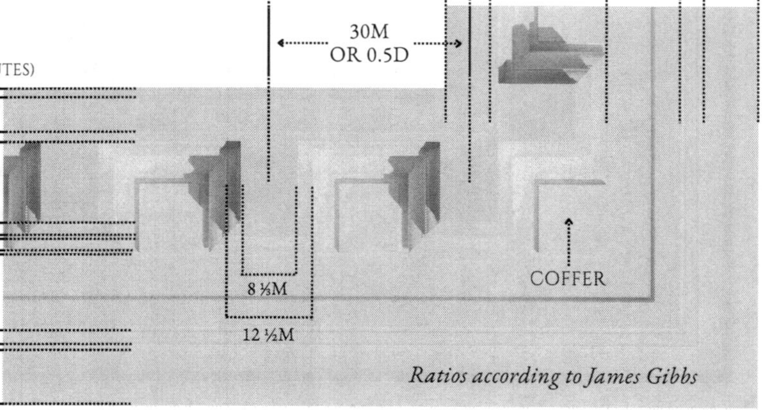

- Note: this page details an Order derived from James Gibbs's system of direct proportionality, to provide dimensions for an Order with a height of 2.5D.

COMPOSITE ORDER VARIATIONS

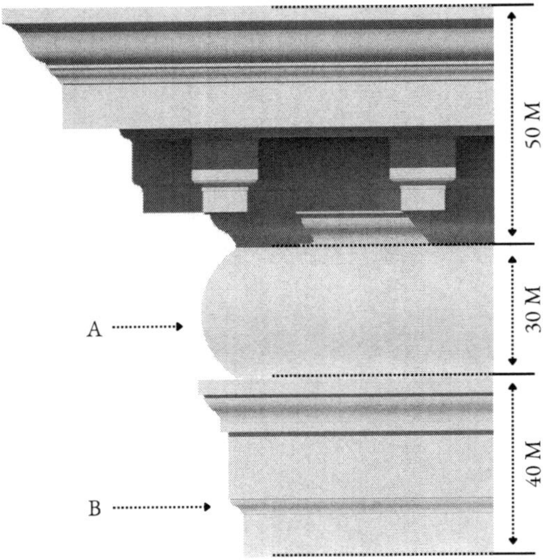

PALLADIO'S COMPOSITE ENTABLATURE
Used at San Giorgio Maggiore

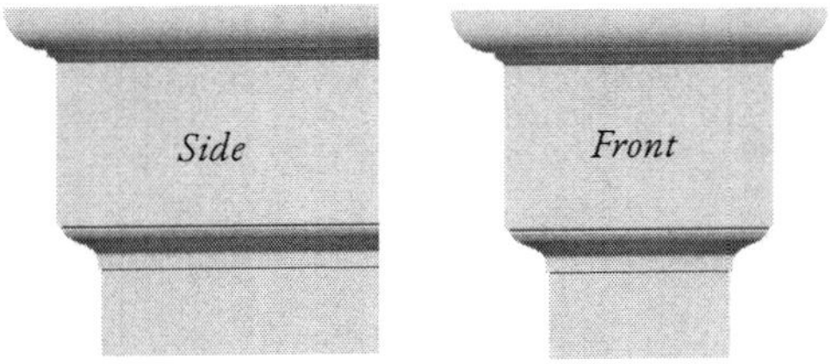

THE COMPOSITE MODILLION

CAPITAL VARIATION WITH SIMPLIFIED LEAVES
Palladio's variation used at San Giorgio Maggiore

- Friezes are often pulvinated (A) or may have a cavetto at the joint between the frieze and architrave, as seen in the Corinthian example on page 79.
- Friezes are often decorated with running acanthus motifs, sculpted figures or text.
- Palladio, as with his Corinthian Order, reduces the entablature height to 2D instead of a more typical 2.5D, and diminishes the height of the frieze (left).
- Whilst the Composite Order has its own base, it most commonly uses the Attic base.
- The Order has its own modillion design, though it often adopts the modillions and entablatures of the Corinthian and Ionic Orders.
- Composite modillions are spaced 1/2 a diameter apart, centre to centre.
- Like the Corinthian Order, all mouldings are usually richly decorated. However, the Order is sometimes rendered plainly: capitals may have simplified leaves, mouldings may be devoid of enrichment and shafts may be unfluted.
- Architraves are typically of two or three fasciae, separated by either astragals or a cyma reversa (B).
- Sir William Chambers writes that Composite cornices may feature modillions that are resemble Doric mutules, although this is extremely rare.

Note: All the 'Roman' variations discussed in the **Corinthian Order Variations (page 79)** and **Ionic Order Variations (page 68)** are also applicable to the Composite Order.

Famous examples: *San Giorgio Maggiore, Venice; Arch of Titus, Rome; Lescot wing, Louvre, Paris; Somerset House, London; Basilica of St John Lateran, Rome; Arch of Constantine, Rome; Palazzo Madama, Turin.*

EXAMPLE OF THE COMPOSITE ORDER

SAN GIORGO MAGGIORE, VENICE (~1566-1610 AD)

Designed by Andrea Palladio in 1566, San Giorgio Maggiore was not completed until 1610 by Vincenzo Scamozzi. It is one of the great masterpieces of Renaissance architecture and a highly influential structure, becoming a model for many church façades across Europe. The grand central pediment, supported by engaged Composite Order columns, is expertly superimposed over a secondary pediment which is supported by smaller Corinthian pilasters.

PART III
ELEMENTS OF CLASSICAL BUILDING COMPOSITION

THE BANQUETING HOUSE, STUDLEY ROYAL (~1732 AD)

INTERCOLUMNIATION

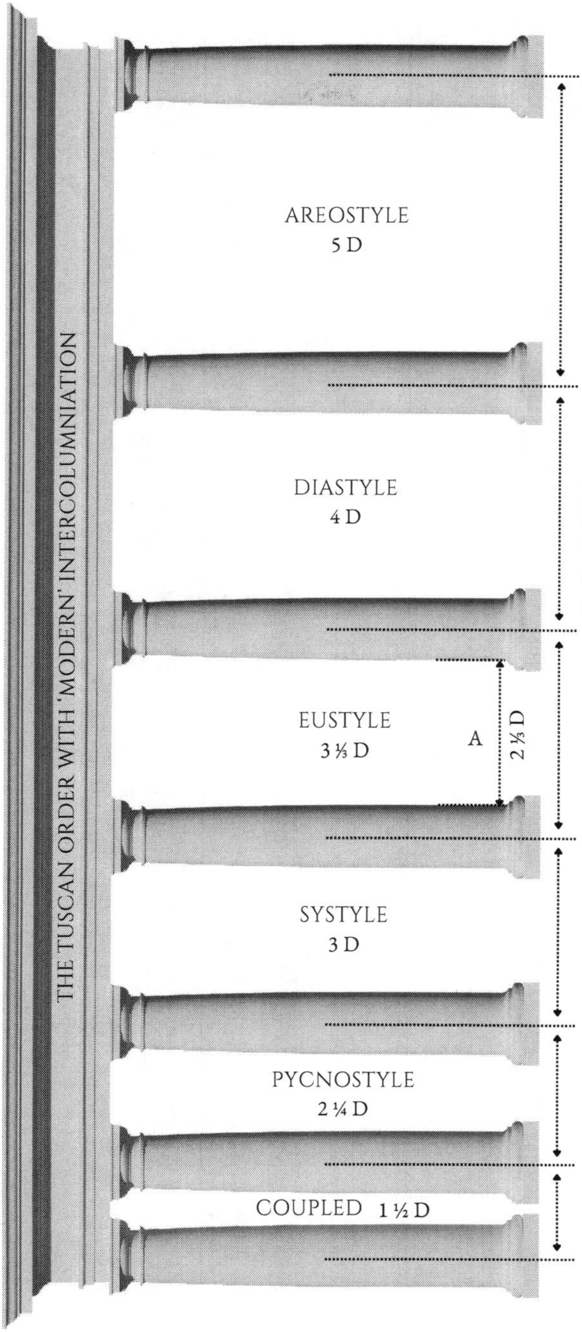

Intercolumniation simply refers to the spacing of adjacent columns, including engaged columns and, generally, pilasters. These spacings are precise, having both structural and aesthetic importance, as columns must be near to each other for the sake of both real and apparent solidity. These spacings are also precise to ensure that there are no gaps or uneven spacings between elements like modillions and dentils.

Like the proportions of the Orders, intercolumniation is measured in column base diameters (see page 42). In the example to the left, the spacings are measured from the centre of one column to the next, though some chose to measure from the sides of the columns (A).

- The Corinthian, Composite, Ionic and Tuscan Orders all use the same intercolumniation spacings based on diameters. Doric spacings are discussed on the next page.
- Traditionally, Tuscan columns are spaced further apart than those of the Corinthian and Ionic Orders.
- Pairs of columns are known as 'coupled' columns. They are spaced only 1.5D apart, centre to centre. Their bases don't quite touch as to avoid overcrowding.
- Eustyle spacing was favoured by the Romans. *Note: Roman Eustyle was measured at 3¼D instead of 3⅓D, and does not work with the Neoclassical placement of modillions as described in this book.*
- Most historic architects view areostyle as too wide.

INTERCOLUMNIATION VARIATIONS

The intercolumniation of Doric columns is determined by the spacing of triglyphs, as each column must align directly beneath one. This results in different diameter spacings from the other Orders.

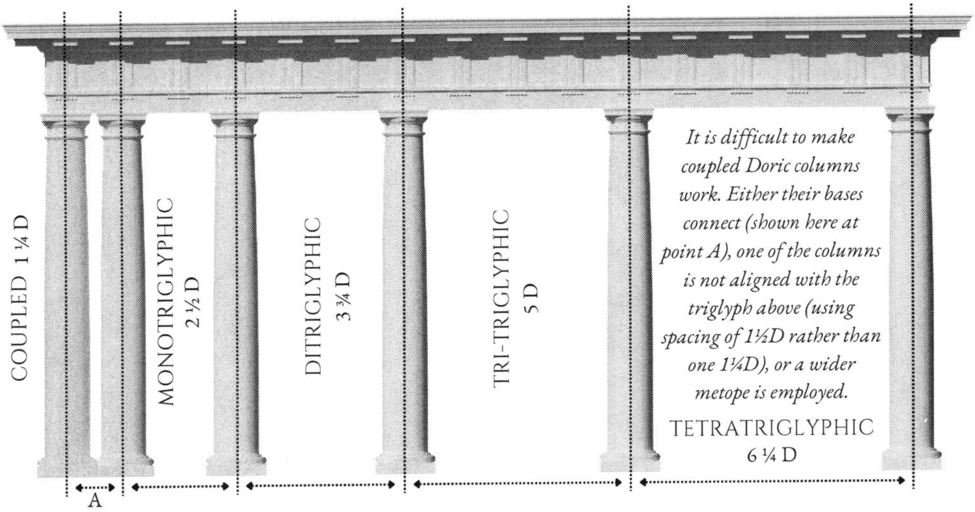

The gap between the two central columns of a portico, particularly in Greek and Roman temples, and later in very large structures, may differ from the rest of the columns (below 4D vs 3.25D). This gives prominence to the entrance, both making it more inviting and correcting the visual illusion that would otherwise make the central columns appear too crowded.

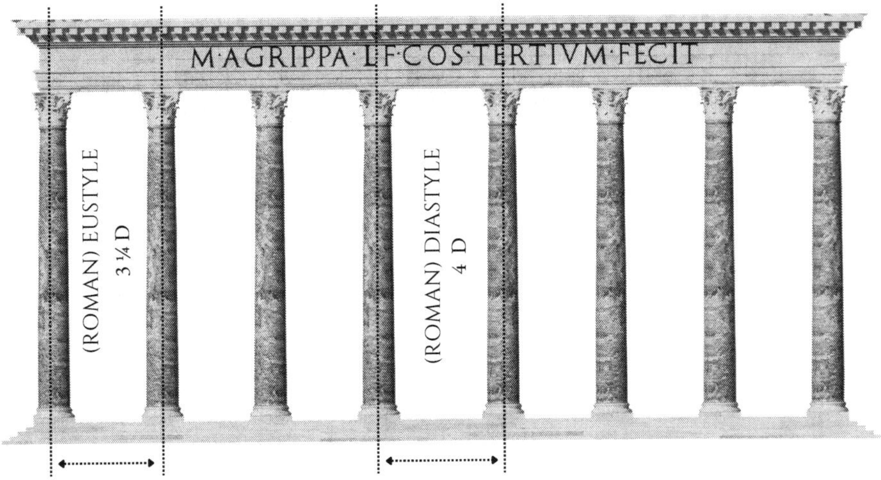

COLUMNS OF THE PANTHEON, ROME (~128 AD)

- Note: there must never be a column directly under the centre of a pediment. This interrupts the eye's natural flow toward the entrance, making a building less inviting and less visually appealing.

SUPERPOSITION

Superposition is the technique of vertically layering columns of different Orders on top of each other across multiple storeys of a building. This is done in one of two ways:

1. Using the same base diameter across all columns, so that each subsequent Order is taller (A). This method is more elegant.
2. Each Order is made to be the same height and so have differing base diameters (B). This method renders the Ionic and Corinthian Orders even slimmer than usual.

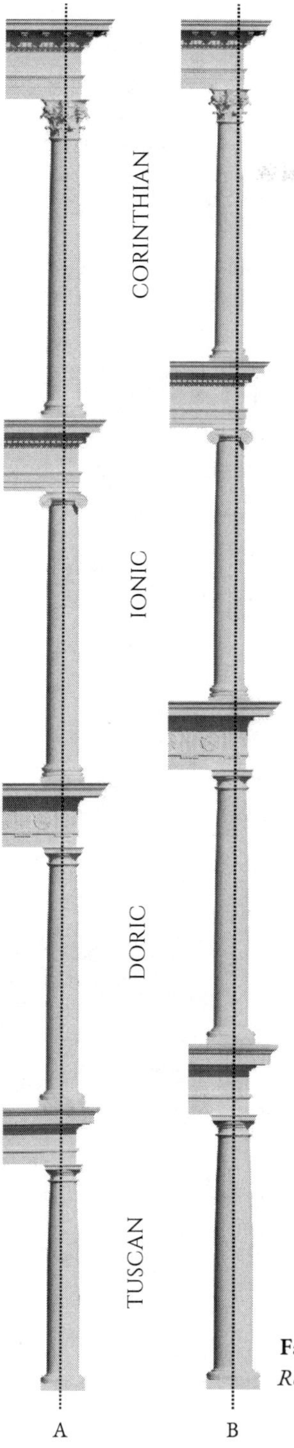

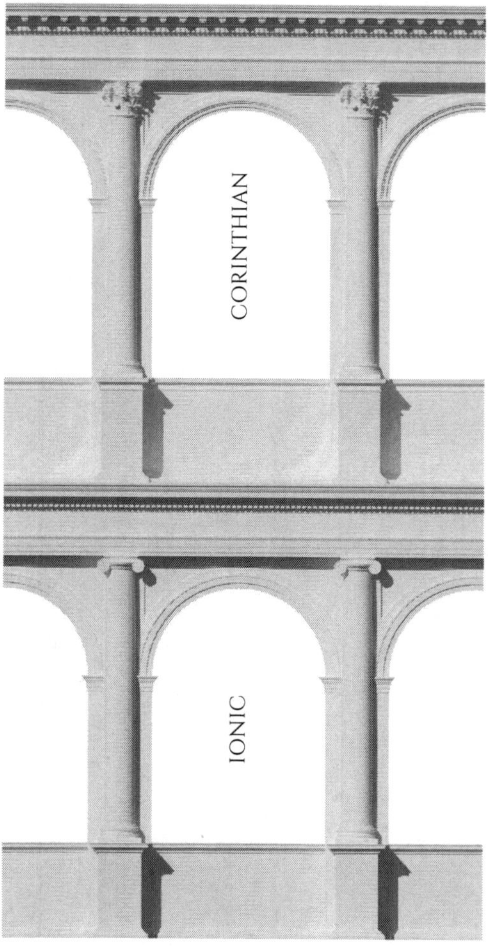

THE COLOSSEUM, ROME (~ 80 AD)
Second & third rows of columns

Famous examples: *The Colosseum, Rome; Theatre of Marcellus, Rome; Biblioteka Marciana, Venice; Banqueting House, London,*

ARCHES

An **Arch** is a curved structural element that spans an opening and transfers the load above it, such as a building, entablature, or arcade, down to supporting piers, walls, or columns. The Romans perfected and systemised the use of arches, typically employing them in structures like aqueducts, bridges, arcades and even doorways. Arches range from purely functional (as in aqueducts) to decorative (doors and windows), and are often rusticated to add visual weight and strength (below).

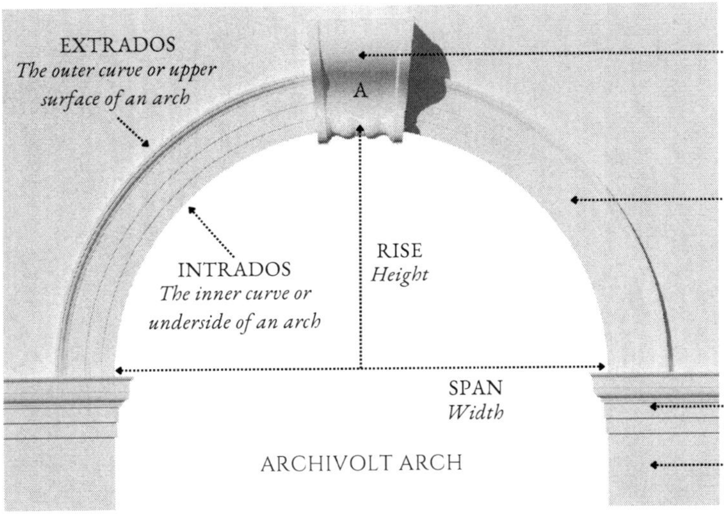

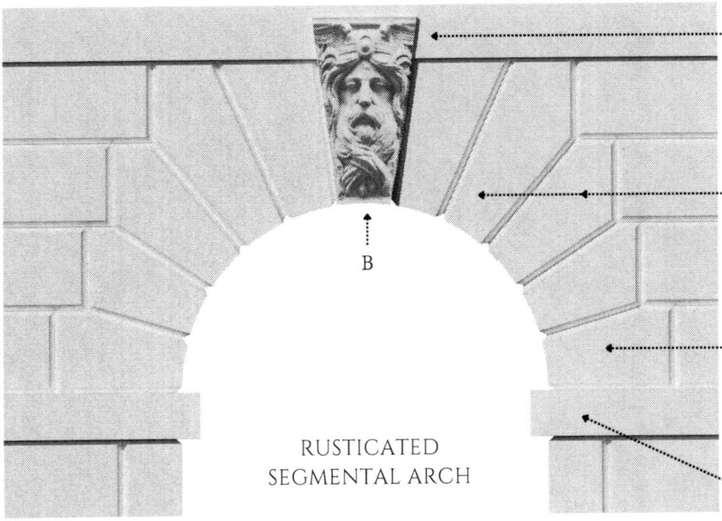

A **Keystone** is the central, topmost stone of an arch. Keystones are usually taller and more projecting than the surrounding stonework, serving as a visual focal point. They may be left plain or decorated in a variety of ways, from corbels (A) to carved faces (B) to rusticated (see page 103).

CLASSICAL ARCADES

Classical **Arcades** are composed of a series of arches placed between engaged columns that support an entablature. They typically form a covered walkway, gallery or structural framework, using the arches' strength to carry the weight above them. Arcades originated in Roman architecture, and were often used in amphitheatres, such as the Colosseum (page 93), and basilicas. Their sizes vary as needed and are typically spaced using column base diameters.

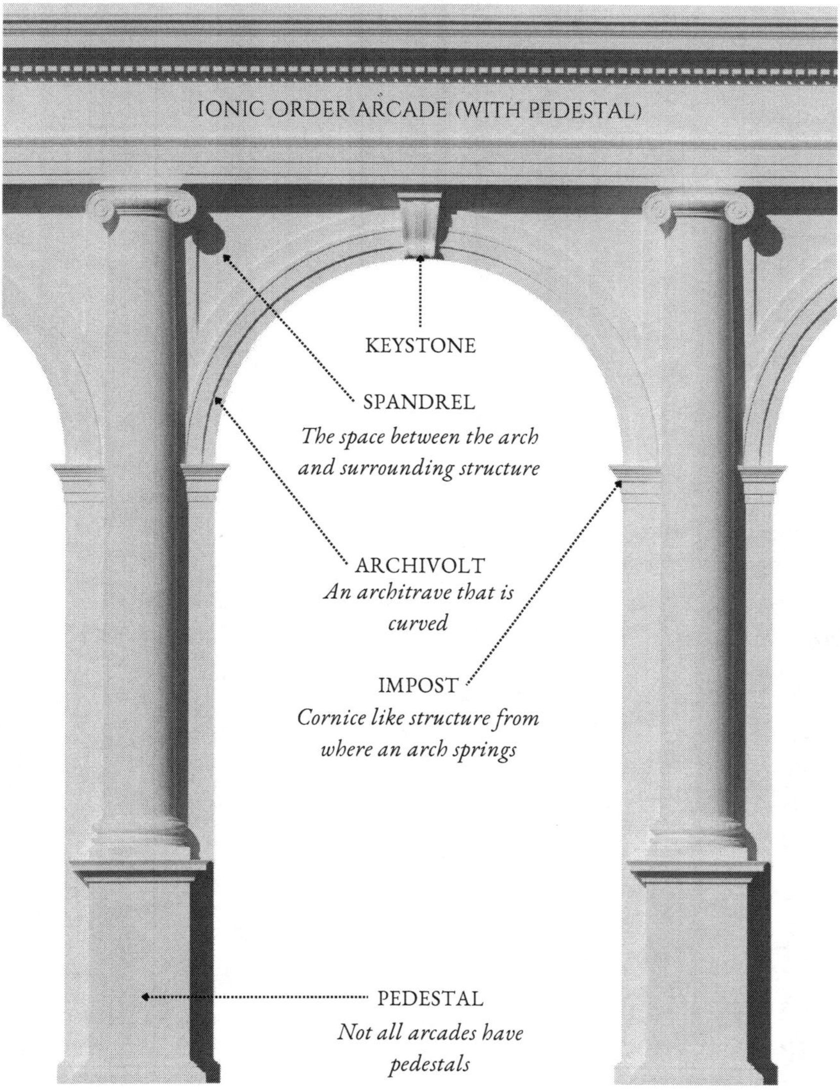

Famous examples: *The Colosseum, Rome; Biblioteka Marciana, Venice; Galeries Royales Saint-Hubert, Brussels.*

ARCADES & COLONNADES

Arcades, though they have many variations (see next page), all feature an impost, the cornice-like structure from which the curved archivolt springs.

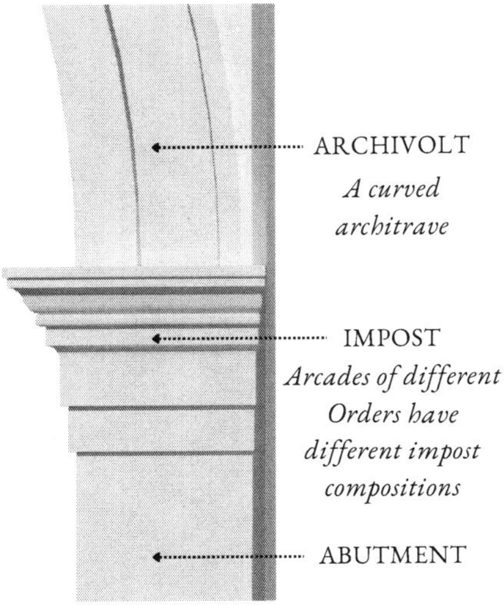

IONIC ORDER IMPOST

A **Colonnade** is a row of columns supporting a structure, usually an entablature. Colonnades are used in similar contexts to arcades, such as for covered walkways, courtyards and civic buildings, and are often decorated with balustrades on top. Unlike arcades, they feature no arches.

ARCADE VARIATIONS

IONIC ORDER ARCADE

PALLADIAN ARCADE

Features the highly popular Palladian motif (expanded upon on page 116)

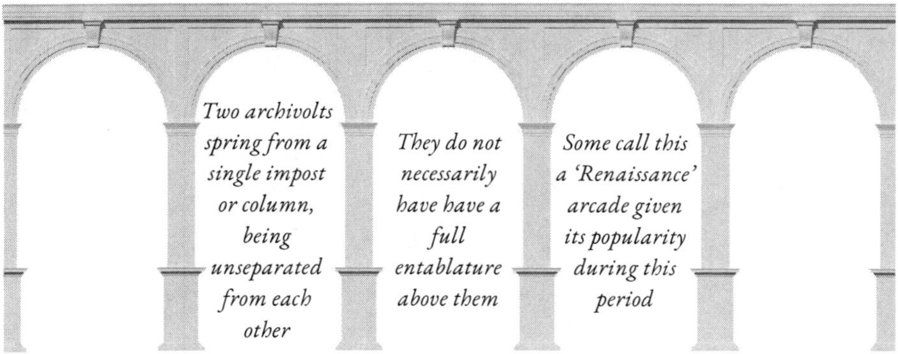

RENAISSANCE ARCADE

PEDIMENT ANGLES

The **main rule** for determining the angle of pediments, known as Vignola's or Serlio's rule, always produces a pediment angle of **22.5 degrees.** It is used for pediments atop doors and porticos alike.

- Firstly, a line is drawn between the widest parts of the raking cymatium (A-Z). At the centre of this line (B), an arc is drawn with a radius equal to A-B. At the lowest point of the A-B arc (C), another arc is drawn from point A to point Z with a radius of (C-A). The top of this second arc, at D, is the apex of the pediment.

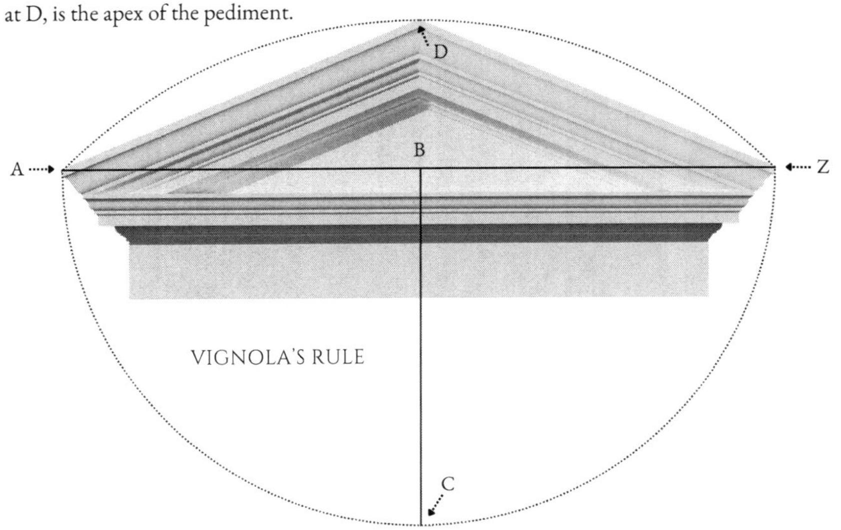

Alternatively, there is Vitruvius's method, suitable for larger buildings and porticos.

- For Corinthian pediments, Vitruvius divides the pediment into **nine** equal parts (measured from between the widest points of the raking cymatium, X), and gives **one** part to the height of the tympanum at the centre line of the pediment (Y). This equals approximately 18 degrees. For Ionic pediments, Vitruvius instead divides the pediment into eight equal parts, giving one part to the height of the tympanum, equalling approximately 19.4 degrees.

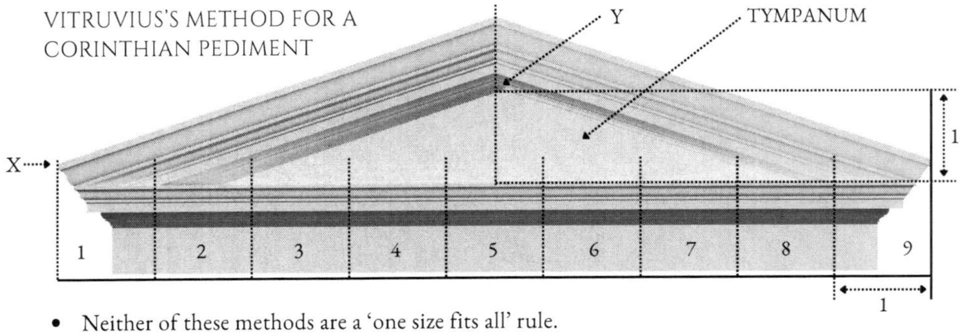

- Neither of these methods are a 'one size fits all' rule.
- Typically, the wider or larger, the portico, the flatter the angle of the pediment, and vice versa.
- Greek structures have shallower angles, typically 12-16 degrees (the Parthenon is 13.5°).

PEDIMENT ANGLES & PORTICOS

Other methods exist for calculating the angles and heights of classical pediments, such as the mathematical example below that is based on the number of columns in a portico. However, in reality, these methods are often inaccurate and do not constitute a systematic rule for all classical structures.

$$\text{Height} = \frac{4}{14 + \text{Number of Columns}}$$

- It is worth noting that classical pediment angles originate from countries with warm, dry climates; therefore, there are examples of steeper pitches used in wetter climates.

- A **Portico** is essentially the façade of a classical temple: a covered entrance or porch supported by columns, with an entablature and pediment, leading to the entrance of a building.
- Temples and porticos constructed with specific numbers of columns have unique names:

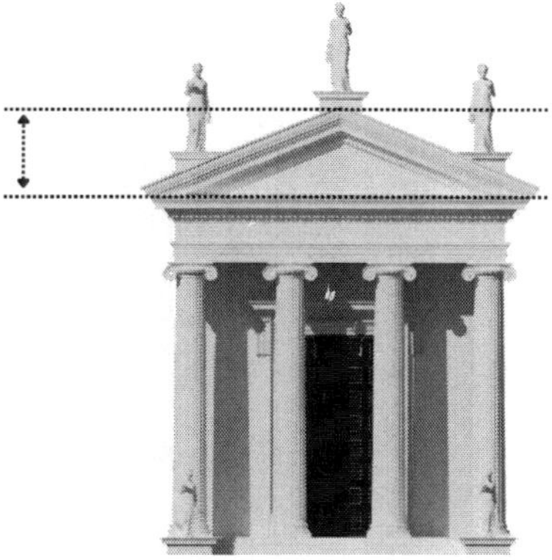

TETRASTYLE

4 Columns: 0.22 Height

Temple of Portunus

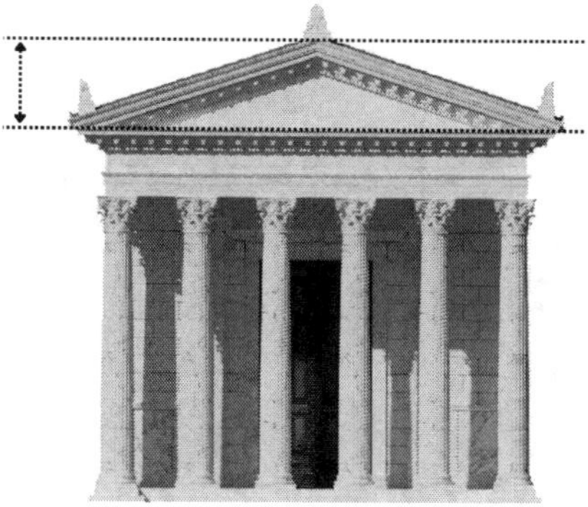

HEXASTYLE

6 Columns: 0.20 Height

Maison Carrée

Note: Heights are calculated (approximately) from the formula above

OCTASTYLE

8 Columns: 0.18 Height

Temple of Castor and Pollux

DECASTYLE

10 Columns: 0.16 Height

Temple of Venus and Roma

PEDIMENT VARIATIONS

There are a huge variety of **Pediment** types. Note: the following variations (except triangular) do not appear on top of temple porticos and are not seen in classical Greek architecture. Instead, these variations are commonly used to decorate the tops of door and window surrounds.

TRIANGULAR/POINTED

- Triangular pediment found in classical porticos, based on roof structures.
- This is the most common variation.

BROKEN

- A pediment that is broken at the apex, leaving the triangular point incomplete.
- Often decorated with urns or busts .

SEGMENTAL

- A curved pediment, sometimes called a round pediment.
- Its shape follows the arc outlined in Vignola's rule on page 98.

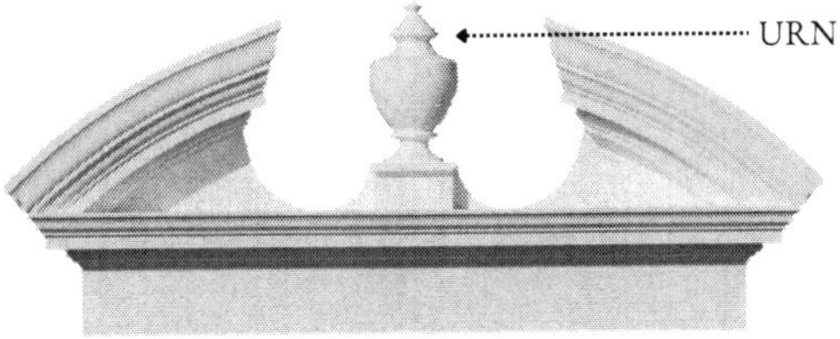

BROKEN SEGMENTAL

- A segmental pediment that is 'broken,' reaching no apex.
- Often decorated with urns or busts.

CONTINUED

- At the outer eaves of the pediment, the cornice and raking cymatium extend horizontally to the sides. This extension is set back slightly, and the cymatium's profile is adjusted accordingly.

PEDIMENT VARIATIONS

STOPPED BASE

- The horizontal cornice at the centre is set back (A) whilst the sides of the frieze project outward in symmetrical blocks (B), beneath which there may be a column.

OPEN TYMPANUM

- Features a stopped base, as above, but no horizontal cornice between stopped bases.
- A decorative element, such as a festoon, is often placed in the resulting space.

SWAN-NECK

- A Swan-neck, or scroll pediment, is a variation of a broken pediment. Its cornice follows an 'S' shape that terminates in volutes or scrolls.
- Typically appear in Baroque architecture and are often decorated with urns, busts or finials.

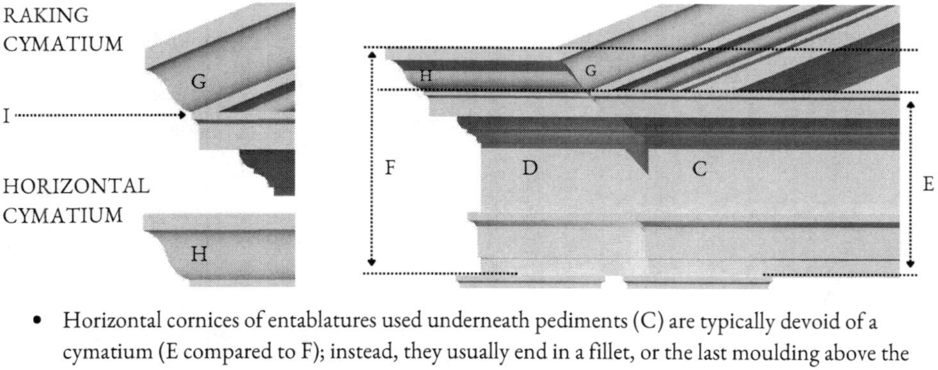

- Horizontal cornices of entablatures used underneath pediments (C) are typically devoid of a cymatium (E compared to F); instead, they usually end in a fillet, or the last moulding above the corona. The cymatium is employed above in the raking cornice as the raking cymatium.
- The curve of the raking cymatium (G) is always at a shallower angle than the curve of the corresponding horizontal cymatium of the cornice (H), as the raking cymatium must run into the horizontal cymatium seamlessly (D - a Tuscan Order).
- The top fillet of the horizontal cornice seamlessly blends into the bottom fillet of the raking cymatium; this is known as a split fillet (I).

PARTS OF CLASSICAL BUILDINGS

DECORATIVE URN

BALUSTRADE

COLOSSAL ORDER

A colossal Order, or giant Order, is a column that extends across the entire façade of a building, spanning multiple floors.

RUSTICATED BASE OR PLINTH

CHATSWORTH HOUSE

STATUE

FINIAL

BALUSTRADE

TETRASTYLE PORTICO

PIANO NOBILE

Italian for 'noble floor'

The main rooms of a building are normally elevated (i.e., one floor up) and typically have the largest windows. This signals the importance of the interior room from the outside.

RUSTICATED BASE OR PLINTH

STOURHEAD HOUSE

RUSTICATION

Rustication is a masonry technique in which stone blocks are deliberately left rough or deeply grooved at the joints to create a bold, textured effect. It is commonly used on the ground floor of buildings to convey strength and solidity in contrast with the smooth upper levels.

- Isodomic rustication is when ashlars (perfectly squared, smooth stones) are rusticated with recessed (square-cut) or chamfered (v-cut) joints between blocks.
- Rustication can also include much rougher, more natural surfaces, such as those with visible tool marks from the stoneworking process or even natural rock faces. Conversely, some styles of rustication employ carefully carved patterns like vermiculation or frost-work (below).
- Rustication is not found in Greek architecture.

CHAMFERED
(V CUT)

CHANNEL
(SQUARE CUT)

ROCK FACED
Usually a split surface, quarried surface or natural rock face.

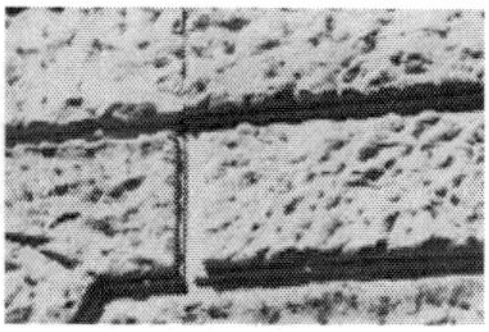

PICKED OR TOOLED
Rough chisel marks are left in the stone.

FROST-WORK
Also called glaciation. Depicts frozen icicles.

DIAMOND
Also called prismatic, features raised pyramids. Popular during the Italian Renaissance.

VERMICULATED
Features irregular curved cut-in sections. From the Latin vermis *meaning 'wormed.' Popular in Neoclassical work.*

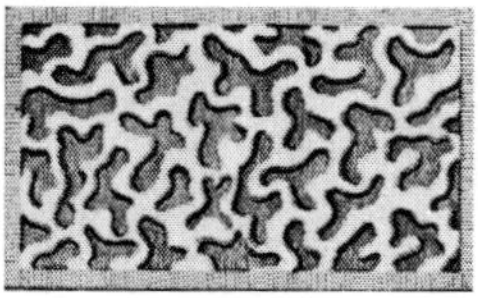

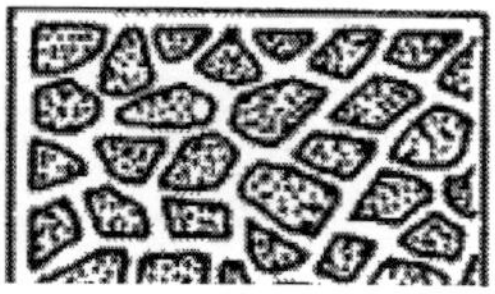

RETICULATED
Often confused with vermiculated. The irregular cut-in sections are not as curved.

RUSTICATION

Rustication not only refers to a masonry finish but also to the treatment of architectural elements that are intersected with rustic elements. In the examples below, both the archivolt and pilasters are treated with rustic elements. Rustication is also used to describe the base of buildings that feature masonry with rusticated finishes, known as a rusticated base or rusticated plinth (A).

- The Romans originally employed the technique, often for practical reasons in aqueducts and city walls, where smooth ashlar blocks were not required, saving time and labour costs.
- The technique was adopted in the Renaissance as an architectural aesthetic. Rustication remained a universal practice from the Renaissance onwards, and is frequently seen in Baroque and Neoclassical architecture.
- Practically, it is generally inefficient, requiring a lot of labour to create the rusticated look.

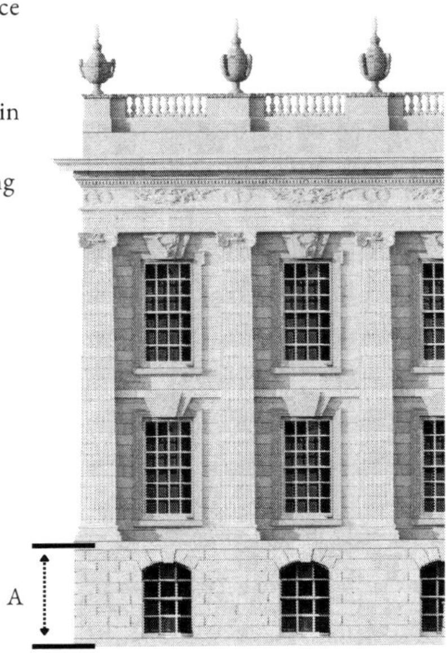

RUSTICATED BASE / PLINTH
CHATSWORTH HOUSE

RUSTICATED DORIC PILASTER

With blocking

RUSTICATED IONIC PILASTER

With chamfering

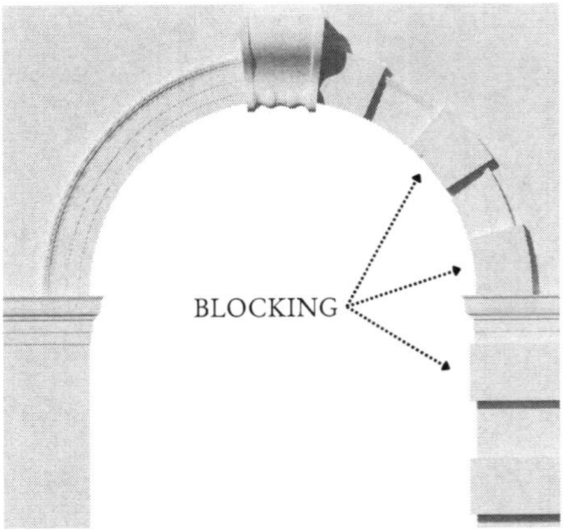

PLAIN ARCH

RUSTICATED ARCH

ARCHITRAVE MOULDING

An **Architrave** moulding, used around doors, windows and other openings, takes its name from the architrave of entablatures, as they originally, and typically still, share very similar profiles and proportions. It serves both a decorative and practical function by covering joints around these openings.

- **The width of an architrave must be 1/6 the size of the opening.**
- This ensures it appears neither too thin and structurally weak nor too large and distracting.

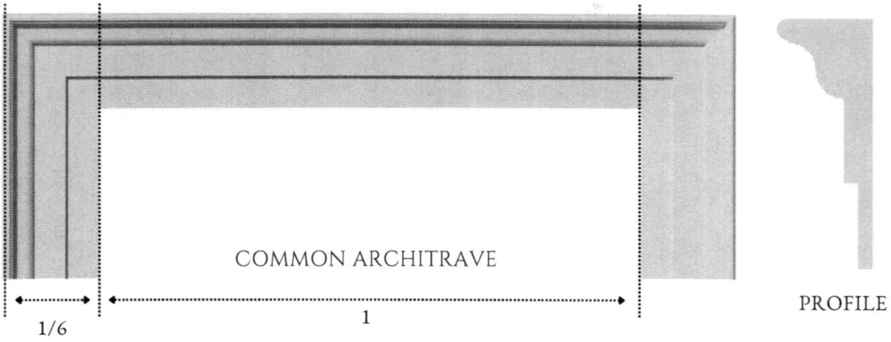

- Two key variations of architrave are the Eared, Lobed or **Lugged Architrave**, and the **Shouldered Architrave.** These are frequently used around ornate windows and doors.
- Designs and profiles can differ significantly, encompassing a wide range of shapes and complexities, particularly for indoor architraves, which are usually more ornate.

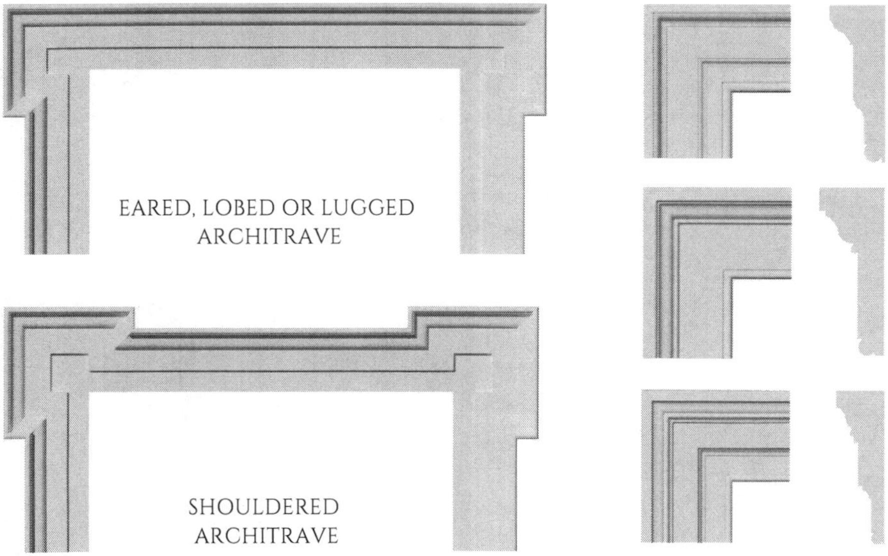

VARIATIONS

THEORIES OF PROPORTION

Proportion Methods: Arithmetic and Geometric

All classical systems of proportion are derived from fundamental geometric and arithmetic principles, using simple numerical ratios and manipulations of basic shapes like circles and squares. Several key methods and proportions are shown on the right and on the next page.

Music

Many classical proportions mirror musical intervals. Ratios such as 1:2 (octave) and 4:3 (fourth) arise from dividing a vibrating string and the resulting change in pitch being a harmonic of the original.

Fibonacci & Golden Ratio

Ratios like 5:8 and 2:3 come from the Fibonacci sequence. As you progress through the series, the ratio of each number to the next gradually approximates the Golden Ratio, 1:1.618.

Myths

It is often suggested that the Parthenon (below) is so beautiful because its proportions align with the Golden Ratio. However, this ratio was likely not used by the ancients and did not appear in architectural texts until the nineteenth century. The Parthenon is more likely based on the simple ratio of 4:9.

Beauty & Harmony

For Vitruvius, architectural harmony was a prerequisite for beauty. Architecture, like music or the human body, had to possess internal proportional order, and classical structures reflect this harmony through their ratios and mathematical balance.

Personal Preferences

Proportions, in many cases, are largely at the discretion of individual architects and their preferences, usually in response to a building's purpose, intended grandeur and size.

Arithmetic Proportions

- 1:1, 1:2, 3:5, 4:9, etc.
- Any simple numbers (typically less than 10) in any ratios.

Geometric Proportions

- Based on certain manipulations of circles and squares.
- Includes irrational numbers like $\sqrt{2}$ (the ratio of the sides of a square to its diagonal) or $\sqrt{3}$.

Musical Intervals

- 1:1, 1:2, 1:3, 3:4, etc.
- Derived from musical harmonics.

Fibonacci Sequence

- 1,1,2,3,5,8,13 etc.
- Simple arithmetic sequence, not dissimilar to regular arithmetic proportions.

Leonardo Da Vinci's Vitruvian man, based on Vitruvius's notes.

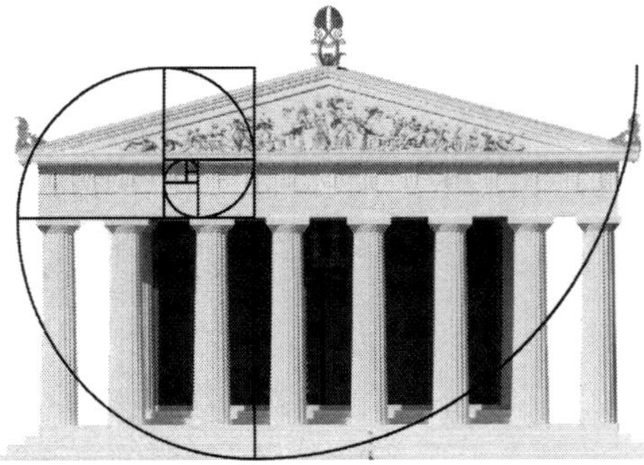

The Parthenon overlaid with a Golden Ratio

PROPORTIONS

The following proportions are commonly found in classical structures and are important for designing rooms, window and door sizes, and other architectural elements. Regardless of the proportions chosen, the most important thing for a harmonious structure is to use consistent proportionality throughout, for example, ensuring that rooms and windows are in proportion.

1:1	16:15	10:9	9:5	6:5	5:4
1:1	*1:1.066*	*1:111*	*1:1.125*	*1:1.2*	*1:1.25*

4:3	45:32	1:√2	3:2	8:5	1:618
1:1.333	*1:1.40625*	*1:1.4142*	*1:1.5*	*1:1.6*	*Golden Section*

5:3	1:√3	9:5	15:6	2:1	7:3
1:1.666	*1:1.732*	*1:1.8*	*1:1.875*	*1:2*	*1:2.333*

PROPORTIONS ACCORDING TO ANDREA PALLADIO

Below is a selection of Andrea Palladio's preferred proportions for room layouts and door and window surrounds.

- Palladio noted his choices favoured and reflected the proportions found in music.
- To reiterate, proportions are often a matter of personal choice.

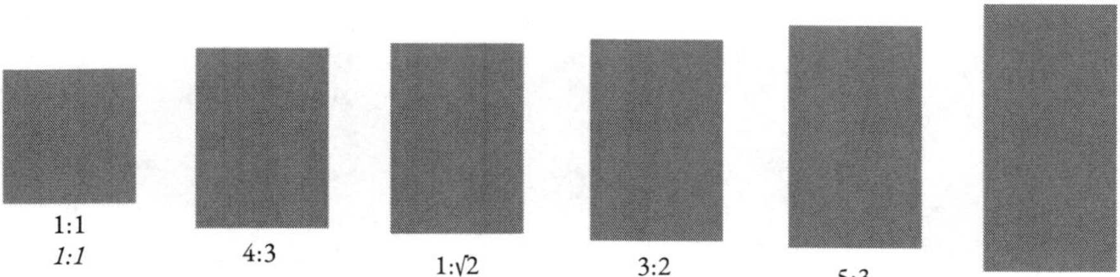

1:1	4:3	1:√2	3:2	5:3	2:1
1:1	*1:1.3333*	*1:1.4142*	*1:1.5*	*1:1.6666*	*1:2*

DOOR SURROUNDS

Door Surrounds are the decorative mouldings and forms around doors, the entrances to buildings. These structures follow the rules of proportion highlighted on the previous and frequently incorporate elements like pediments, architraves and rustication. Their general rules are:

- The proportions of door openings are nearly always **2:1, 2⅙:1** or **2⅓:1**.
- Door openings are often in proportion to the base diameters of the columns used in the main structure. For example, a doorway may be two column diameters wide.
- Door surrounds typically have entablatures above them, with an architrave, frieze and cornice in simple ratios such as **7:6:8, 5:4:5, 4:3:5, 10:9:11, 1:1:1** and many others, rather than always using the standard entablature proportions outlined in Part II.
- Architrave surrounds are **1/6** the size of the opening, with the frieze and cornice therefore proportioned to this size. These sizes are again also often proportional to column-base diameters.
- Doorways are frequently rusticated, to emphasise their visual and architectural importance.
- The main decorative door or entrance of a building is called the frontispiece.
- The main entrance of a structure, as with the principal windows of the piano nobile (main floor), is typically larger and more ornate. As with the rest of the building, size, scale, ornamentation and use of the Orders convey importance.
- Door surrounds typically have the exact same decorative elements and formats as window surrounds.
- The following variations are largely post-Roman (e.g. Baroque and Neoclassical); Greek architecture did not use these forms.

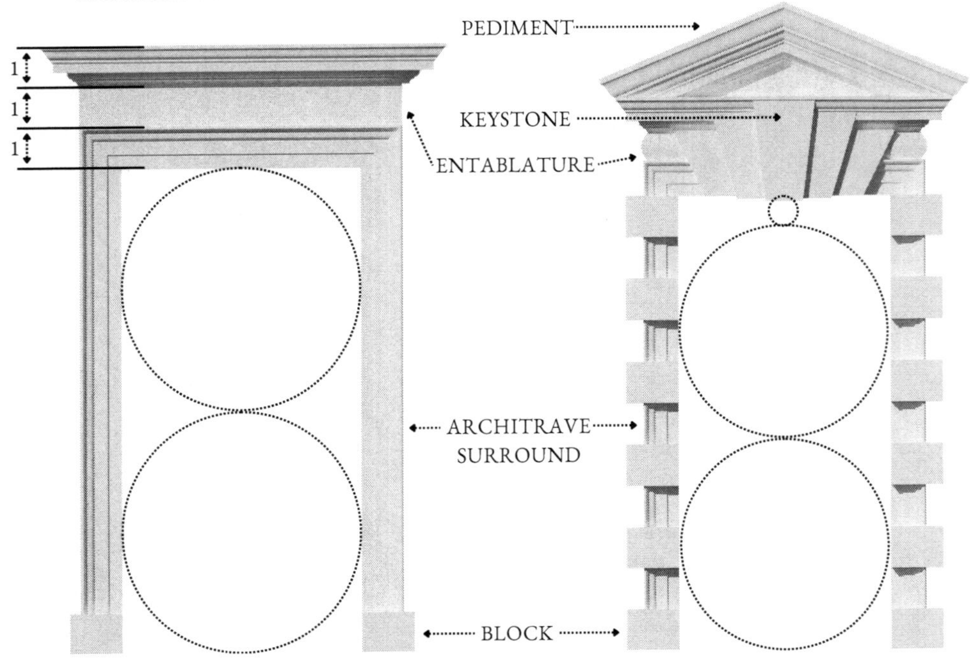

SIMPLE DOORWAY
2:1

RUSTICATED DOORWAY
2⅙:1

DOOR SURROUND VARIATIONS

Note: Numbers represent ratios of elements

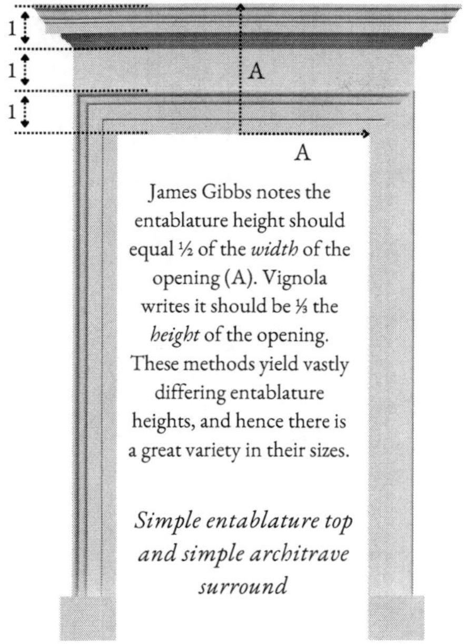

James Gibbs notes the entablature height should equal ½ of the *width* of the opening (A). Vignola writes it should be ⅓ the *height* of the opening. These methods yield vastly differing entablature heights, and hence there is a great variety in their sizes.

Simple entablature top and simple architrave surround

Note: Changes of scale

Rusticated with chamfered blocks

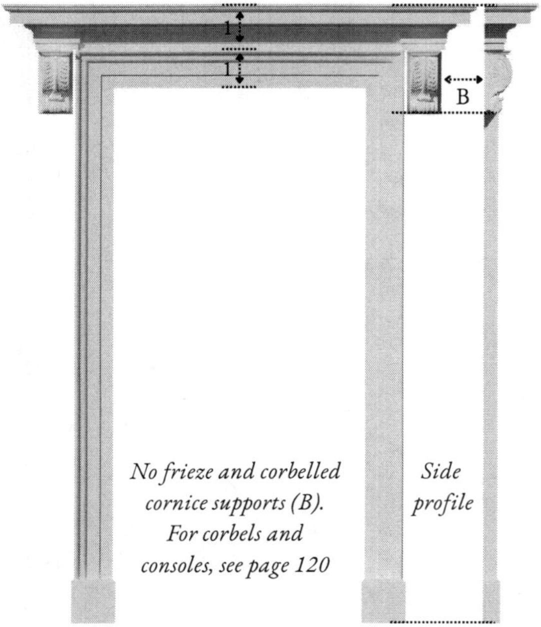

No frieze and corbelled cornice supports (B). For corbels and consoles, see page 120

Side profile

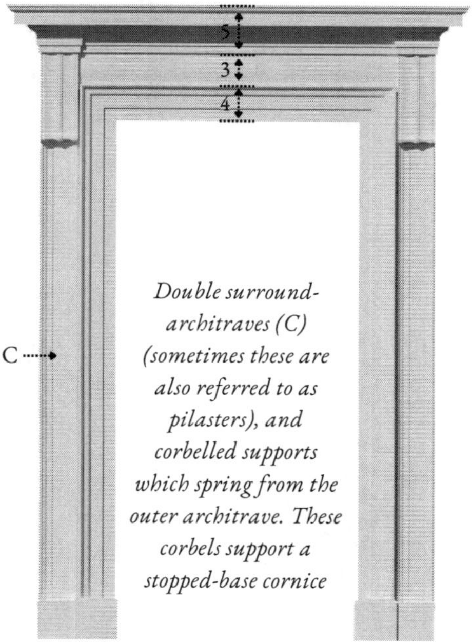

Double surround-architraves (C) (sometimes these are also referred to as pilasters), and corbelled supports which spring from the outer architrave. These corbels support a stopped-base cornice

DOOR SURROUND VARIATIONS

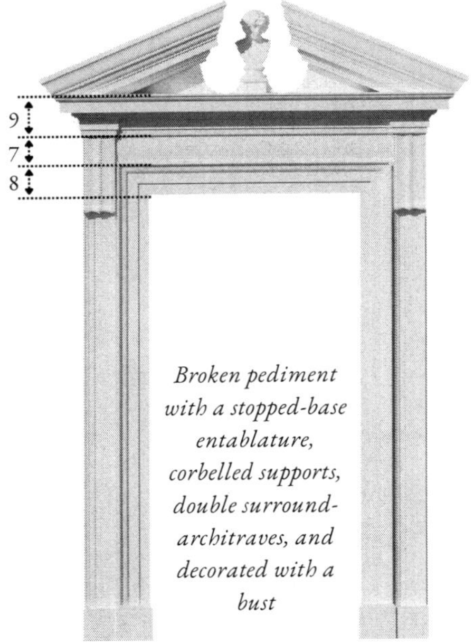

Broken pediment with a stopped-base entablature, corbelled supports, double surround-architraves, and decorated with a bust

Note: Changes of scale

Note: Numbers represent ratios of elements

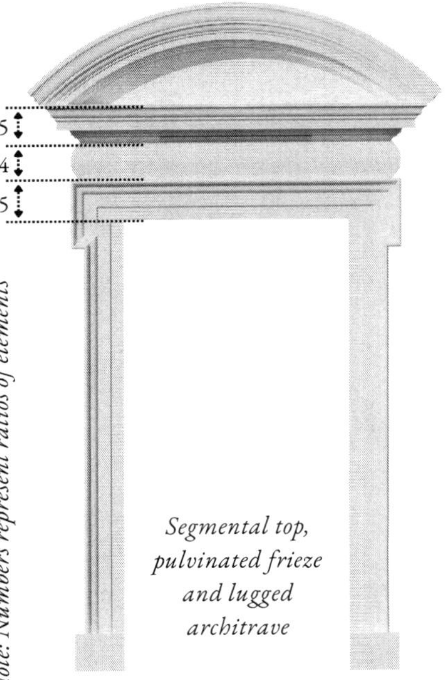

Segmental top, pulvinated frieze and lugged architrave

Columned supports to the sides of the architrave surround, with a pediment atop. For ***Aedicules****, see page 117*

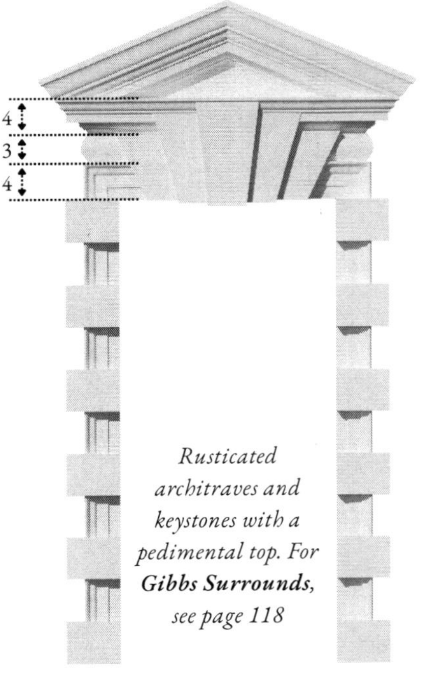

Rusticated architraves and keystones with a pedimental top. For ***Gibbs Surrounds****, see page 118*

WINDOW SURROUNDS

Window Surrounds are the decorative mouldings and forms around windows, which admit light into a building. They use the same forms and decorations as door surrounds but are not limited by the more specific proportions required for door openings. Instead, they may follow any of the proportional dimensions listed on page 107. The rules for windows and window surrounds are:

- Windows are commonly proportioned with simple ratios, like **1:1**, **3:2**, **2:1** and **1:√2**.
- Principal windows of the piano nobile (main floor) are typically the largest and most ornate.
- Their architrave surrounds should be **1/6** the size of the opening.
- They utilise the same decorations and forms as door surrounds, often featuring entablatures and pediments, with the architrave, frieze and cornice of these entablatures usually proportioned in simple ratios such as **7:6:8, 5:4:5, 4:3:5, 10:9:11, 1:1:1** and others, rather than always using the standard entablature proportions outlined in Part II.
- Unlike door surrounds, window surrounds are often placed on top of pedestals and balustrades.
- Typically follow the principle of graduated fenestration, the practice of diminishing window sizes with each ascending story of a building (elaborated on page 115). Windows in attic storeys and upper floors are usually proportioned in 1:1 ratios.
- They can be completely round (called an oculus) or have arched tops (below).
- The base of a window is called a sill and is shaped with a slope on its top face to shed water away from the opening. Sills are often supported by decorative corbels.
- The glass parts of a window are called panes or lights. The solid dividing parts are known as glazing bars.
- The following variations are largely post-Roman (e.g. Neoclassical, and Baroque); Greek architecture did not use these forms.

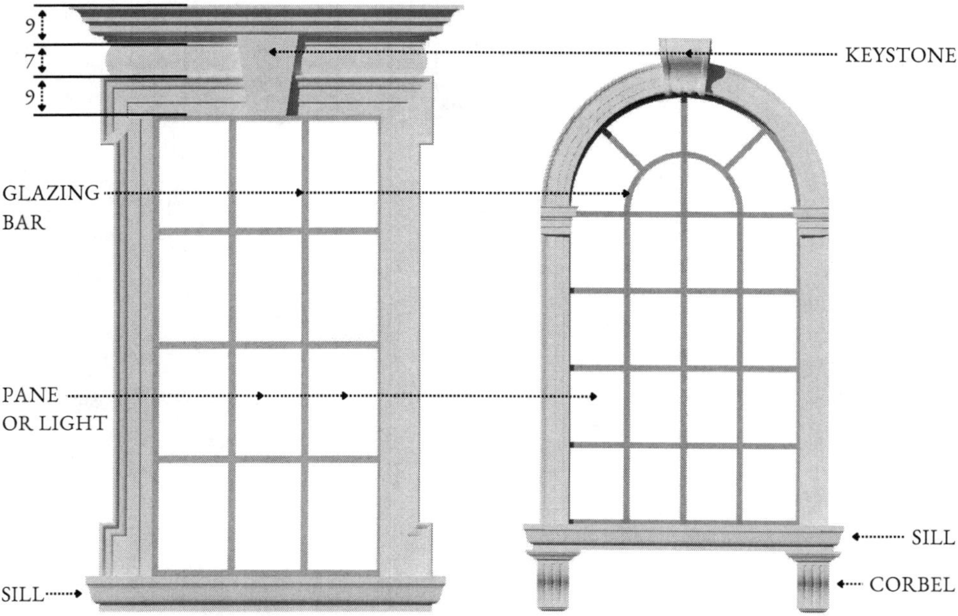

ORNATE 12 LIGHT WINDOW

FAN OR ARCHED WINDOW

WINDOW SURROUND VARIATIONS

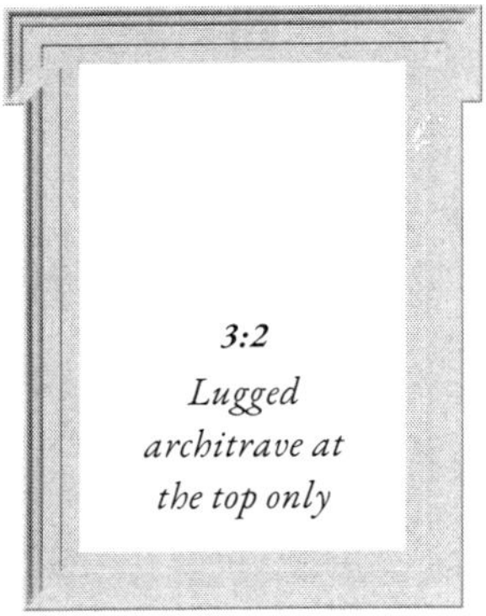

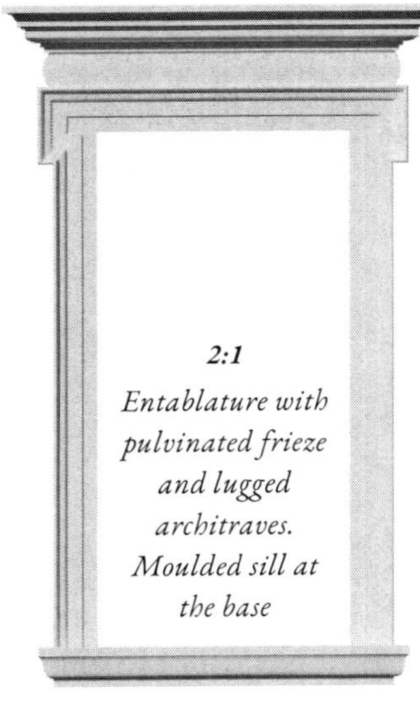

Note: Changes of scale

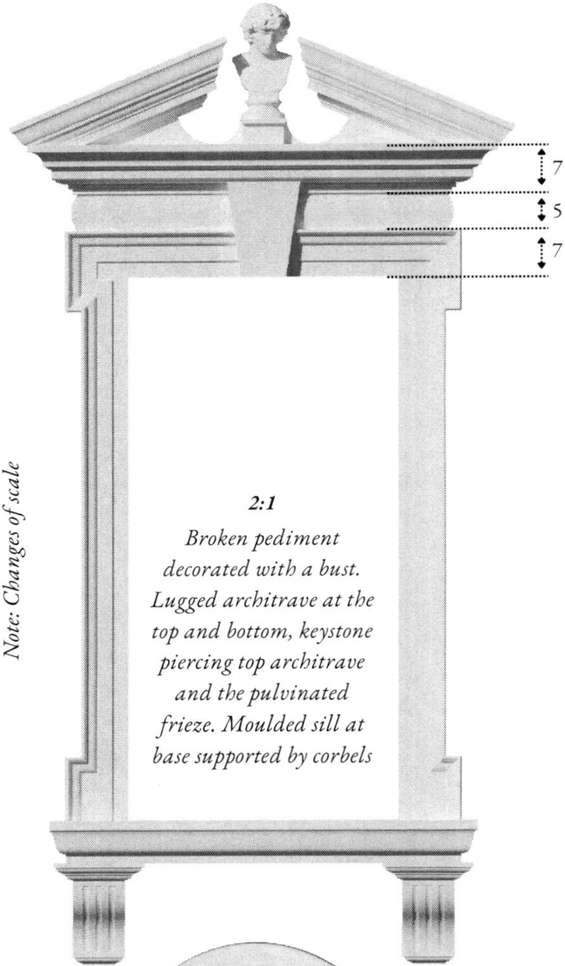

Note: Numbers inside windows represent the opening's proportions. Numbers next to entablatures represent ratios of their elements

WINDOW SURROUND VARIATIONS

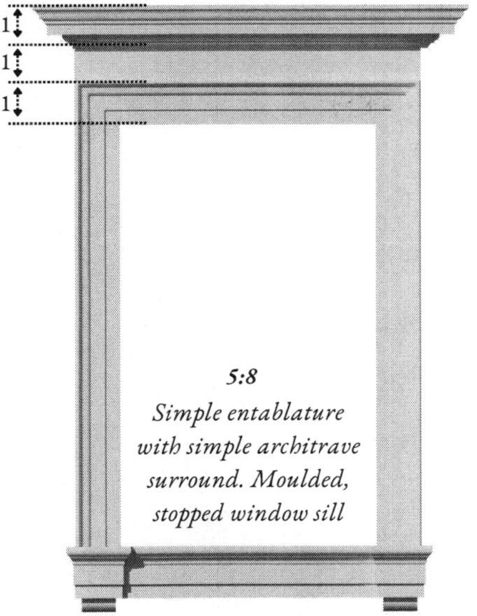

5:8
Simple entablature with simple architrave surround. Moulded, stopped window sill

Note: Changes of scale

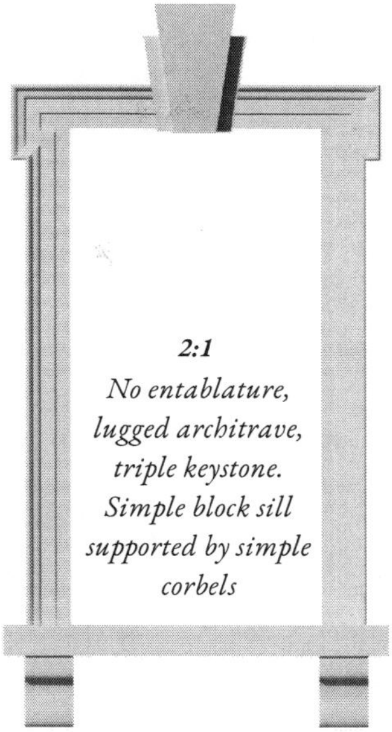

2:1
No entablature, lugged architrave, triple keystone. Simple block sill supported by simple corbels

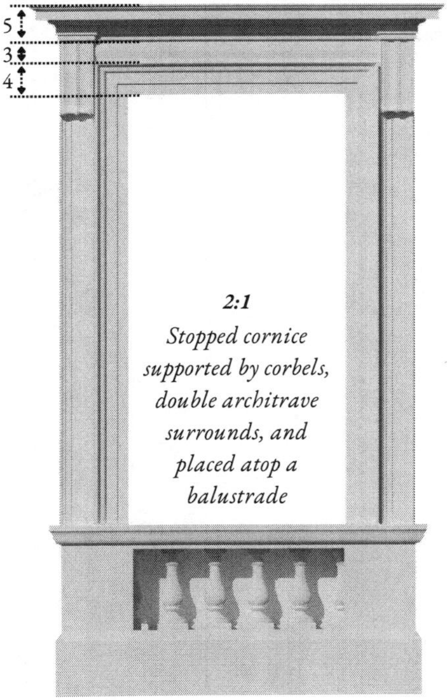

2:1
Stopped cornice supported by corbels, double architrave surrounds, and placed atop a balustrade

Note: Numbers inside windows represent the opening's proportions.
Numbers next to entablatures represent ratios of their elements

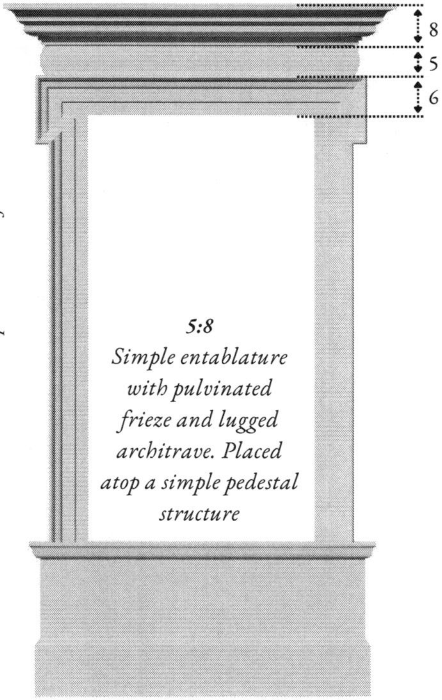

5:8
Simple entablature with pulvinated frieze and lugged architrave. Placed atop a simple pedestal structure

RUSTICATED AND ARCHED WINDOW SURROUNDS

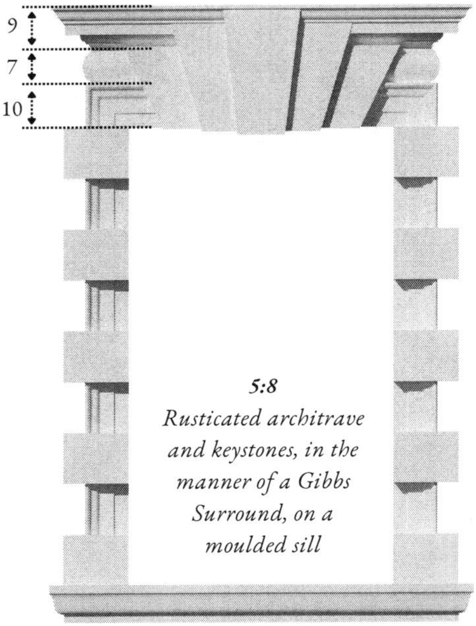

5:8
Rusticated architrave and keystones, in the manner of a Gibbs Surround, on a moulded sill

Note: Changes of scale

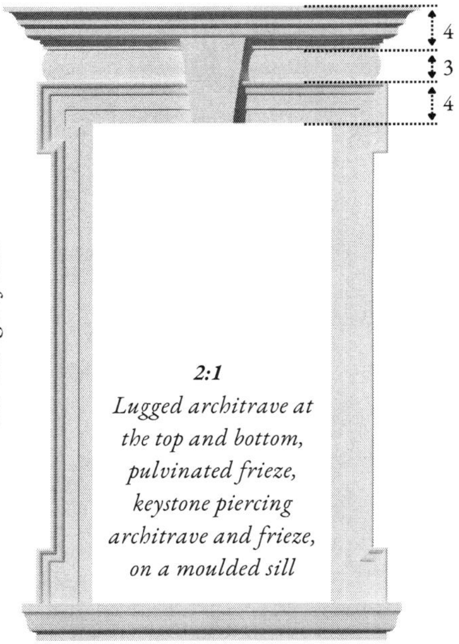

2:1
Lugged architrave at the top and bottom, pulvinated frieze, keystone piercing architrave and frieze, on a moulded sill

1:√3
Rusticated with chamfered blocks and segmental flanking voussoirs, on a moulded sill

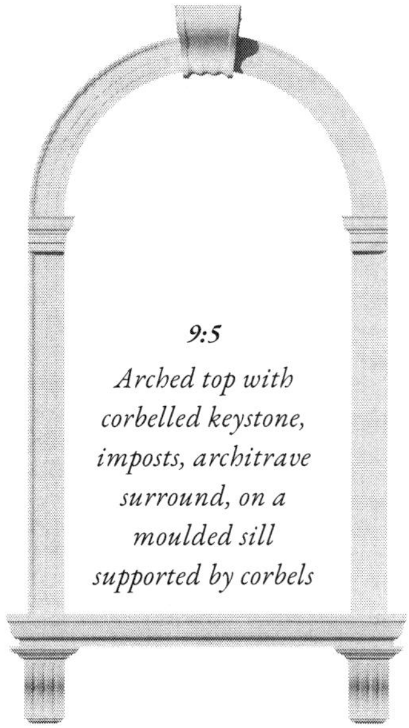

9:5
Arched top with corbelled keystone, imposts, architrave surround, on a moulded sill supported by corbels

Note: Numbers inside windows represent the opening's proportions. Numbers next to entablatures represent ratios of their elements

GRADUATED FENESTRATION

Graduated Fenestration is the reduction in window size, spacing and ornamentation with each ascending storey of a building. This creates a visual hierarchy, emphasises the importance of the principal rooms of the piano nobile and lends a sense of elegance and refinement to the façade.

- Common progressions (top to bottom) include series such as 1:1, 1:√2, 1:√3, 2:1, or 1:1, 3:2, 2:1. Ratios like these allow window panes to maintain a consistent size and proportion across a façade (left).
- The term fenestration derives from the Latin *fenestra,* meaning 'window.'

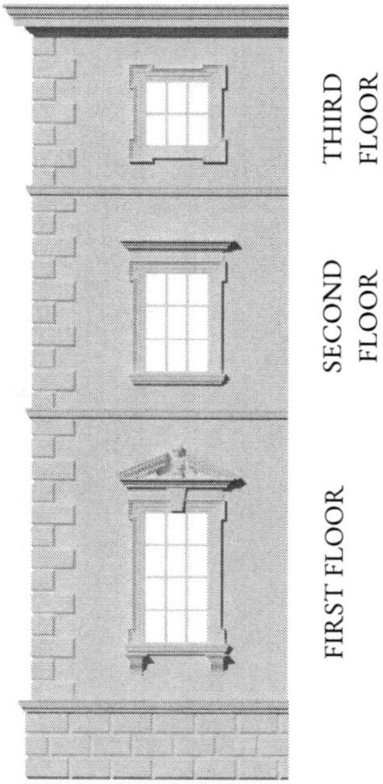

NEOCLASSICAL FAÇADE

VENETIAN WINDOW

A **Venetian Window**, commonly called a Palladian window, is one of the most recognisable motifs in classical architecture. It is named for its frequent use in Venice and by Andrea Palladio, and is typically used as a window or within arcades (page 97). The form consists of a tripartite window featuring a large central arched opening flanked by two smaller rectangular openings, framed by pairs of columns or pilasters. The entablature above these columns supports the central arch. The columns are typically of the Ionic Order, usually placed atop a pedestal base and sometimes rusticated.

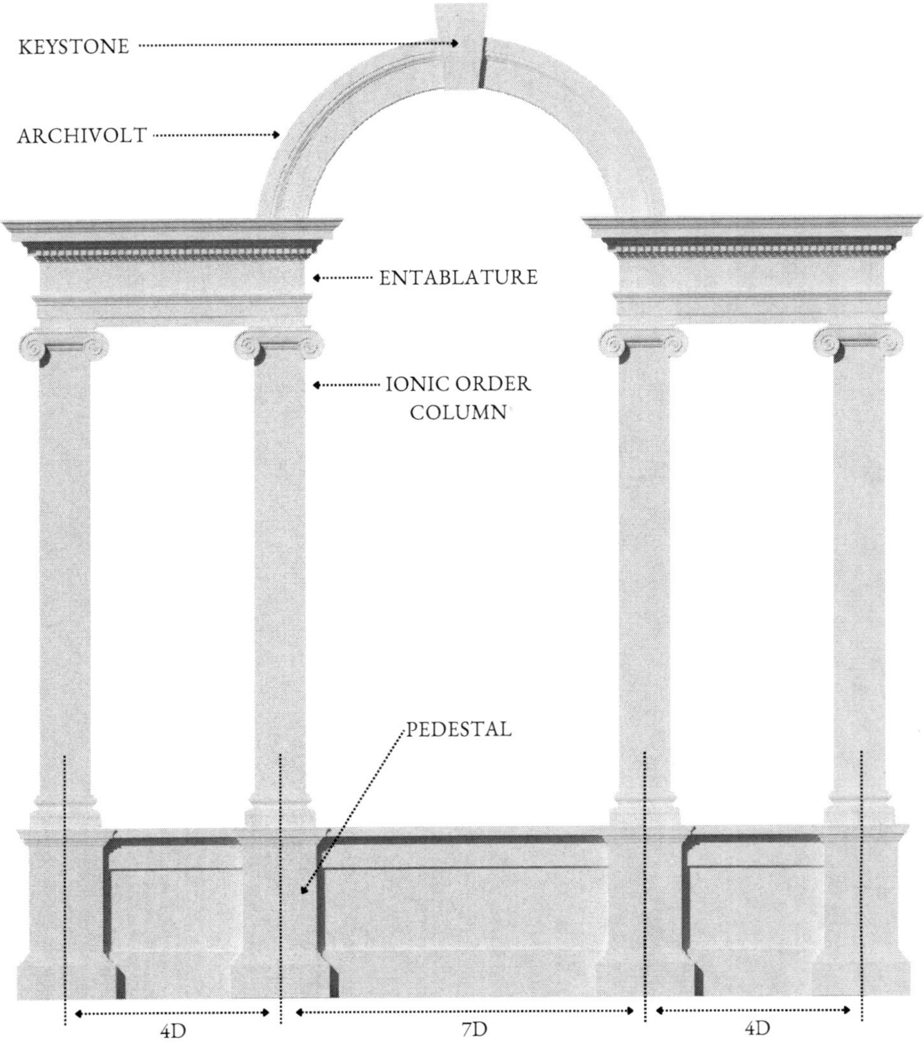

- It is also commonly called a 'Serliana' or a Serlian arch, after the Italian architect Sebastiano Serlio.

AEDICULE

An **Aedicule** is comprised of an architrave surround framed by two columns or pilasters, with an entablature and pediment above. Commonly used around the windows and doors of grand structures, they are particularly popular in Renaissance and Baroque architecture. Aedicules originated in Roman architecture, where they were small, temple-like shrines. The Latin *aedicula* means 'small building.'

- The example below features Corinthian columns, though any of the five Orders may be used.
- While the aedicule below is set on a pedestal, as is commonly done for window surrounds and shrines, they are not used for doors.

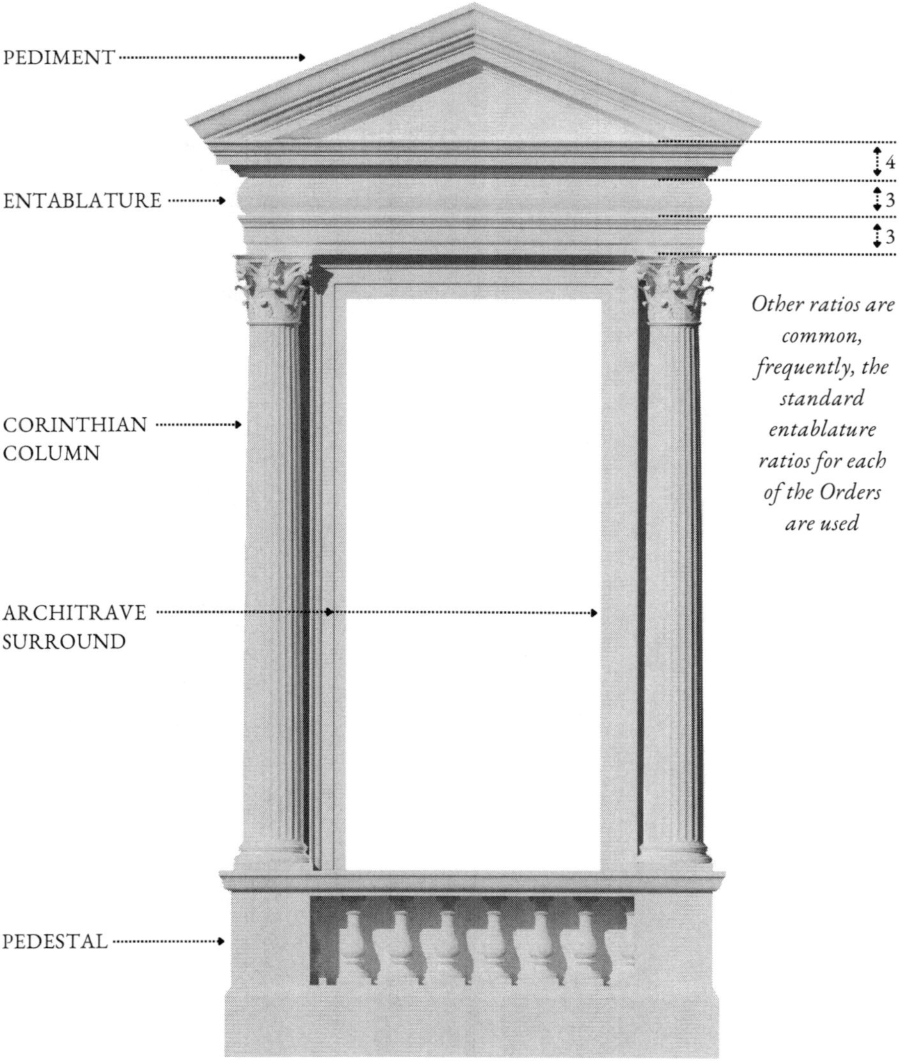

GIBBS SURROUND

A **Gibbs Surround** consists of square or rectangular blocks that intersect the architraves at the sides of an opening at regular intervals. The keystone (A) and flanking voussoirs usually project into the horizontal upper part of the architrave surround and continue into the frieze and cornice above. They are usually topped with a pediment (below), though this is not always the case (page 114). It is a highly distinctive motif used for both door and window surrounds.

- The form is named after James Gibbs who, though not its inventor, used the motif frequently.
- It originated in the Renaissance and became highly popular in Baroque architecture.
- The blocks may also be placed to the sides of the architrave surround instead of intersecting it.
- A Gibbs surround is a variation of a rusticated door or window surround.

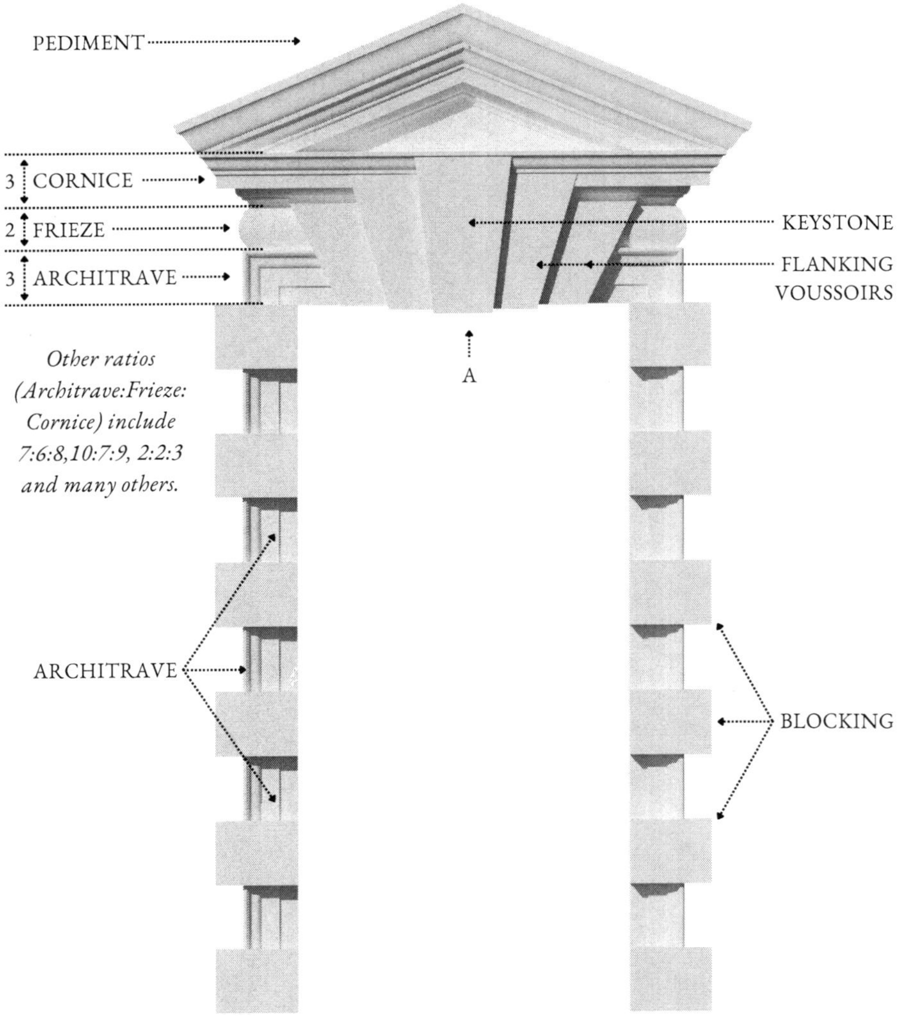

BALUSTRADES, PARAPETS & ATTICS

Single *Double/Mirror* *Squared*
BALUSTERS

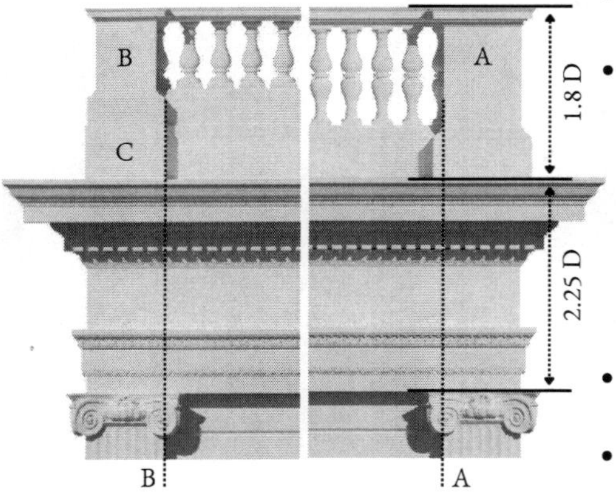

The example above is of the Ionic Order, with an entablature height of 2.25D. The balustrade above this is proportioned at 4/5 of the entablature, making it 1.8D tall.

Technically, any structure above an entablature is called an **Attic.** These often take the form of a balustrade (a row of balusters ending in pedestals), a parapet (a solid wall; often with the same profile as a pedestal), or an attic storey when the building continues upward with rooms.

- Balustrades are made tall enough to be clearly visible from underneath, past the projecting cornice.
- Typically, balustrades are **4/5** the size of the entablature they are set on, though ratios of 1:1 are sometimes used.
- The pedestals of balustrades are placed in line with the columns of the entablature below.
- The die of the pedestal should line up with the top of the columns shaft (B), resulting in larger balusters and pedestals. Alternatively, the plinth of the pedestal (A) should line up with the top of the columns shaft; in this case it is common for a small parapet wall to support the balustrade (C). This method results in smaller balusters and pedestals.
- Balusters are spaced at ½ the diameter of their widest section, from the widest section.
- The pedestals and rails of balustrades often use the pedestal forms associated with each of the five Orders, featuring profiles of varying form and complexity.
- Balusters themselves vary greatly in their design.
- Balusters always remain vertical when placed on angled surfaces (D).
- Pedestals of balustrades are frequently decorated with statues, urns and finials.

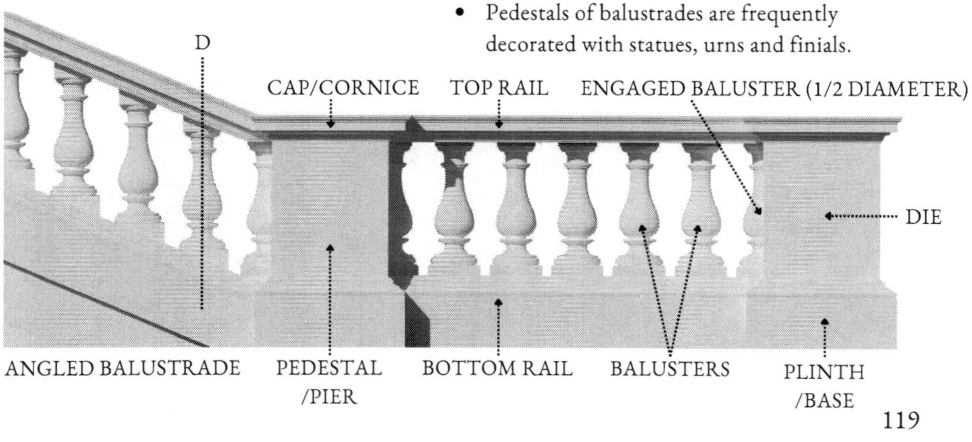

CORBELS, CONSOLES & NICHES

A **Corbel** is a structural, integral projection from a wall used to support heavy loads like beams or arches. A **Console** is a decorative scroll-shaped bracket attached to walls, typically used to support lighter loads like cornices or to embellish elements such as keystones, particularly in highly ornate styles, such as Baroque architecture. Consoles are often referred to as corbels and the terms corbel and console are often used interchangeably. Though all consoles are a type of corbel, not all corbels are consoles. A modillion, the small bracket found in series beneath Corinthian cornices, is a sort of small console.

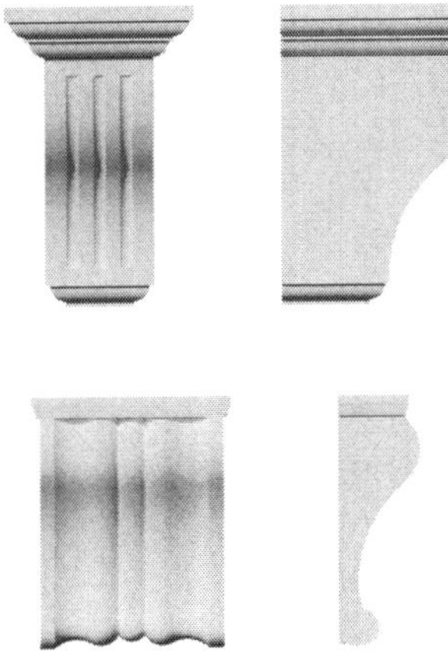

CLASSICAL CORBELS

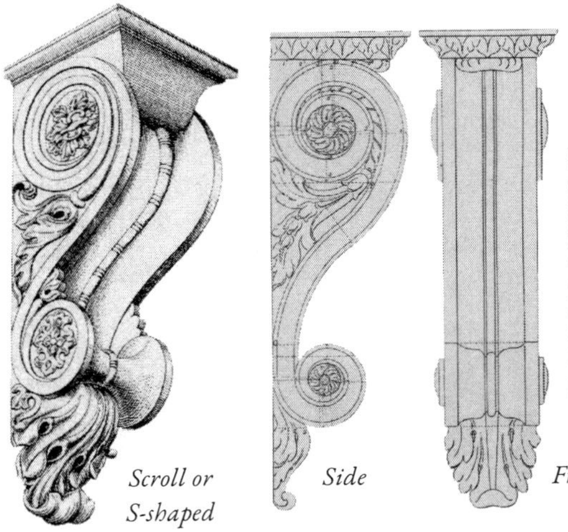

CLASSICAL CONSOLES

NICHE

A **Niche** is a recessed, semi-circular space or cavity set into a wall, typically with an arched top, designed to house statues or urns. Niches are often framed by mouldings or structures akin to window surrounds. They add visual depth and ornamentation to building façades, often reflecting acts of devotion or patronage associated with the structure.

- Sometimes called an architectural niche.
- The example on the left is a 'shell-headed' niche.

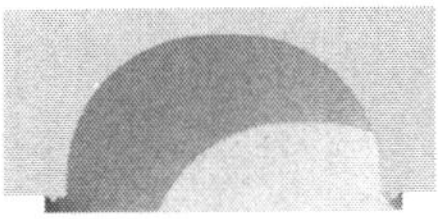

CROSS SECTION

NICHE WITH STATUE

STRING COURSE & ARCHITRAVE-CORNICE

A **String Course** is a horizontal band or moulding, often slightly projecting, that runs across a building's façade. String courses typically mark structural transitions, for example, delineating between a rusticated plinth and the rest of the building or marking divisions between storeys. The term originates in construction practice, where every few layers of stonework were levelled to a string line.

An **Architrave-Cornice** is essentially an entablature without a frieze (right). It is often used at the top of buildings to provide a strong visual termination where a full entablature is not necessary, yet is more visually prominent than just a cornice alone. Note: cornices alone are frequently used at the top of classical buildings.

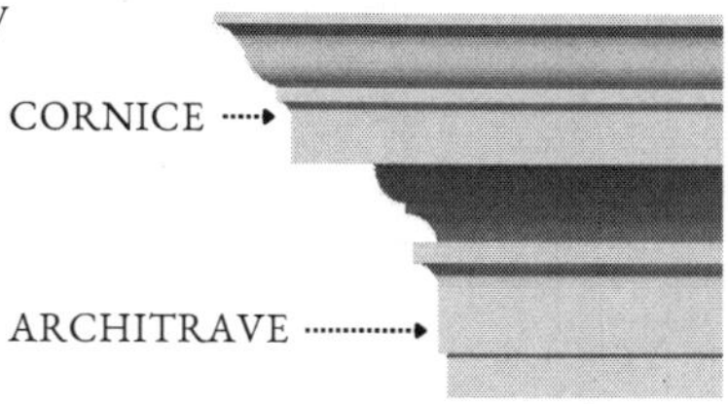

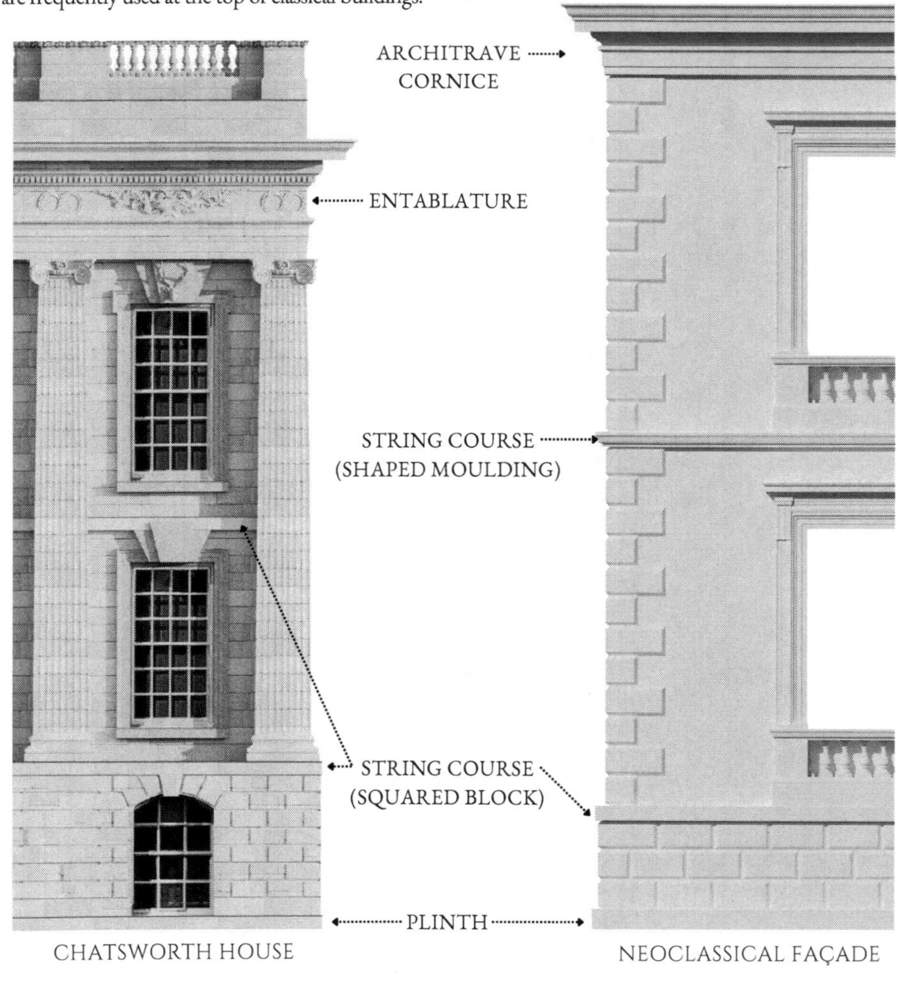

CHATSWORTH HOUSE

NEOCLASSICAL FAÇADE

ACROTERIA

The term **Acroterion** (plural *acroteria*) originally referred to the small pedestal or plinth placed at the apex and sides of a pediment in classical Greek and Roman architecture. In the present day, the term more commonly refers to the decorative ornaments placed on these pedestals, notably anthemion acroteria. The term may denote both the ornaments and the pedestal.

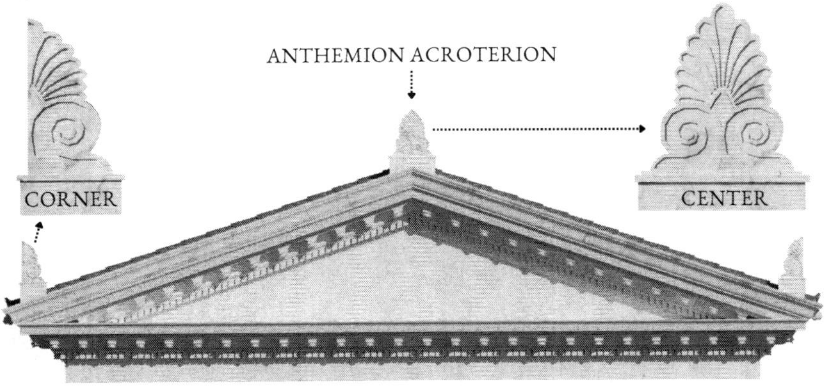

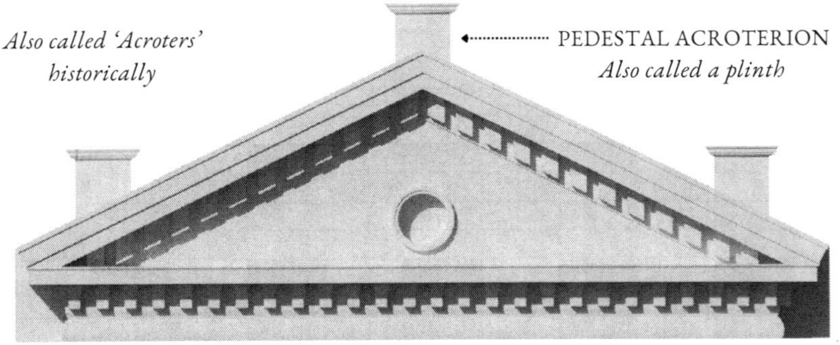

- Acroteria most commonly feature variations of the anthemion motif but may also include sculptural figures, such as people or creatures like eagles and sphinxes.

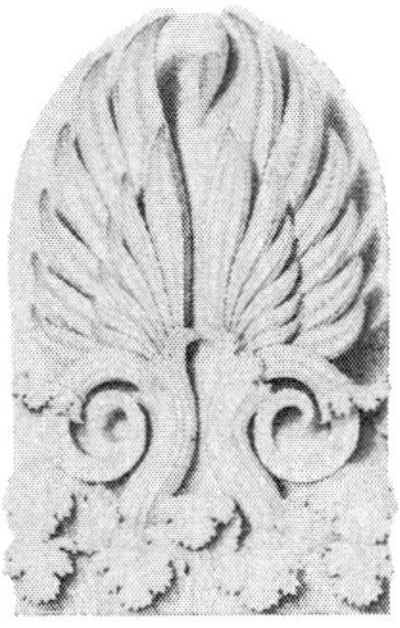

ORNATE VARIATION

(Antefix of the Parthenon)

ORNATE VARIATION

ORNAMENTATION

On the following pages is a collection of decorations commonly found on classical structures.

ANTEFIX

- An antefix is a decorative vertical ornament placed along the lower edge of a tiled roof to conceal the ends of the roof tiles and prevent water infiltration, particularly in Greek and Roman architecture.
- They usually feature anthemion motifs (see the antefix on the previous page).
- Antefixes also refer to an attachment to a horizontal cymatium, typically featuring lion heads (see Maison Carrée).

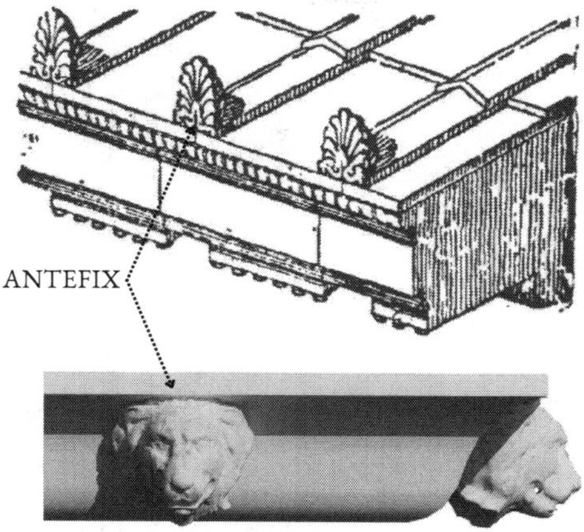

FESTOON

- Also called a garland or a swag, they typically contain arrangements of fruits, flowers and leaves.
- Feature primarily on flat areas, such as friezes, but may also decorate the volutes of Ionic capitals.

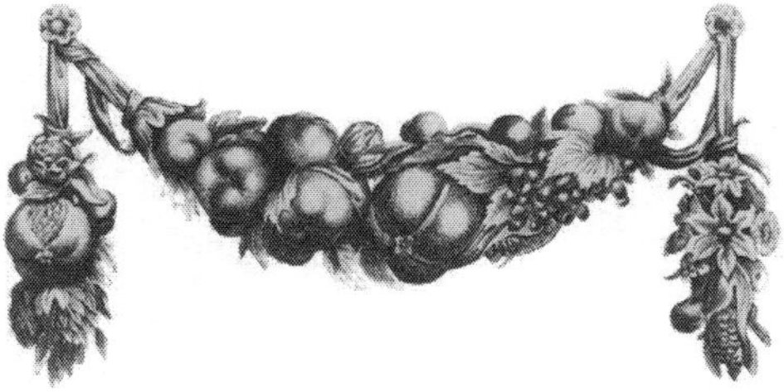

CARYATID

- A sculpted female figure that serves as an architectural support, taking the place of a column to uphold an entablature.
- The most famous caryatids are those of the Erechtheion in Athens.
- A male caryatid is called an 'atlas' or a 'telamon'.

The 'Daughters of Athens' from the Erechtheion, Athens

Caryatid supporting an entablature

ORNAMENTATION

URN

- Decorative vase-like ornament featuring a curved body (top) and a narrow neck (base).
- Usually found on pedestals and adorning balustrades.

FINIAL

- A spherical, ball-shaped crowning feature, of varying complexity.
- Like urns, they are often on gateposts, pedestals and balustrades.

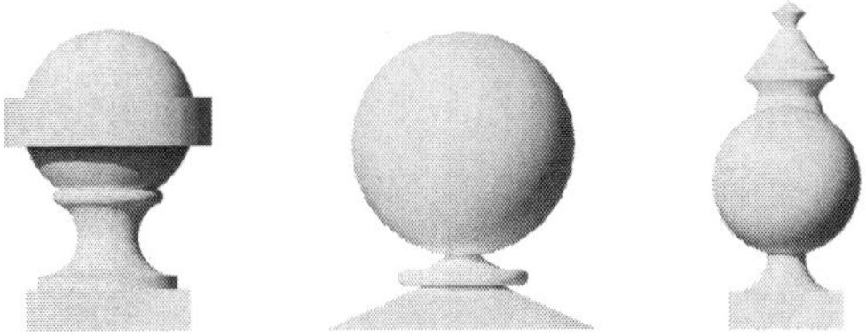

STATUE

- Sculptural representation of people, often in relation to the building's purpose or dedication, typically featuring mythical figures, gods or public figures.
- Like urns and finials, they are frequently used on top of pedestals, balustrades, and porticos.
- Typically stone or bronze.
- A statue of just the head and shoulders is called a bust (page 100).

ROSETTE

- Circular, stylised rose-like ornaments carved in relief, typically featuring radiating petals and acanthus leaves.
- Primarily used in coffers and capitals.

Neoclassical

Baroque

Roman

Rosette inside a coffer

CLASSICAL COFFERS

Coffers are square or rectangular insets found on the soffit or arches, cornices, domes, ceilings and sometimes underneath architraves, fitting to both flat and curved surfaces. They are typically decorated with rosettes and are occasionally octagonal, oriented diagonally or stretched to fit a dome. A feature that has coffers is described as coffered (e.g. a coffered ceiling), and the technique is known as coffering.

SOFFIT OF A COFFERED ARCH (THE ARC DE TRIOMPHE, PARIS)

COFFERS OF A CORINTHIAN CORNICE (WITH ROSETTES)

COFFERS OF THE PANTHEON, ROME

COFFERED CEILING (WTH ROSETTES)

DOMES, CUPOLAS & ATTIC STOREYS

A **Dome** is a hemispherical roof structure, often supported by a series of arches beneath it, designed to span wide spaces. Domes were made possible by the engineering innovations of Roman concrete, most famously demonstrated by the Pantheon in Rome, and later came to epitomise classical grandeur and opulence. The interiors of domes are often highly decorated, featuring coffers, arches and elaborate paintings.

- Domes typically feature an oculus or lantern at their apex to admit light into the building.
- A **Cupola** is a small, dome-like structure placed atop a building, often crowning a larger dome or roof. Cupolas serve both aesthetic and functional purposes, commonly acting as a roof lanterns to admit light and provide ventilation to the building below.
- An **Attic storey** (A) is a storey that is above the main entablature of a building (B).

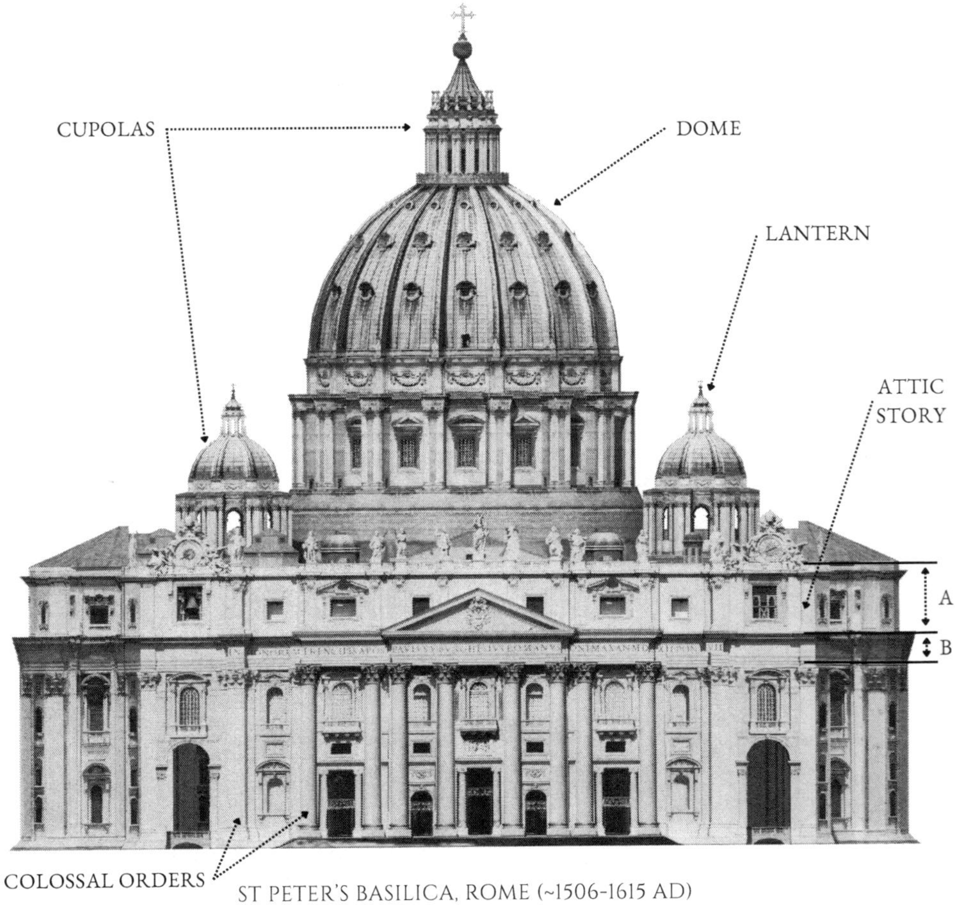

ST PETER'S BASILICA, ROME (~1506-1615 AD)

Famous examples: *US Capitol, The Pantheon, St Peter's Basilica, St Paul's Cathedral, Les Invalides, Villa La Rotunda.*

CLASSICAL TEMPLE LAYOUTS

Below are the most common architectural floor plans of Greek temples. Many Roman temples also followed these formats. Variations of prostyle and peripteral temples are the most common in both Greek and Roman architecture.

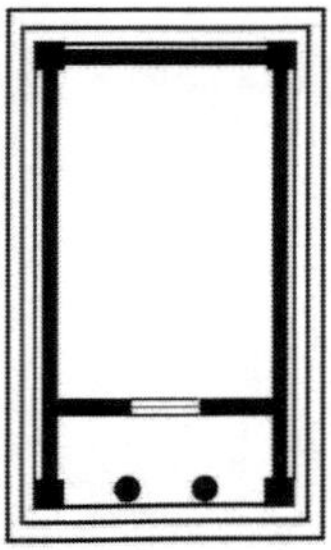

ANTA
Treasury at Delphi

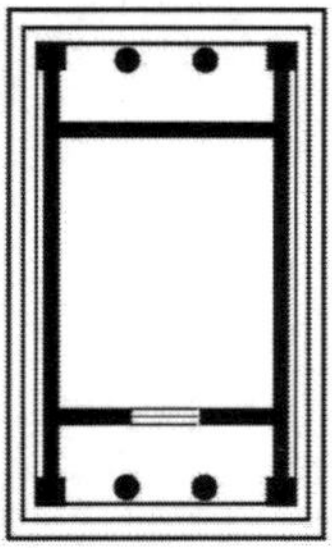

DOUBLE ANTA

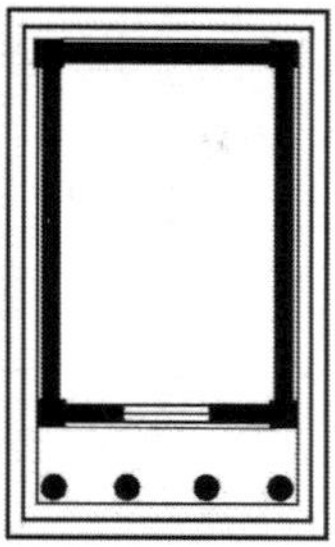

PROSTYLE

AMPHIPROSTYLE
Temple of Athena Nike

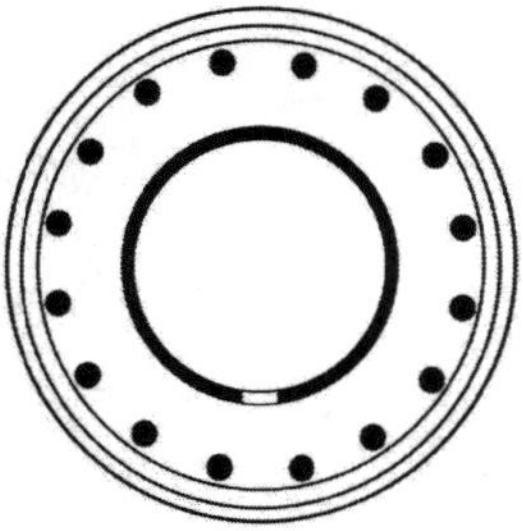

THOLOS

- Rarely found
- Akin to a 'rotunda' - a round classical building.

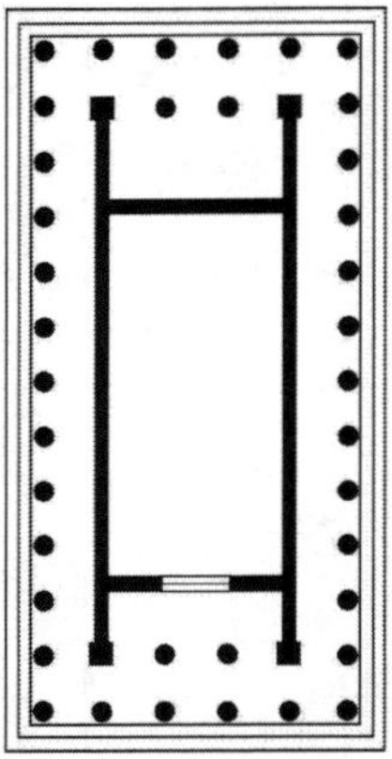

PERIPTERAL
Parthenon
Temple of Hephaestus

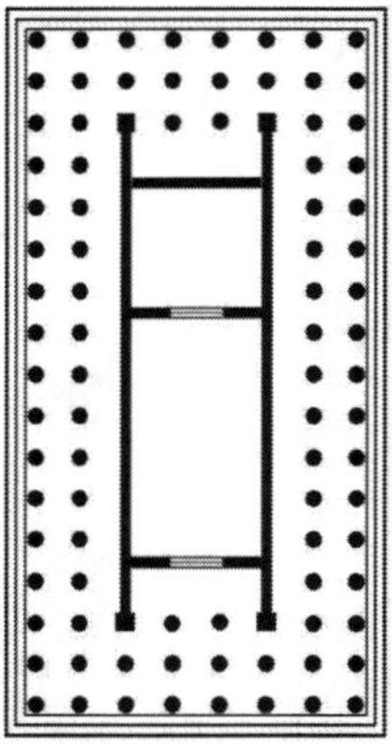

DIPTERAL

PSEUDOPERIPTERAL
Maison Carrée
Temple of Portunus

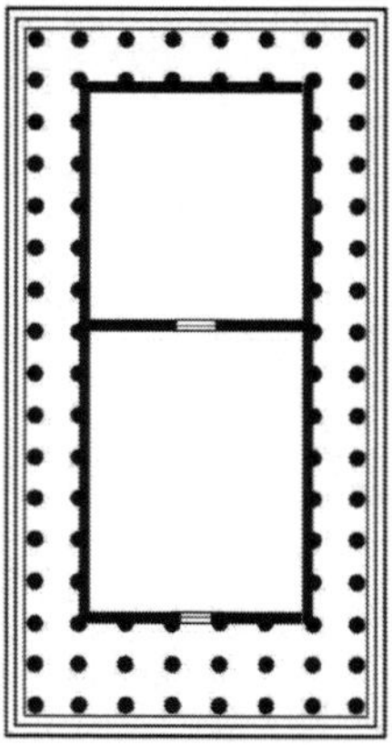

PSEUDODIPTERAL

PART IV
GENERAL RULES FURTHER READING GLOSSARY & INDEX

GENERAL RULES

A concise collection of standard rules and classical architectural principles for effective use in contemporary practice:

- The Orders are proportioned using the base diameter of their column shafts.
- Tuscan (1:7): used for simple, rustic and utilitarian structures.
- Doric (1:8): Association with the 'masculine,' order, and militarism; often used for door porticos.
- Ionic (1:9): Association with the 'feminine' and elegance; commonly used for civic, public and religious buildings.
- Corinthian and Composite (1:10): the most ornate Orders, used for the grandest and most monumental structures.
- Columns should have entasis. The top of their shafts is 5/6 of the base.
- Entablature is typically 1/4 the height of the column.
- A pedestal is usually 1/3 to 3/10 the height of the column.
- Columns are spaced in relation to column base diameters, a system known as intercolumniation. Eustyle is a historically favoured spacing, with columns spaced at 3⅓ diameters apart to the column's centres.
- Pediment angles are typically 22.5 degrees, though very large structures or Greek Doric temples should have shallower angles.
- Mouldings are arranged in specific orders to create desirable shadow patterns and to protect the structure they form from weathering.
- A column must never be placed directly in the centre of a pediment.
- The thinnest parts of the entablature (bottom of the architrave and frieze) should align with the top of the shaft of the column below.
- Architraves for door and window surrounds are 1/6 of the width of the opening.
- Door proportions are typically between 2:1 and 2⅓:1.
- Window openings are proportioned anywhere between 1:1 and 2:1, commonly 1:1, 3:2, 1:√2, 5:8, and 1:√3.

FURTHER READING

ROMAN

- **Vitruvius** (~1st Century BC)
  De Architectura - Ten Books on Architecture (~1st Century BC)

RENAISSANCE

- Sebastiano Serlio (1475-1552) - Note: of historical significance, but less useful for today
  The Fourth Book of Architecture: the rules of the five orders of building (1537)
- **Giacomo Barozzi da Vignola** (1507-1573)
  The Five Orders of Architecture (1562)
- **Andrea Palladio** (1508-1580)
  Four Books of Architecture (1570)
- Vincenzo Scamozzi (1552-1616) - Note: of historical significance, but less useful for today
  The Idea of a Universal Architecture (1615)

ENGLISH

- **James Gibbs** (1682-1754)
  1) *The Rules for Drawing the Several Parts of Architecture (1732)*
  2) A book of architecture : containing designs of buildings and ornaments (1728)
- **Sir William Chambers** (1723-1796)
  A Treatise on the Decorative Part of Civil Architecture (1791)
- **Abraham Swan** (1725 - 1768)
  The British Architect: Or, The Builders Treasury of Staircases (1745)
- **Batty Langley** (1696-1751)
  1) *The Builder's Complete Assistant (1738)*
  2) *The City and Country builder's and Workman's Treasury of Designs (1741)*

AMERICAN

- **Asher Benjamin** (1773-1845)
  The Architect: Or, Practical House Carpenter (1843)
- **William R. Ware** (1832-1915)
  The American Vignola: A Guide to the Making of Classical Architecture (1904)

ORNAMENTATION

- **G.E. Walters** (Firm c. 1900)
  Catalog of Capitals, brackets and compo ornament for exterior and interior decoration (1900)
- **Franz Sales Meyer** (1849-1927)
  Handbook of ornament; a grammar of art, industrial and architectural designing (1900)

GLOSSARY & INDEX

A

Abacus	The flat square slab on top of a capital.	***16***
Abutment	Structural support at the sides of an arch or vault.	***94***
Acanthus	A plant whose leaves are highly stylised and used to decorate Corinthian and Composite capitals as well as various mouldings.	***30, 34***
Acroteria	Small pedestals decorated with sculpture or palmette found on the edges and top of a pediment.	***14, 122***
Aedicule	A type of architectural frame for an opening, made of a two columns supporting an entablature and pediment, and an architrave around the opening. Originally a sort of shrine.	***117***
Amphiprostyle	A form of temple layout.	***127***
Angular	Ionic capital variation with angled volutes on all sides. *See Scamozzi Ionic capital.*	***64***
Angulated	Ionic capital variation with two pulvinar volutes at ninety degrees to each other and an Angular/Scamozzi volute mediating between them.	***69***
Anta	An extended wall end, equivalent to a pilaster in Greek architecture. Plural: *Antae.* A temple with antae is called *in antis.*	***23***
Antefix	Decorative block used covering tile joints on a temple's roof. Or, an attached sculpted figure (e.g. lion) attached to a Cyma.	***123***
Anthemion	Floral motif depicting a stylised honeysuckle plant. Often used for Acroteria and Antefix.	***34***
Annulet	Small square moulding, variation of the term Fillet. See *Fillet.*	***n/a***
Apex	The top of a pediment.	***n/a***
Apophyge	The cavetto like curve found at the top and bottom of a column's shaft.	***19***
Araeostyle	Intercolumniation - column spacing where columns are 5 diameters apart to their centres.	***91***
Arch	A curved symmetrical structure spanning an opening.	***94***
Arcade	An arcade is a series of arches supported by columns or piers, forming a covered passageway, corridor, or open gallery.	***95***
Architrave	The lowest part of the entablature. Also refers to the mouldings around a door or window - which often share a similar profile to the architraves from entablatures.	***17, 105***
Architrave-Cornice	An entablature where there is no Frieze.	***121***

GLOSSARY & INDEX

A

Archivolt	An architrave that follows the curve of an arch.	***94***
Arris	Sharp edge where two surfaces (flat or curved) meet *(e.g. flutes).*	***26***
Ashlar	Perfectly smooth masonry in square or rectangular blocks.	***103***
Astragal	A small convex moulding with a circular profile.	***28***
Atlas	Male figure used as a supporting column - the male equivalent of caryatid.	***n/a***
Attic	A small upper story, parapet, or wall above the main entablature of a building.	***119***
Attica	The area surrounding classical Athens.	***n/a***
Attic base	A column base used in the Doric, Ionic, Corinthian, and Composite orders. Primarily identified by the two Tori (see Torus) with one Scotia (see Scotia) in between them. The Attic base is the most common of all the column bases.	***19, 66***
Attic storey	A floor above the main entablature of a building.	***126***

B

Baluster	Small ornamental columns, pillars or posts supporting a rail in a balustrade.	***119***
Balustrade	A series of balusters capped with a top and bottom rail. Often used on top of entablatures, balconies and roofs.	***119***
Baroque	Ornate, dramatic European style (~1600 to 1750) following classical principles and highly decorative interiors.	***11***
Base	The lowest part of a column, for support.	***19***
Beading	An enrichment for a bead or astragal, consisting of repeated spheres.	***32***
Bead-and-reel	An enrichment for an astragal, consisting of alternating beads (spheres) and reels (spools).	***32***
Bed-mould	The mouldings between the underneath the corona in a cornice. Usually a cavetto, then ovolo then a dentil band.	***17***
Blocking	Decorative rectangular masonry pieces that project from the main structure, such as in a *Gibbs surround*, or a *rusticated* arch.	***103***
Bolster	Cushion-shaped form behind the volutes of a Pulvinar Ionic capital.	***64, 69***
Boss	Ornamental knob or protrusion, often carved with flowers.	***74***

GLOSSARY & INDEX

B

Broken Pediment	A pediment that split or interrupted at the apex - and does not form a point.	***100***
Bucrania	Ox skull motif symbolising sacrifice, often on friezes - particularly of the Doric Order. Also spelled *Bukrania*. Plural: Bucranium.	***53***

C

Cable flute	The partial refilling of the flutes on the lowest third of a column, with a decorative moulding, usually a round rod.	***27***
Canalis	The gap (channel) between two of the fillets of the face of an Ionic volute.	***64***
Cap	Alternative name for the cornice or top of a pedestal.	***20, 119***
Capital	The top of a column that supports the entablature. Often ornately decorated.	***16***
Cartouche	An ornate frame around a design or inscription.	***n/a***
Caryatid	A sculpted female figure that serves as an architectural support, taking the place of a column or pillar to uphold an entablature.	***123***
Caulicoli	Stem-like decorations that are beneath the volutes of Corinthian capital, and hold up the third layer of acanthus leaves.	***74***
Cavetto	A concave moulding, with a profile of one quarter of a circle.	***28***
Cella	The inner area of an ancient temple.	***n/a***
Chamfer	A bevelled edge connecting two surfaces in a smooth transition.	***103***
Classical	Typically refers to Greek and Roman architectural principles.	***n/a***
Coffer	Sunken panel (usually square, rectangular or octangular) in a ceiling or dome, often decorated with rosettes. may also be found in the soffit of a Corinthian cornice and underneath an architrave.	***125***
Colossal Order	A colossal order is an architectural order where columns, pilasters, or engaged columns extend over two or more stories of a building.	***102, 126***
Colonnade	A colonnade is a row of evenly spaced columns supporting an entablature or arches, often forming a covered walkway or part of a larger architectural structure. Does not have any arches.	***96***
Column	A vertical architectural support consisting of a base, a shaft, and a capital.	***14, 15***
Composite Order	The fifth Order of architecture. It combines the volutes of the Ionic order capital with the acanthus leaves, and proportions of the Corinthian order (1:10). Sometimes called the Roman Order.	***82***

GLOSSARY & INDEX

C

Console	An projecting ornamental bracket or corbel, often with a scroll-shaped profile (ogee curve) used to support elements above it.	*120*
Coping	Protective cap or covering atop a wall.	*n/a*
Corbel	A projecting bracket used to support a beam, arch, or other heavy structure above it. May be ornate like a console.	*120*
Corinthian Order	One of the three Classical orders. the Corinthian is the most ornate, characterised by slender, fluted columns (1:10 ratio) and a capital decorated with acanthus leaves and small volutes.	*72*
Cornice	The uppermost section of an entablature; projecting, horizontal and usually very decorative.	*17*
Corona	The main projecting flat and vertical part of a cornice.	*17*
Coupled	Intercolumniation - column spacing of 1½ diameters apart.	*91*
Crepidoma	Stepped base of a Greek temple, consisting of a stylobate and a stereobate.	*14*
Cupola	Small dome atop a building or roof	*126*
Cyma Recta	S-shaped moulding with a convex then concave profile.	*28, 29*
Cyma Reversa	Reverse S-moulding with a concave then convex profile.	*28, 29*
Cymatium	Top moulding of a cornice or capital.	*17*

D

Decastyle	A temple front that consists of 10 columns.	*99*
Dentil	A dentil is a small, rectangular block that forms a continuous, evenly spaced row of dentils, typically found in the cornice of the Ionic and Corinthian orders.	*35*
Dentil band	A row of dentils that are not fully separated - a block of material remains in the upper section between the dentils.	*35*
Denticular	Containing dentils. *I.e. Denticular Doric Entablature.*	*59*
Diameter	The width of a column (of any Order) at the base, which is used to proportion the Orders, and building layouts.	*42*
Diastyle	Intercolumniation - column spacing of 4 diameters apart (centres).	*91*
Die	The central block, or plain central part of a pedestal.	*20*
Diminution	Archaic/alternative word for entasis - the tapering of a column's shaft upward.	*24*

GLOSSARY & INDEX

D

Dome	A curved, hemispherical roof structure.	***126***
Door Surround	The moulding or architectural frame surrounding a door.	***108***
Doric Order	The oldest of the Classical Orders, with simple entablatures, plain capitals, decorative friezes and with 1:8 column ratios.	***50***
Drip	Projecting moulding designed to shed water, often underneath the corona in a cornice.	***38***
Drum	Cylindrical section of a column shaft or dome base.	***21***

E

Echinus	Moulding profile, sometimes called a Greek ovolo, with a quarter round, or egg-like profile with a notch at the top. and is typically found underneath an abacus in a Doric or Ionic capital.	***16***
Egg-and-dart	Ornamental motif (for ovolo profile) alternating egg shapes with dart-like forms. Originally thought to represent the opium poppy.	***31***
Elevation	The vertical view (from the front or sides) or drawing of a building's façade.	***n/a***
Engaged Column	A column partially embedded in a wall (usually ⅓ - ½ of its diameter), projecting outward.	***21***
Entablature	The horizontal structure above columns, consisting of an architrave, frieze, and cornice.	***17***
Entasis	Slight convex curve in a column shaft, usually starting ⅓ of the way up the column. Corrects a visual illusion for straightness.	***24, 25***
Epistyle	Another term for an architrave. typically only referred to in classical Greek and Roman structures.	***n/a***
Eustyle	Intercolumniation - column spacing of 3 ⅓ diameters (modern) apart (to the columns' centres).	***91***
Extrados	Outer curve or surface of an arch.	***94***

F

Façade	The exterior face of a building, particularly the primary front that faces a street or public space.	***n/a***
Fascia	A flat, horizontal band in an entablature or moulding, akin to a very large fillet. If divided, the divisions are called upper and lower.	***29***
Festoon	Also called a swag, is a hanging garland or decorative drape often found on friezes and typically contains fruit of floral motifs.	***123***

GLOSSARY & INDEX

F

Fibonacci	Mathematical sequence used in proportion or design (1, 1, 2, 3, 5, etc.).	***106***
Fillet	Narrow, flat band used to separate mouldings or flutes. Occasionally called an annulet or a listel.	***29***
Finial	Ornamental top of a spire, balustrade, pedestal, or other structure. Often a ball.	***124***
Fleuron	Floral or leaf-like ornament, often at the centre of a design. Also *Boss.*	***74***
Fluting	Vertical grooves or channels which are cut perpendicularly to a a columns' shaft.	***26***
Frieze	The middle part of an entablature, often plain but may also be highly decorated (acanthus, bucrania, figures etc.) depending on the architectural Order and time period.	***14, 15, 17***
Frontispiece	The decorative main entrance to a building. Sometimes refers to the whole main façade also.	***108***
Frostwork	A form of *rustication* that features decorative carving resembling icicles. Also called glaciation.	***103***

G

Geison	Alternative name for a cornice or projecting moulding in classical Greek architecture.	***57***
Georgian	Architectural style (1714 - 1830) during the reigns of the British monarchs George I to George IV. Chiefly, it denotes Palladianism, but encompasses late Baroque and Neoclassical work of the time.	***12***
Gibbs Surround	A door or window surround that consists of a series of square or rectangular blocks either paralleling or interrupting the side architraves of an opening's frame. The surround also typically has a pediment, and was popularised by James Gibbs.	***118***
Glazing Bar	Bar dividing a window into smaller panes of glass	***111***
Glyph	The perpendicular channels cut in the triglyphs of the Doric frieze.	***52***
Golden Ratio	Proportion (approximately 1:1.618) used for aesthetic harmony.	***106***
Graduated Fenestration	Windows decreasing in size as you move upward on the façade of a building.	***115***
Greek	Architectural style of ancient Greece, emphasising simplicity and proportion. Frequent use of the Doric and Ionic Orders, and no use of arches or domes.	***10***

GLOSSARY & INDEX

G

Greek Key	Distinctive ornamental pattern of continuous, interlocking geometric lines. A form of running moulding.	*33*
Greek Leaf	Leaf-like motif in originally found in Greek moulding for cyma profiles. Does not contain acanthus motifs.	*31*
Greek Ovolo	*See Echinus.*	*28*
Griffin	Mythical creature (lion body, eagle head) used in decorative sculpture.	*n/a*
Guilloche	Ornamental pattern of interlaced, circular motifs in continuous bands.	*33*
Guttae	Small pyramids or cones in Doric entablature, immediately underneath the triglyphs. They represent wooden pegs that would have held beams in place in the pre-stone, wood Doric temples. Also called *drops.*	*52*

H

Helix	A small volute, or scroll, located under the abacus of a Corinthian capital. A Corinthian capital will have a total of 16 Helices. If the helices cross over each other, they are called *interlocked.*	*74*
Hexastyle	Temple or structure with six columns across the front.	*99*
Hypaethral	A temple that is uncovered, or open to the sky - without a roof.. According to Vitruvius.	*n/a*
Hypotrachelion	The upper part (alternative name for necking) or groove in the shaft of a (Greek) Doric column.	*n/a*

I

Impost	Block or cornice, which is on top of a pier or an abutment at the springing point of an arch and in turn supports the arch.	*94, 96*
Insulated	A column that is standing alone, as in not *engaged* or a *pilaster.*	*21*
Inter-columniation	Spacing between columns, measured in diameters.	*91*
Intrados	Inner curve or underside of an arch.	*94*
Ionic order	One of the five Orders of Architecture. Characterised by capitals with large volutes and columns with a 1:9 ratio.	*62*
Isodomic	Masonry with uniformly cut, evenly laid blocks - akin to *ashlar.* Isodomic rustication refers to blocks that have their edges chamfered or that have square channels cut into them.	*103*

GLOSSARY & INDEX

K

Keystone	The central and the the highest stone of an arch. Often large and projecting further than the rest of the voussoirs, and is often more decorated.	*94*

L

Laurel	Decorative motif of laurel leaves (bay leaf), symbolising victory.	*32*
Light	Window pane or glazed opening.	*111*
Lugged Architrave	Also called lobed or eared architrave, is an architrave with sideways projecting, extensions at the top of the surround.	*105*

M

Metope	The interval panel or square space between the triglyphs in the Doric frieze, often decorated.	*53*
Minute	One sixtieth of a *Diameter*. An architecture fraction or measure. When the lower diameter of a column divided into sixty parts, each part is so called a minute.	*42*
Modillion	Ornamental bracket under a cornice, typically in Corinthian and Composite Orders.	*35, 36*
Module	Standard unit of measure. 1) The same as a diameter (60 minutes)- the diameter of the lowest part of the column. 2) Half a diameter (30 minutes) - several authors confusingly refer this way.	*42*
Monolithic	Structure or element made from a single block of stone - typically a monolithic column.	*21*
Moulding	Decorative strip with a shaped profile, used in transitions and for ornamentation. The main mouldings are the *Cavetto* and the *Ovolo-* from which the *Cyma Recta* and *Cyma Reversa* are derived. All mouldings may be "enriched" - meaning decorated with ornate motifs such as *Roman Leaf, Egg and Dart,* or other patterns.	*28*
Mutulary	Relating to, or containing Mutules. Mutules in a 'Mutulary Band.'	*51, 59*
Mutule	A flat, projecting, cantilevered bracket or block under a Doric cornice. Like a triglyph, they are usually with decorated with guttae. It is akin the modillions of the Corinthian and Composite Orders.	*52*

GLOSSARY & INDEX

N

Necking	Narrow vertical band or moulding of a Tuscan or Doric capital. It is between the *Echinus* and the *Astragal*.	***16***
Neoclassical	An 18th–19th-century style reviving classical Greek and Roman forms, rejecting the excessive drama of Baroque architecture, and the more monumental than Palladian architecture.	***12***
Niche	Recessed space in a wall, often for a statue or ornament.	***120***

O

Octastyle	an edifice having eight columns in front.	***99***
Oculus	1) Circular opening or window in a wall or dome, admitting light. 2) The centre of an Ionic volute, also called an *eye*.	***112*** ***64***
Ogee	Describes S shaped mouldings - cyma reversa or cyma recta. Traditionally, just a cyma reversa.	***29***
Open Tympanum	A pediment that does not have a complete horizontal cornice underneath it.	***101***
Order	A certain assemblage of parts subject to uniform established proportions including a column, capital, and entablature.	***40***
Ornament	Decorative element enhancing architectural features, such as a statue on a balustrade, or an acanthus scroll in a frieze.	***123, 124***
Ovolo	A convex moulding with a quarter-circle, or an egg-shaped profile.	***28***

P

Palladian	Architectural style (~1715 and 1760) based on the works of Andrea Palladio. Employs classical authenticity, simplicity, symmetry and the use of portico fronts.	***12***
Palladian Motif	A Venetian window. *See Venetian Window.*	***116***
Parapet	Low wall along the edge of a roof or balcony.	***119***
Patera	Circular, shallow dish-like ornament, often with floral or radial designs, typically found on friezes.	***53***
Pedestal	Base supporting a column, statue, or other element. Consists of a base, die, and a cap.	***20***
Pediment	Triangular or curved gable above an entablature, or opening.	***98***
Pier	A vertical load-bearing structural support element.	***n/a***
Peripteral	Temple surrounded by a single row of columns on all sides.	***127***

GLOSSARY & INDEX

P

Peristyle	Columned porch that surrounds a building or courtyard.	***n/a***
Piano Nobile	Principal floor of a building, often elevated and grandly designed.	***102***
Pilaster	Flat, rectangular version of a column that is attached to a wall, often decoratively.	***22***
Pillar	An isolated, vertical structure used in architecture or construction to serve an aesthetic or structural purpose in a building.	***n/a***
Plan	Horizontal drawing or layout of a building's design.	***n/a***
Plinth	Square base or block supporting a column, wall or ornament.	***15, 20***
Podium	Raised platform or base supporting a building or columns.	***15***
Porch	A covered, exterior space, usually attached to a building's entrance.	***n/a***
Portico	Covered entrance with columns supporting a roof.	***99***
Posticum	The porch area in the back front of an Greek temple.	***n/a***
Profile	Outline or cross-sectional shape of a moulding or structure.	***n/a***
Proportion	Balanced relationship of dimensions in architectural design.	***41, 106***
Pronaos	The front porch area of an Greek temple.	***n/a***
Prostyle	Temple layout with columns only at the front, forming a portico.	***127***
Psuedo-peripteral	A temple layout with engaged columns on sides, mimicking a peripteral design.	***127***
Pulvinar	Cushion-like element, often referring to the bolster in Ionic capitals.	***64***
Pulvinated	Curved or bulging, often describing a convex frieze or moulding.	***68***
Pycnostyle	Intercolumniation - column spacing of 2 ¼ diameters apart (to the columns' centres).	***91***

Q

Quarter Round	A moulding with a quarter round profile, the same as an *Ovolo*.	***28***
Quoins	Masonry blocks at the corner of a wall (exterior), often pronounced.	***n/a***

GLOSSARY & INDEX

R

Rail	Horizontal bar or moulding, often part of a balustrade.	***119***
Raking	Sloping, as in the angled cornice of a pediment.	***14, 15, 101***
Regula	Short band or block beneath the taenia in a Doric frieze, with guttae.	***52***
Renaissance	Architectural style (14th–17th-century) reviving classical forms.	***11***
Rise	Vertical height of an arch or vault from springing to apex.	***94***
Rococo	Architectural style (18th-century) that is a more extreme version of *Baroque,* with ornate, playful, and asymmetrical decoration.	***11***
Roman	Architectural style of ancient Rome (5th century BC - 4th century AD) that is characterised by the use of the five classical Orders, incorporating arches, domes and vaults.	***10***
Roman Leaf	Decorative leaf motif featuring acanthus. Roman interpretation of the *Greek Leaf* ornamentation.	***31***
Roman Order	The same as the Composite Order.	***83***
Rope Twist	Ornamental pattern resembling twisted rope or cable.	***32***
Rosette	Circular, rose-like ornament, often in relief.	***124***
Rotunda	A (classical) building which is completely round.	***127***
Rusticated Base	Lower part of a wall with rough, textured stonework.	***104***
Rustication	Masonry with textured (natural stone) or recessed (chamfered) joints for a rugged effect.	***103***
Running Moulding	Flat decorative mouldings that made of interlocking patterns.	***33***

S

Scima or Sima	Alternative spelling of Cyma.	***n/a***
Scotia	Concave moulding with an elliptical profile used in bases of columns.	***19, 28***
Section	Type of drawing that provides a vertical cross-section view of a building or structure	***m/a***
Segmental Pediment	Pediment with a curved top instead of triangular. The curve is a segment of an arch.	***101***
Shaft	Main cylindrical body of a column, between the base and capital.	***14, 15***

GLOSSARY & INDEX

S

Shouldered Architrave	Architrave with upward and outward (shoulders) projections at the top or at the corners.	***105***
Soffit	Underside of an arch, cornice (underneath a corona), ceiling, architrave, or other projecting element.	***17, 125***
Solomonic Column	Column with a twisted spiral shaft (typically Baroque).	***21***
Span	Horizontal distance between supports of an arch or beam.	***94***
Spandrel	Triangular space between an arch and its rectangular frame.	***95***
Sphinx	Mythical creature (lion body, human head) used in decorative sculpture.	***n/a***
Spiral Fluting	Column fluting with a twisted or helical pattern.	***27***
Springer	Lowest stone of an arch, where it begins to curve.	***94***
Statue	Sculpted figure, often used as architectural decoration.	***124***
Stereobate	The two lower two steps in the *Crepidoma,* found in the bases of Greek temples.	***14***
Stoa	Covered walkway or portico, often used as a public The word Stoicism is derived from Stoa.	***n/a***
Stopped Fluting	Column fluting that only starts approximately ⅓ of the way up the column.	***27***
String Course	Horizontal band or moulding running across a façade. Historically used to ensure the building remains level.	***121***
Style	Greek word for column. Hence the nomenclature used in Intercolumniation.	***n/a***
Stylobate	Topmost step of a temple's crepidoma (Greek temples) on which the columns are placed.	***14***
Superposition	Where successive storeys of a building have different architectural Orders. E.g. Corinthian on top of Ionic on top of Doric.	***93***
Swan-Neck Pediment	Pediment with S-shaped curves at the top, resembling a swan's neck.	***101***
Systyle	Intercolumniation - column spacing of 3 diameters apart (to the columns' centres).	***91***

GLOSSARY & INDEX

T

U

V

GLOSSARY & INDEX

V

Volute	Spiral scroll, characteristic of Ionic and Composite capitals.	***64***
Voussoir	Wedge-shaped stone forming part of an arch.	***94***

W

Wash	Sloping surface or bevel used to shed water. Often found on top of cornices and on window sills.	***38***
Window	Fenestrated opening of a building.	***111***
Window Surround	The moulding or architectural frame surrounding a window.	***111***

FINIS

DOWNLOAD 3D MODELS - CLASSICAD™

Feel free to visit ClassiCad™ where you can explore and download a growing collection of proportionally accurate 3D models of the five Orders.

https://app.classicad.co.uk/

EDUCATIONAL USE

Please contact **ed@anvilsquare.co.uk** for information regarding high quality downloads of the book for educational and institutional use.

PINTEREST

Feel free to visit our Pinterest, where there are hundreds of saved images relating to all aspects of classical architecture - from historical etchings of the five Orders to photos of real-life examples.

https://uk.pinterest.com/ASQClassicalArchitecture/

QR CODE REVIEW

Thank you for reading and for your support!

If you have a moment, I'd truly appreciate it if you could leave a review on Amazon. Your feedback helps me understand what you enjoyed and how I can create even better books for you in the future.

NOTES

CLASSICAL ARCHITECTURE IN 30 MINUTES

Printed in Dunstable, United Kingdom

75447443R00085